ALTERNATIVE HARDY

Alternative Hardy

Edited and introduced by
Lance St. John Butler

Lecturer in English Studies
University of Stirling

MACMILLAN

First published 1989

Published by
THE MACMILLAN PRESS LTD
Houndmills, Basingstoke, Hampshire RG21 2XS
and London
Companies and representatives
throughout the world

Typeset by Wessex Typesetters
(Division of The Eastern Press Ltd)
Frome, Somerset

Printed in Hong Kong

British Library Cataloguing in Publication Data
Alternative Hardy.
1. Fiction in English. Hardy, Thomas,
1840–1928—Critical studies
I. Butler, Lance St John
823′.8
ISBN 0–333–42769–6

For Alice

Acknowledgements

The poem on p. 122 'Not Ideas about the Thing but the Thing Itself'
is reprinted from *The Collected Poems of Wallace Stevens* by kind
permission of Alfred A. Knopf, Inc., and Faber and Faber.

Contents

Notes on the Contributors

Christine Brooke-Rose is an English experimental novelist who lives in Paris, France, where she is Professor of English and American Literature at the University of Paris VIII.

Lance St. John Butler is Lecturer in English Studies at the University of Stirling, Scotland. He is the author of *Thomas Hardy* (1978) and the editor of a previous collection of essays, *Thomas Hardy After 50 Years* (1977) as well as author of *Samuel Beckett and the Meaning of Being* (1984).

Jagdish Chandra Dave is Lecturer in English on the staff of the Government Colleges of Gujarat, India. He is the author of *The Human Predicament in the Novels of Thomas Hardy* (1985).

Annie Escuret is Lecturer at the Université Paul Valéry, Montpellier, France. She is the author of a doctoral thesis on Hardy ('L'Oeuvre romanesque de Thomas Hardy (1840–1928: Lectures)'). She has published articles on Hardy, Burgess, Coppard, Naipaul and Dubus.

Patricia Ingham is Senior Fellow in English at St. Anne's College, Oxford. She has written the definitive analysis of how *Jude the Obscure* evolved during composition, as well as several other articles and chapters on Hardy, particularly his language. She is at present writing a new study, *A Feminist Reading on Hardy*.

Howard Jacobson lectured in English at the University of Sidney, Australia; supervised at Selwyn College, Cambridge; and, until he gave up teaching to be a full-time writer, lectured at the Wolverhampton Polytechnic. He is the author of *Shakespeare's Magnanimity* (with Wilbur Sanders), *Coming From Behind, Peeping Tom, Redback* and *In the Land of Oz*.

Jean Jacques Lecercle was educated at the Ecole Normale Supérieure and Trinity College, Cambridge. He is currently Professor of English Language and Literature at the University of Nanterre. He is the author of *Philosophy through the Looking-Glass: Language, Nonsense, Desire* (1985).

J. Hillis Miller is Distinguished Professor of English and Comparative Literature at the University of California at Irvine. He has published a number of books on nineteenth- and twentieth-century English and American literature: most recently, *The Linguistic Moment: From Wordsworth to Stevens* and *The Ethics of Reading: Kant, de Man, Eliot, Trollope, James, and Benjamin*. He is at work on a continuation of *The Ethics of Reading*, a study of a series of shorter fictions, tentatively entitled *Versions of Pygmalion*.

Henri Quéré is Professor of English Literature at the University of Lille III, France and a member of the Groupe de Recherches sémio-linguistiques (Ecole des Hautes Etudes en Sciences Sociales, Paris). He has written a doctoral thesis on narration in the modern novel, and has published a variety of essays and articles in literary and semiotics journals, both in France and abroad. He is currently working on the problems of figurative language and is also interested in advertising and the media.

Michael Rabiger, now teaching in the Film/Video Department at Columbia College, Chicago, left school at 17 to pursue film editing. He is the director of 25 films, mostly for the British Broadcasting Corporation. He became interested in Hardy in 1968 after the BBC rejected a Hardy documentary idea and research proved addictive. He is the finder of the Hoffman papers and the author of several articles on Hardy, as well as two books, *Directing the Documentary* and *Directing the Fiction Film*. He is currently working on a biographical study of Hardy.

Janie Sénéchal is Maître-Assistante at the University of Lille III, France. She has written a doctoral thesis on the problems of enunciation and narration in the novels of Thomas Hardy. She has published various essays on Thomas Holcroft, Thomas Hardy and melodrama.

Introduction

Lance St. John Butler

All great writers speak in new ways to different generations. Hardy does this, and additionally seems extraordinarily capable of keeping the loyalty of what might be called his traditional readership while at the same time impressing the various schools of criticism as they emerge. In recent years his poetry has revealed depths and dimensions at one time unsuspected. His novels have proved even more elusive, complex and challenging than was thought only a few years ago. Affinities have been suggested the interpretative power of which is surprising only in that it had been overlooked before. Equally, Hardy's own life continues to fascinate and to offer previously half-seen facets to fresh eyes.

Thus the new languages of criticism—semiotic, structuralist, poststructuralist—the feminist revision of literary meaning, political and religious interpretations, a more adventurous style of biographical enquiry, all these have been applied to Hardy in the last ten years. Hillis Miller has a brilliant deconstruction of *Tess of the d'Urbervilles* in *Fiction and Repetition*, Patricia Ingham has produced her *Feminist Hardy*, Jagdish Dave has offered a convincing analogy between Hardy and oriental thought in *The Human Predicament in the Novels of Thomas Hardy* and Howard Jacobson has taken outrageous, hilarious and revealing liberties with the meaning of certain episodes in Hardy's life in *Peeping Tom*.

These, and other studies of a similar kind, have emerged since I collected the essays published as *Thomas Hardy After Fifty Years* in 1977. Then, approaching the half-centenary of Hardy's death, Hardy studies were in a healthy state but since then they have developed as strongly as one could possibly have expected and it seems appropriate, now in the late eighties, to offer a showcase that brings together some of the more exciting examples of these insights.

Two things distinguish the contributions to this volume: they are written by those who have proved themselves to be at the forefront of new thinking about Hardy, whether in Britain, France or North America; and they share a disregard for conventional disciplinary boundaries.

These qualities are made apparent by even the briefest summary. Thus Jean Jacques Lecercle is a linguist and critic of philosophy, Christine Brooke-Rose is an experimental novelist, Michael Rabiger a film and television director and theorist. Patricia Ingham presents us with *Jude the Obscure* and the two versions of *The Well-Beloved* as a trilogy of the utmost significance for our understanding of Hardy at the end of his career as a novelist; Hillis Miller discovers a Hardy who uses the central literary trope most revealingly in some of the obscurer corners of his work; Jagdish Dave convincingly pursues his thesis that it is with Buddhist eyes that we can best understand the complex metaphysical and moral standpoint of Hardy the poet. For Annie Escuret Hardy becomes a revolutionary comparable with Turner while, on another plane altogether, Henri Quéré and Janie Sénéchal offer a model Greimasian analysis of a few crucial paragraphs that should help us to see, finally, how it is that Hardy constructs his patterns of narrative possibility. The freedom which I find so exciting in all this is perhaps best exemplified by Howard Jacobson's contribution in which a superb range of insights are achieved from apparently unpromising material.

Criticism, after all, has been liberated too, and there is some hope that it may be able to retain both its new-found freedom, which has given it a new status and prestige, and its commitment to human values.

This volume presents a series of contrasts offering a number of alternative Hardys. This is as it should be. As Annie Escuret demonstrates, Hardy is one of the prophets of the new world-view that holds that there are no definitive or originary things, there are only versions of things. This view is not, of course, new at all, as a glance at Sartre or the Buddhist tradition will demonstrate.

Lance St. John Butler
Université de Pau, France
University of Stirling, Scotland

1

The Violence of Style in *Tess of the d'Urbervilles*

Jean Jacques Lecercle

There is a sense in which we must begin our reading of *Tess of the d'Urbervilles* with the last paragraph. But not the obvious sense. For it is too trivially clear that the closing paragraphs of the novel provide material for a retrospective reading and give both meaning and direction (*sens* in French) to the story, so that the whole novel is pervaded with emotional tension towards its catastrophic ending. What strikes one in the last paragraph, however, is not so much the climactic event on which it is the commentary as the violence of Hardy's style. The physical violence of Tess's death (which is not described) is displaced not only to the symbolic black flag (and indeed the word 'hang' which is the meaningful centre of the description is only present in the last chapter concealed within the apparently innocuous clause 'till the horizon was lost in the radiance of the sun hanging above it'[1]) but to the violence of the language. In spite of Hardy's notorious disclaimer in the *Life*[2], there is stylistic violence in the famous sentence 'the President of the Immortals . . . had ended his sport with Tess'. The allusion is to a Promethean song of revolt against tyranny and torture[3]; the definite description for Zeus, taken out of its original context, takes on sardonic overtones, and the metaphor of the hunt is one of inherent violence. What we have is an explosion of anger, irony giving way to sarcasm and rage, an instance of verbal violence, as if the pent-up energy of a narrator who so far had kept his distance has suddenly been liberated.

Neither the suddenness of this violence nor the narrator's previous distance should be overstressed, although the last paragraph does contrast with the subdued and symbolic rendering of the execution itself. But the retrospective reading of the novel which this ending, like all endings, provokes, will show the importance not only of violence in *Tess* — for although violence is not absent from most of Hardy's novels, the amount we find here is rather overwhelming: a rape, a murder, an execution, etc. — but also of the connection between violence and language, both as a theme (I shall try to show that to a certain extent this is a novel about language) and as a practice — I shall try to show that the violence of style is Hardy's main object in *Tess*.

I

The omnipresence of violence in *Tess* is often interpreted as tragic. In fact, the allusions in the last paragraph seem to point towards this. The President of the Immortals is clearly a tragic God, passing sentence for a fault which he himself has engineered. This is why Tess, a tragic heroine, although she is responsible for her deeds, remains a pure woman. And if one objects to this by drawing attention to the rather disrespectful tone which turns Zeus into the chairman of a limited liability company, we can answer by pointing to that well-known passage in *The Return of the Native*:

> The truth seems to be that a long line of disillusive centuries has permanently displaced the Hellenic idea of life, or whatever it may be called. What the Greeks only suspected we know well; what their Aeschylus imagined our nursery children feel.[4]

Even if tragedy proper is no longer possible, even if the tragic catastrophe has become a melodramatic *fait-divers*, even if the heroic sufferings of the aristocrat have been superseded by the banal love sorrows and *crime passionnel* of a peasant girl, the tragic rhythm and the tragic sense of violence are still with us. And it is, as we know, not really possible to reduce Tess to a mere servant girl, seduced and deserted. In fact, the interpretive devices we can use for Greek tragedies seem to apply quite aptly to Hardy's 'tragic novels'. *The Return of the Native*, for instance, has the formal structure of a tragedy according to Aristotle's categories — five of the six parts correspond to the five acts of a tragedy, and one is even entitled 'The Discovery'. In the case of *Tess* the origin of the story is to be found in the world of classical tragedy.[5] One can argue that the ending has a truly cathartic effect, and Tess appears to be the *pharmakos* of the tale — she suffers the catastrophe, she undergoes a reversal on her wedding night, although the true experience of *anagnorisis* seems to be reserved for Angel. It appears, therefore, that Hardy is using a tragic structure in both novels, even if less clearly so in *Tess*.

I would like to show, however, that this traditional interpretation is open to counter-arguments. The first is that the ending is not truly tragic. In the literal sense, of course, the novel does *not* end, since the final words are '(they) went on': the closure is also an opening. This is in no way impossible as the ending of a tragic text: once the crisis has been overcome, life goes on. Or, if we interpret this in the terms of the folk-tales with which *Tess* shares certain characteristics, 'they lived happily ever after'. After the vicissitudes of the quest, the end of the text is the beginning of an uneventful and therefore uninteresting life which the heroes fully deserve. In this case, however, the hero's princess having just been executed for murder, this uneventful life will have to be spent with another woman: we are leaving equilibrium and getting dangerously close to Freudian repetition. It is not only a question of making the best of things after the catastrophe, for the woman who replaces Tess by Angel's side is not only her sister but also, Hardy insists, her replica.[6] Is this another instance of Hardy's irony, a Hegelian repetition of tragedy as, if not farce, at least petty-bourgeois bliss? I am not sure, for *Tess* is not only riddled with repetitions, but the novel as a whole is the repetition of an *Ur-text*. If the ending opens up the possibility of a compulsive repetition of the plot — of Angel neurotically repeating with Liza-Lu, should he find her wanting, the traumatic scene of his separation from Tess — it also stresses, more importantly, the fact that the text is part of a chain of texts, each rehearsing, with due change of emphasis, the preceding one. There is, of course, no sequel to *Tess*, but the novel is the end-product of a series of texts. It repeats — in the tragic mode — two comic pieces: a poem, 'the Ruined Maid', and a shorter story, *Romantic Adventures of a Milkmaid*.[7]

In the poem, there is a straightforward inversion of judgment and expectations: the maid's ruin is obviously the cause of her success, and the innocent narrator is rebuked for hoping to attain the same elevated state ('"You ain't ruined!" said she'). In the story, we find a series of elements that are repeated, displaced or inverted in *Tess*: a socially powerful and wealthy man, whom the maid saves from suicide (instead of murdering him), and who unwittingly almost ruins her happiness; and a marriage followed by immediate separation (but this is due to the maid's rejection of her husband). Woman as the victim of social pressure, the wrong man first, whose lingering presence poisons the atmosphere, an unconsummated marriage: Hardy's imagination plays with these themes, and his text repeats itself in the system of their displacement. The main displacement is an anti-Hegelian one: the light comedy of *quid pro quo* turns into potentially tragic violence, the romantic milkmaid's happy end into catastrophe. But what turns into tragedy is not so much the plot itself (which is ambivalent — material for either a comic or a tragic version) as the narrator's language. The tragedy is not in the repetition of elements of the story but in the narrator's rage. The maid's ruin is no longer taken light-heartedly, and yet it is the same ruin. Two things have changed, which both have something to do with style — the heroine's situation, her style of life (which includes her relation to her own language), and the narrator's attitude, his style. The tragic violence is a stylistic one.

The second counter-argument is that the heroine of *Tess* is not a good *pharmakos*. True, she is the victim or the agent of violence, but it is always *at the wrong moment*. This is where comedy is repeated as tragedy. The *quid pro quo*, the missed opportunity, the wrong occasion are well known devices or themes of comedy. In Hardy's 'tragic' repetition they are translated into chance and the blindness of fate. Yet this is no mere transposition into tragedy: something of the comic origin remains in the repeated element, which means that in *Tess* the potentially tragic event occurs in the wrong (ironic) context.[8] Thus, if we compare *Tess* to the model of all tragedies, the story of Oedipus, several differences strike us. At the early stage in the story when Oedipus causes violence — by killing his father — Tess is the victim of violence: she is raped. When she in her turn becomes a murderess, it is not the direct consequence of a tragic error — as it is in the case of Oedipus, whose decision to leave Corinth turns out to be the wrong one — but rather a long term effect, more like a catastrophe than a direct result of *hamartia*. Tess wanders, like Oedipus, but her wanderings occur too early. Instead of following the catastrophe (when Oedipus flees to Colonus), most of her peregrinations, with the exception of the final flight to Stonehenge, occur well before it. There is one event, however, which seems to occur at the right moment: a journey away from home, at the beginning of the tale, a chance meeting on the road (Oedipus kills his father at a crossroads) and the death of a creature named Prince, followed by self-accusations and a sense of guilt, which are patently ominous ('Her face was dry and pale, as though she regarded herself as a murderess.'[9]). Only it is not her father she kills, but the family horse — an ironic displacement again. More generally, Tess is not a good *pharmakos* because she is a victimiser as well as a victim — much more so than a classic *pharmakos*. We are tempted to reverse the usual description and show that Tess destroys Alec's life (even before she murders him, she is the — albeit innocent — cause of his religious relapse) and brings pain and sorrow to Angel — she it is who forces him into emigration, with the subsequent illness and suffering. This deliberately biassed summary of Tess's actions is meant to show that she is not only the object, but also the subject of violence.

It could be argued, perhaps, that my second counter-argument is unconvincing, that it shows, on the part of Hardy, not so much ignorance or rejection of the rules of tragedy as a deliberate flaunting of them: what is known in pragmatics as the 'exploitation' of rules. Displacing all the tragic elements, ironically inverting them, is a way of recognising their force. But I think that much more than this is at stake. For the violence caused by or inflicted on the *pharmakos* is determined and limited by the tragic structure. It takes place in the tragic structure of events at certain moments only; the *pharmakos*'s own violence is often relegated to a mythical past, and the tragedy concentrates on his or her violent expulsion. Not so, as we have seen, in *Tess*: there violence becomes reversible, as if the contagious violence of the world of René Girard's sacrificial crisis could never end.[10] Only there is no sacrificial crisis in *Tess* but a whirl of violence, in which everybody is caught. This, again, seems to point to language — what I am describing is a situation of possession. Tess is caught in violence as the native speaker is possessed by his or her language, with no possibility of escape. Tess's prison-house is not only the violence of a male-dominated society, of the clash between social classes in a changing Wessex, it is also the prison-house of language, which inflicts violence on the subject, and is an insidious source of violent actions.

The first two counter-arguments point to language in a rather indirect fashion. The third is more directly concerned with it. For tragedy, too, assigns an important place to certain uses of language: the ambiguity of omens and prophecies, the inscription of his fate in the hero's name (*oidos pous* 'swollen foot'; *oida* 'I know'), the verbal battle of *stichomythia*, the dramatic irony and delusion of the angry speech. The first items are present in *Tess*, but the last is missing: there is no linguistic *hubris*, no expression of the tragic hero's blind anger, as in Oedipus's famous speech (or, closer to us, in the exhortations of Sir Leicester Dedlock in *Bleak House*, when Inspector Bucket pays the part of Tiresias). Not that the novel is lacking in instances of dramatic irony ('What a fresh and virginal daughter of Nature that milkmaid is'[11]), but they are disseminated all through the text, they are too numerous and too insistent to be mere elements of the tragic structure. This I take to mean that language in *Tess* is too central to be only the tool of tragedy: it is rather the content, or the reality, of the tragedy of Tess. I will try to show that the contradiction which lies at the bottom of the novel is that between two languages and two cultures, between Tess's dialect and the dominant language in her world, the Queen's English. Of course, there could still be a tragic interpretation of this: the novel as tragedy is an imaginary solution to this contradiction, exactly as Levi-Strauss interprets the myth of Oedipus[12] as a solution to the contradiction between two concep-tions of the origins of man. But again, *Tess* will not be limited by the structure of tragedy: the novel refuses to resolve the contradiction between two experiences of language; on the contrary it unfolds it, develops it to the full, pursues it to its bitter end. Tragic violence is temporary and announces equilibrium: not so the violence of language in *Tess*.

In the last paragraphs, I seem to have eaten my cake and yet attempted to have it. I have tried to show that violence in *Tess* is not mere tragic violence, and yet I have also shown that the novel has practically all the elements of a tragedy. *This* contradiction is only apparent: it is accounted for by the textual work Hardy does on classical tragedy, a system of displacements not unlike those of the Freudian dreamwork. The outcome is the disappearance of the tragic structure in the dissemination of its elements (this is where we must take the passage from *The Return of the Native* mentioned above at face value: tragedy is no longer possible). Having discarded its structural limits, violence contaminates everything, because of its links with language. The young woman is no scapegoat, but rather the embodiment, both as subject and object, of this violence. My counter-interpretation is that what she embodies is the violence of language.

Although the rest of this chapter will be an attempt to substantiate this thesis, that is, to account for the violence/woman/language nexus, a provisional definition of the phrase 'the violence of language' is in order. The first meaning it can be given is literal: certain implicit speech acts in the novel are violent (slogans, like 'THY, DAMNATION, SLUMBERETH, NOT'; the words of various quarrels, but also the insidious words of seduction). The second is social: the language of the heroine is subject to repression by the dominant idiom — this repression often takes pedagogic form. Tess, in Althusserian terms, is submitted to a process of interpellation which transforms her into a subject at the expense of her native language and culture. The process is rife with symbolic, if not physical violence. The theme of possession by language indicates the unavoidable character of this violence (ideology interpellates all individuals, without exception, into subjects).

My thesis is that the main object of the novel is this 'becoming violent' of language, to use a Deleuzian phrase. From this point of view, 'Tess' is the name for a 'collective arrangement of utterance',[13] i.e. a style as expression of a culture and a collective mode of discourse: a style of life (which is fast disappearing, because a victim of the violence of historical change), a style of speech (*'la femme, c'est le style'*: the essence of Tess is in her language, and what happens to it) and of course also, *en abyme*, a style of writing (the famous question of Hardy's style). The rest of the essay will deal with violence in relation to these two notions: woman and style.

II

The link between women and violence is a general one in Victorian fiction, where women are the main objects of physical, social and symbolic violence. Bertha Rochester has come to be regarded as the symbol of this situation. And the last page of *Jane Eyre*, in which Jane, who had obviously gained the upper hand on a slightly damaged Rochester, goes back to the conventional role of a submissive child-bearer, can be interpreted as a compromise, imposed on Charlotte Brontë's velleities of emancipation by the dominant ideology. (The refusal of any such compromise is what makes *Wuthering Heights*, in comparison, so modern.) What we usually find in Victorian novels is not so much a series of episodes in which women are the victims of violence, although these are not lacking, as a narrative structure based on their exclusion as independent individuals, separate from their gender role. Such a structure, which refuses women the position of subjects, is based

on symbolic violence. Thus, Thackeray's satire of the marriage
market as a form of oppression is well known. But we soon realise
that even his denunciation relies on this narrative structure of
exclusion. The structure has often been described as the following
system of positions:

Mother

Spinster   (woman as subject)   Whore

Virgin

The path of moral (and social) success goes from virgin to mother:
the heroine is rewarded with it in the happy ending. Two cul-
de-sacs branch off: respectable failure (becoming a spinster) or
disreputable and temporary success, followed by retribution (the
story of Becky Sharp). And of course the system is organised
around its absent centre, i.e. the position claimed by Jane Eyre
before the compromise, that of a woman who is a subject in her
own right, mistress of her words, her body, and therefore her fate.
The habitual repression of this centre explains the quasi-oxymoron
in the subtitle of *Tess*.[14] How can a 'woman' be 'pure'? The answer
is problematic only if this narrative structure is implicitly accepted.

Thus, *Tess* may be read as a reaction and a protest against this
narrative structure. In spite of another of Hardy's notorious
disclaimers ('Melius fuerat non scribere'), we must take the oxymoron in the subtitle as announcing the reinstatement of the absent
centre in its position. And we understand why the story is one of
violence: it is the story of Tess's attempt to occupy the position,
and of the violence imposed on her by social expectations which
oblige her to fulfil the roles in the structure: the unmarried and
therefore unlawful mother; the whore (the pressures of society on
the Durbeyfield family and of Alec on her combine to force Tess
into this position); the spinster — or rather the deserted wife. This
kind of interpretation insists on Tess's brave struggles, but also,
conversely, on her passivity, on her fatalism ('"If you wish", she
answered indifferently. "See how you've mastered me!"' — this
is her reply to Alec when he kisses her on their parting in Chapter
12[15]): she is the object of the violence of society.

But this interpretation does not take into account a certain
structural excess: Tess is not limited to one or two of the positions,

but occupies them all in succession. So it appears that the structure is not merely the reflection of a state of affairs existing outside the novel (in 'Victorian society', or in 'Victorian ideology'). The opposition between men and women, the various moments of which it spells out, turns out to have a chronological or narrative and a semiotic value. For the story unfolds as, in her peregrinations, Tess moves along the various positions of the structure, according to what Levi-Strauss calls the irreversible time of history or story.[16] But the opposition also has semiotic value (the various positions of the structure open up a field of differences, in the reversible time of myth or structural analysis). It is part of a series of oppositions around which the text is woven, and which can all be subsumed under the general opposition between nature and culture. First comes the opposition between history (Wessex is caught in the general change of English society in the Victorian period) and folklore (old Wessex was a self-contained world, ignorant of change and following the natural rhythm of the seasons). Then, there is the opposition between town and country — I do not claim to be the first to notice the contrast between 'd'Urber*ville*' and 'Durbey*field*', but I would like to point out that the first of these names is both insistent and coherent ('ville' repeats 'urbs'), while the second is unstable and incoherent, which hints at the fact that the world of nature, of fields and hedgerows and old families, is subject to the violence and corruption of change. Third, we find the opposition between popular literature (there are obvious elements of melodrama in *Tess* — recognitions, missed opportunities, chance meetings and a woman who pays, as in Miss Braddon's *Lady Audley's Secret*) and the high literature of classical tragedy. And last, there are also the two opposed languages already mentioned.[17]

The whole series develops the opposition between nature and culture: women, popular literature, folklore and dialect are all 'natural'. It is not only Tess who is exploited and destroyed in the novel, but the world of nature, dominated by culture and changing under its impact: landscapes, traditional social relations and customs, ways of speaking. The woman's 'closeness to nature' in a man-made world (in itself a reflection of the dominance of sexist ideology) makes Tess the vessel of natural emotion soon to be tinctured by cultural experience: the experience of meeting the dominant culture of the urban middle class.

In order to show how the opposition between nature and culture

structures the story in *Tess*, I shall offer the semblance of a
Greimasian 'semiotic square',[18] in which the structure of feminine
roles outlined above is combined with the two axes of nature and
culture. In a pastiche of Greimas, we could say that the position
which Tess occupies in the novel is determined by her relation
with men, and so by the semic opposition between wife and
mistress. Tess occupies not so much one of the four positions
produced by the square as a compromise between two of them:

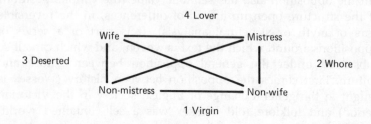

According to the narrative/chronological reading of the structure,
position 1 is the point of departure — Tess as we see her in the first
chapter. Position 2 corresponds to the situation of Tess in her
relation to Alec; 3 and 4 represent her situation in relation to Angel
after her marriage and in the final flight to Stonehenge (where the
wife, recognised as such and no longer deserted, becomes her
husband's mistress — a success story for Mills and Boon, only
caught in Hardy's ironic world, i.e. dominated by the usual sense
of doom). It is indeed clear that the plot of the novel can be
described as a journey from one of these positions to another. Let
us briefly follow Tess. Her first step, from 1 to 2, is a false start. In
her second step, from 2 back to 1, she is given a second chance
('Phase three: the Rally' — each of the steps corresponds loosely
to a 'phase' of the novel): she acquires that false virginal appearance
which strikes Angel. The third step, from 1 to 3, is 'the consequence'. Success, (the Mills and Boon story) would have meant
going straight from 1 to 4: this is made impossible by the preceding
move from 1 to 2. Her fourth step, which goes from 3 to 2, is the
relapse (Alec is not the only one to experience this: his anticipates
hers), the sign of failure. The fifth and last step, from 2 to 4, might
be called using Hardy's discarded subtitle, 'Too late beloved'.

So far, this is not much more than a summary of the plot, strictly
corresponding to Hardy's explicit intentions. But I would like to
make three remarks, thus beginning to interpret the structure

'semiotically', as a logical space. First, Hardy is indeed exploiting (in the pragmatic sense of the term) the ideological narrative scheme presented above: the important pole of motherhood has been replaced by the 'lover' position, which can be interpreted as the reappearance of the absent centre. Secondly, he is also exploiting a simple melodramatic story, a pre-Mills and Boon success-through-love novel: the 'absent centre' has reappeared not as the centre (in terms of which the other positions are given), but in the ideological position of the pole of success, the position which the heroine occupies in the happy ending. This imposition of chronological direction on a logical space is typical of the ideological conception of narrative on which Hardy is dependent but which he is also attempting to subvert. Thirdly, the two axes along which the steps are taken represent the opposition between nature and culture. We can define a horizontal axis of exclusion, of culture (from 'deserted' to 'whore': the expulsion of the woman–scapegoat by the cultural laws governing marriage and by the moral laws of society: it is Angel's narrow-minded morality, the result of cultural training, not natural impulse, which eventually forces Tess along that path), and a vertical axis of nature, where the virgin, conforming to the natural laws of the heart and to the natural affections of the body becomes a lover — and this potential is what Angel fails

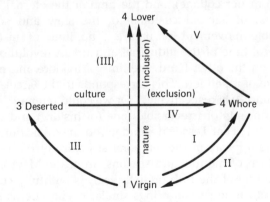

STEPS: I False start
           II Second chance
         III Consequence
       (III) Success
        IV Failure
         V Too late beloved

to recognise in Tess: had he listened to his natural impulse, he would have realised that Tess is truly, although the mother of an illegitimate child, 'a virginal daughter of nature'. I therefore propose the improved diagram shown on page 11.

Two things are apparent in this. One, the axis of nature is the axis of success and happiness, the axis of culture one of unhappiness and failure (any movement away from the vertical axis causes unhappiness). The logic of Tess's relapse is the logic of the cultural axis, the logic of exclusion. Two, the axis of culture functions as a bar which Tess cannot cross, except at the moment of her death: culture and history kill her. This is to show that I have not strayed from my subject, that the relation between the two axes is one of violence. Going from the chronological interpretation of the diagram (a sequence of moves) to the 'semiotic' one (a field of differential positions) shows that the text functions as a locus for contradictions. As the term 'contradiction' indicates, the violence in the text has something to do with language.

Let us, for instance, go back to the still rather sketchy notions of 'history' and 'folklore'. The first step is to realise that in *Tess* there coexist two conceptions of time: the time of tragic tension, disruptive change and violence, the historical–cultural time of the uprooting of a part of rural society (as appears in Mrs. Durbeyfield's removal from her cottage); and the time of the eternal return of the seasons, of age-old customs, of the slow and sometimes imperceptible movement of nature. The time of history, the chronological time of the industrial and urban revolution on the one hand; on the other hand, the time of folklore and myth, the cyclical time of repetition. This corresponds to the Greek concepts of *Chronos* and *Aiôn* respectively.[19] Or we could refer again to Levi-Strauss's concepts of irreversible time (of history) and reversible time (of myth). That Tess is dependent on the cyclic time of myth and folklore appears in the temporal structure of the novel. The regular return of months and seasons, from the May of the first year to the July of the fifth or sixth year, is faithfully chronicled, and each returning season brings similar events, i.e. is endowed with symbolic meaning — rape in September, the death of Tess's child in August, her own execution in July: summer is the season of violence and death. The cyclic time also appears in the repetition of the episodes (for instance in the repetition of her fall with Alec). That she is also caught in the irreversible time of history, where the past cannot be undone, and the present is dominated by the tension towards the tragic catastrophe, appears in the *fuite en avant* of her adventures, as well as in the fact that her seduction is the ironically dissymmetric repetition of her aristocratic ancestors' infamous deeds:

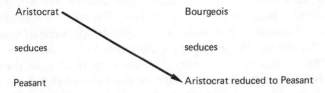

Aristocrat   Bourgeois

seduces   seduces

Peasant   Aristocrat reduced to Peasant

The arrow indicates that the repetition is oriented: historical time is a constant displacement.

But Tess's link to folklore is not limited to time. In a passage which has attracted little attention, Tess tells dairyman Crick about her belief in ghosts: 'I do know that our souls can be made to go outside our bodies when we are alive . . . A very easy way to feel 'em go . . . is to lie on the grass at night and look straight up at some big bright star; and by fixing your mind upon it, you will soon find that you are hundreds and hundreds o' miles away from your body, which you don't seem to want at all.'[20] This instance of Tess's participation in the beliefs of her people, in their folklore, finds curious corroboration in the description, by the Italian historian Carlo Ginzburg, of the sixteenth-century sect of the *benandanti*,[21] who claimed to leave their bodies at night and to 'walk in defence of Good', fighting witches with wands of sorghum (and indeed we recall that the Marlott club 'lived to uphold the local Cerealia' and that 'every woman and girl carried in her hand a peeled willow wand'[22]). Ginzburg sees in this a survival, in Christian times, of old fertility rites: Tess is a link in an immemorial religious chain, she is steeped in the traditions of the countryside ('a daughter of Nature' is what a *benandante* is, a resurgence of Demeter). There is no question here of picturesque folklore for antiquarians like Parson Tringham, but a deep impregnation by a culture and its language.

But Tess is also subjected to the violence of history, in the light of which this culture disintegrates: 'all that is solid melts into air', to use the Marxian phrase. For history is violence. It breaks into the rhythms of traditional life (cf. the celebrated threshing machine scene in Chapter 47, complete with Hellish steam engine and minor devil in the shape of the engineer), it enters into Tess's life

by effraction, by a sort of rape, it uproots her family and in the
end destroys her. Her execution, both final and irreversible, is the
very illustration of historical time. The movement of the novel goes
from a folk-opening, in the Cerealia scene, to a historical closure.

This opposition between folklore and history has a linguistic
equivalent. There are two voices in *Tess*. The voice of folklore (the
dialect, of course, but also the proverbs like 'All is fair in love and
war', the clichés, the metaphors, the customs and the stories that
form the culture of the countryside: the voice of Mrs. Durbeyfield
with her Complete Fortune Teller, or the voice of dairyman Crick
telling the story of Jack Dollop) and the voice of history —
the Queen's English, the voice of education, of established and
enlightened religion and morality, the voice of industry and
commerce, useful knowledge and progress: Alec and Angel, each
in his different tone, speak this language). The tragedy of Tess is
that she is crushed between these two voices: she speaks English
at school, and dialect at home, she is made to learn English, and
is duly subjected to linguistic and pedagogic violence — this is one
of the outcomes of her seduction. No wonder that, when Angel is
falling in love with her, he offers to teach her, and in particular to
teach her *history*. No wonder Alec, when he meets her again,
exclaims: 'Who has taught you such good English?''[23] In the novel,
as in Tess, two cultures and two languages clash: this violence is
at the unstable centre of Tess's world.

The difficulty with this interpretation is that it makes Tess too
much of a victim, too much the object of violence, whereas I would
like to take into account the fact that she is also the subject of
violence.

In fact, the role of women in *Tess*, in their relation to violence,
might be the object of two types of interpretation. The first is
structuralist: Tess is an essentially passive character, she submits
to events, she moves around Wessex not so much as the agent of
her actions but rather as the patient of other people's actions. In
structuralist terms, she is in the position of the 'empty square' (*case
vide*), the element in the structure which, meaningless itself, moves
from position to position and gives them meaning by establishing
a network of relationships. The best fictional instance of this is Jo
in *Bleak House*. He keeps moving on, he is nobody, has no family,
no past, no future, he 'knows nothink'. As a character, he is a
complete blank. But by moving on, he establishes connections
between places and people, he weaves a web of relationships

between the numerous characters in the novel. He gives them meaning by marking their place in the overall structure; he also gives them, of course, smallpox — an apt symbol. Tess, as we know, also moves on. She it is who goes to Alec; she visits Angel's home in Emminster, she tramps the roads of Wessex. Her peregrinations delineate the spatial structure of Wessex: home bases (Marlott, Trantridge, Emminster), places of convergence, where the main characters meet when they leave home (Talbothays, the hub of the universe, and its opposite, the Hell of Flintcomb Ash), and places of divergence, where the characters part or are separated by fate (Kingsbere, Sandbourne, Stonehenge). And of course the meaning assigned by Tess's moves is not restricted to places. Alec and Angel are also given their roles as Tess moves on: the seducer, the lover, the estranged husband. Let us remember Tess's passivity when faced with Angel's decision to part with her. Hardy insists that she might have kept him had she made a gesture. This is the essence of the 'empty square' character: her passivity forces other characters to act, to reveal what they are, to assume their position in the narrative structure.

But here it appears that Tess's passivity is illusory, and I pass on to my second interpretation. What circulates in *Tess* is more than a mere 'empty square', it is rather a quantum of energy, a source of violence, which is always trying to breach the limits of its territory, to break out (she succeeds in doing so right at the end, after the murder, when her potential violence has at last erupted: neither Stonehenge nor Wintoncester is in the deep heart of Wessex ('South Wessex') that is the landscape of the rest of the novel). The meaning Tess gives to the other characters as she seeks them out is that she brings out the physical or moral violence which was inherent in them. This is why *Tess* is not a tragedy. We must read Girard backwards. The movement of the story does not go from a primitive form of law (the sacrifice) to our modern version ('Justice was done'), but rather, regressively, towards the pagan origins of our society (in this sense Tess *is* a *benandante*), towards the violent origin of justice in sacrifice. Tess is the sacrificed witch; she tears the veil of the civilised morality of modern society and provokes a regression to the original, founding violence. She is an *antipharmakos*, whose function it is to revive the forgotten sins of the city, to re-establish the reign of chaos in the midst of the cosmos.

This is a schizoanalytic interpretation.[24] Tess's wanderings are

read as a *fuite en avant*; she follows her lines of flight, is deterritori-
alised and attempts to reterritorialise herself. In other words, her
actions can be interpreted along two different lines. Either one
sees her as repressed and kept in her place by society, the victim
of the brotherhood of men, 'triangulated', i.e. safely imprisoned
within the bounds of a social and family role (the metaphor is both
geographic and psychoanalytic) — a paranoid reading. Or one sees
her as struggling for the free expression of her desire, breaking
the bounds of authority (for instance, in her relations with the
established church), following the lines of her destiny — a schizophrenic reading. In the former case, the character of Tess is
interpreted in terms of lack (the passivity of Tess as a victim); in
the latter, in terms of excess (the excess of Tess's desire, of her
flight, of her violence). That both interpretations are correct can
be shown by a comparison between *Tess* and a contemporary text,
Dracula. For the position of women in *Dracula* — undoubtedly a
sexist piece — is ambiguous. They are placed on the usual pedestal
(cf. Van Helsing enthusing over the purity of 'madam Mina'), and
put down with the utmost cruelty, as appears in the sadistic
destruction of Lucy the vampire, a collective rape by the (latently)
homosexual group of positive characters. Women in fact are the
weak link in the human chain: their sexual attraction (in both the
subjective and the objective sense) makes them Dracula's natural
allies. Thus, Dracula fails to vampirise Jonathan Harker when he
has him safely in his power, but repeatedly attempts to vampirise
his wife in the most dangerous circumstances. What *Dracula*
expresses is the male fear of the violence that is in women, the
violence of blood and sex, a fear which is expressed, through
typical projection, in the numerous scenes of rape that make up
the novel. Going back to Tess, we realise that in a way she too is
in the position of Lucy. The themes of blood (with the symbolic
use of the colour red), of contamination and of the chase can also
be found in *Tess*. She too is up against a group of men bent on her
destruction, even if they are not as conscious of it as they are in
Dracula. Ancestral tombs, rape in the autumn mist, unholy religious
ceremonies (the baptism of the child): this is the world of Lucy the
vampire.

I am fully aware of the excessive character of my comparison.
But this excess is precisely what I want to point up: it is not only
in the interpretation, but also in the text, where its violence is felt
everywhere. In the terms of Deleuze and Guattari, the construction

of a hierarchic social, moral and religious order (the metaphor for which is the tree) is always threatened by the anarchic branchings and the violent tearings of Tess's rhizomatic progress.[25] Nowhere is this schizophrenic breaching of frontiers more apparent than in language.

III

I have at last reached the centre of my argument: violence in *Tess* is primarily linguistic. We have in fact already encountered several instances of such violence. Let us go back to the pedagogic violence of Angel's teaching (that there is such a thing needs to be proved). Tess is peeling lords and ladies, an old custom in her culture, and ironically expresses the truth about the situation: 'I meant there are always more ladies than lords when you come to peel them.'[26] Angel replies: 'Never mind about the lords and ladies. Would you like to take up any course of study — history for instance?' In this scene, a pre-linguistic semiotic activity, a game which does not need elaborate language, is repressed by the articulate language of the dominant culture. Exactly as the unspoken past, which flows in Tess's veins, must be replaced by the spoken past, history as 'a course of study'. Angel's question, in spite of appearances, does not allow Tess any choice: it is preceded by an imperative, and takes on the force of an order (if she wants to reach Angel's elevated position, to be worthy of him, she *must* abandon her culture and her language, she must study). We are entering the world of Deleuze and Guattari's 'signifying semiotics', as opposed to the 'pre-signifying semiotics' of dance and gestures, where the origin of the sentence is the slogan (the imperative mood, or the performative verb implicit in the deep structure of all sentences), where there is no direct speech, only the repetition, as indirect speech, of collective slogans. 'THY, DAMNATION, SLUMBER-ETH, NOT. 2. PET.ii.3.'[27] What is striking about this sentence is the commas that separate the words, thus turning them into the repetition, or quotation, of authoritative speech, in short into a slogan (and the authority which transforms the sentence into an injunction is duly mentioned). The conception of language which we find in Deleuze and Guattari's *Mille Plateaux* (especially in *plateau* no. 4, 'The four postulates of linguistics') provides an account of violence in language. One of the aspects of post-Saussurian linguistics which they criticise is the postulate of a standard language. This theoretical linguistics disregards dialectal variations, whether social or geographical, for it needs to study a stable object. What Deleuze and Guattari point out is that there is no stability in language, that it is a violent and unstable mixture of dialects. I shall add one more source of violence. Another of the postulates of theoretical linguistics, which they do not attack directly, is that of synchrony: for its object to remain stable, linguistics must disregard diachronic variations (or at least carefully separate the two fields of study). But a synchronic state of the language is an abstract construct. In reality, what we find — and this is particularly obvious in *Tess* — is an unstable mixture of various historical layers of language, all combining into a corrupt whole.

The postulate of a standard language has to be abandoned when we realise that a natural language is a battlefield for the struggles between a *major* and various *minor* dialects.[28] Thus, Kafka writes in German, the major dialect of the Austrian empire, but from the linguistic position of a Czech Jew; Yiddish and Czech struggle against the dominant German to produce Kafka's own dialect, his style. In the same way, Tess has to express herself in a no-woman's speech, situated between the dialect of her forefathers and the English of her men. Hers is a situation of minority, by which we must also understand her personal and social minority, her position of irresponsibility as a child or a woman — but also the fact that she and the likes of her are historically 'in a minority', expelled from their traditional territories by the invasion of the urban 'majority'. And this also has consequences for the language of the majority: it threatens and destabilises it. English, far from being reducible to a 'standard language' is the totality of major and minor dialects. If the minor dialect of Wessex is repressed or destroyed by the Queen's English, the process can also be reversed, and both Alec and Angel lose some of their linguistic sense of superiority in their contact with Tess. There is a clash, a source of uncertainty to all concerned, a source of violence also. Angel's adoption of the Wessex phrase, 'a drop of pretty tipple' (p. 155) shocks his brothers, who have been to Cambridge. Tess's description of her family origins, 'we have an old seal, marked with a ramping lion on a shield . . . and we have a very old silver spoon' is corrected by Alec: 'A castle argent is certainly my crest . . . And my arms a lion rampant' (p. 34). The technical terms of heraldry come from the French, whereas Tess's 'mistakes' have a distinctly English sound.

The violence of language — nothing as picturesque as rape or murder, of course — apears here in the following nexus: blood (the origin) — language (French vs English) — sex (one of the meanings of 'rampant', so my edition informs me, is 'lustful').

The postulate of a synchronic *langue* must also be abandoned if we realise that language is subject to historical forces, that it is always uttered by a collective arrangement of utterance, in a historical conjuncture: the slogan which provides the deep structure for a sentence is historically determined. Instead of a stable synchronic structure, we have an unstable diachronic process of 'becoming' (*devenir*), subject to the violence of corruption.

This is apparent in *names*. One may recall here Derrida's theory of the violence inherent in proper names.[29] This instability is obvious in the very title of *Tess* — it is not only the subtitle which reminds us of an oxymoron. If Tess Durbeyfield is a corruption of Teresa d'Urberville, we must note that the title combines the nickname (an instance of corruption) and the archaic name. And we can try and follow this process of linguistic corruption: the unchanged element is the syllable *urb*, which contains the 'ur' characteristic of Tess's dialect: 'the characteristic intonation of that dialect for this district being the voicing approximately rendered by the syllable UR, probably as rich an utterance as any to be found in human speech' (p. 9). Here, the situation is reversed: far from being a corruption of pure English, the dialect appears as the rich *Ur-sprache* in which meaning is preserved ('as rich an utterance'), exactly as the country girl is the true descendant of the archaic nobility, much more so than the *nouveau riche* impostor who has appropriated her name, or the petty-bourgeois who dominate her world. So there is violence in proper names. Tess's name is the locus of a struggle for appropriation (of her name by Alec, of her person by the ancient d'Urbervilles, whose name governs her destiny) in a process which Deleuze and Guattari might describe as one of deterritorialisation/reterritorialisation: being chased from Marlott, obliged to seek work elsewhere, to move from the almost ancestral cottage, as the third life comes to an end, finding one's ancestors by camping in the family vault at Kingsbere.

The phrase 'the corruption of language' is ambiguous between an objective and a subjective genitive: language corrupts, it is corrupt or corrupted. There is violence in both cases. Language corrupts Tess: the contrast between the opening scene, where she keeps silent, and the explanation scene, when she tells Angel at last, is striking. Words do not favour Tess: they create misunderstanding, and in spite of appearances explanations are the opposite of a clarification. They only induce in Angel an unnatural — because culturally determined — hardness of heart. It is when he is 'taken in' by Tess's appearance, by her behaviour, by her gestures, that Angel is *intuitively* right. The explanation scene clears that 'mistake' only by replacing it with a deeper mistake. Far from expressing the truth of the matter, language is the bearer of hypocrisy and illusion. The consequences are duly violent.

But language corrupts because it is corrupt. Tess is not an actor in a synchronic system of communication, a linguistic cosmos, exchanging messages and performing felicitous speech acts. She has to come to terms with the chaos of linguistic corruption. It is not only her name which undergoes the process: customs disappear, words change meaning (the 'lords and ladies' passage is a good example of this — and of Hardy's ironic skill — for 'the terms LORD and LADY, which nowadays refer to high positions of the social order, must originally be seen in the context of an agricultural society: OE *hlāford* and *hlǣfdige* were compounds with *hlāf* 'bread' as their first element'[30]). Perhaps the exact term is 'corrupted' rather than 'corrupt'. For it is ironic that the dialect, which is being superseded by the national tongue for obvious historical reasons, should be less corrupt, less subject to change (because the time of folklore is *aiôn* and not *chronos*), closer to the English of Chaucer and Shakespeare than modern speech. Tess's name is 'corrupt', her blood is tainted because the energy of her line is spent (this is Angel's vision of 'old families'), but her speech is closer to the origins and to nature than Alec's or Angel's. This is her contradiction — the core of the linguistic violence to which she is subjected; on the one hand, she is caught in historical change, the corrupt descendant of a long line of ancestors; on the other hand, she has remained close to nature, and is corrupted — as her dialect is corrupted — by culture and history.

At this point it appears that linguistic corruption is (a) the tenor of a metaphor, the vehicle of which is decay and rottenness, and (b) the vehicle of a metaphor, the tenor of which is moral corruption. The tenor: linguistic corruption is embodied in images of decay (the tombs, the recurrent mention of the old d'Urbervilles) which offer a concrete version of the abstract corruption of language and society. The vehicle: linguistic corruption is the outward sign of the moral corruption which cankers the main characters. Alec, with his sensuousness and his lapses, is corruption incarnate: the serpent does not bother to disguise himself. Angel, a serpent in angel's garb, embodies the sly corruption of pride, narrow-mindedness and conventionality: his temptation is all the more devastating as it is offered with the best of intentions. Confronted with this double serpent, what can Tess, a daughter of nature, do, except be a daughter of Eve, and follow her mother's advice (and Mrs. Durbeyfield is always ready with ill advice). The very first letter of her name, in the shape of a cross, the cross of St Anthony, a saint celebrated for his temptation, but also in the shape of a gallows, indicates her fate — it is not only inscribed in her speech, but in the writing of her name.

In the light of Deleuze and Guattari's analyses, I can now propose a better definition of the phrase 'the violence of language'. It has literal meaning (the illocutionary force of the slogan which is to be found beneath every utterance), symbolic meaning (language is an unstable rhizome-like proliferation, rather than a hierarchically ordered tree-like structure; it is subject to the corruption of diachrony). And it is itself contradictory and unstable, for the violence of language has two sources: the paranoid violence of triangulation, which interpellates the individual into a subject; and the schizophrenic violence of the subject's attempt at liberation, when he or she crosses the frontiers, follows his or her lines of flight. This is why Tess is not only the object, but also the subject of violence.

So the violence of language is central in *Tess*. But it does not only concern the heroine: an obvious *abyme* makes it also the violence of the author's style. For Tess's linguistic and social minority, which determines her subject position, is close to Hardy's. Her difficult relation to language is paralleled in the contradiction of Hardy's style. What Tess embodies is perhaps not so much the position of women in late Victorian times: the social minority of the heroine becomes a metaphor for the minority of the author's writing, for the struggle of his style against the major, i.e. established, literary English. Seen in this light, the plot of the novel is a reflection of Hardy's linguistic strategy.

There is indeed a striking parallel between Tess's relation to language and Hardy's. She is torn between two languages and two lives, he is torn between three lives and several languages, as a well-known passage in his autobiography notes: 'his inner life

. . . might almost have been called academic — a triple existence unusual for a young man — what he used to call, in looking back, a life twisted of three strands — the professional life, the scholar's life and the rustic life.'[31] As in *Tess*, the languages which correspond to the three lives, tend to clash. Tess, as we have seen, they destroy — with Hardy, according to the critics, they threaten his style. A common type of criticism of Hardy is that sometimes he writes well, and sometimes atrociously. He himself was conscious of this 'stylelessness': he wanted to improve his style, and for that purpose read Addison and *The Times*, much to the scandal of the academic critic.

And it is certainly true that Hardy speaks several languages, that, to use his own metaphor, his text is woven of several strands of discourse. There are at least two Hardys: the speaker of dialect — often with rich comic or dramatic effect — and the reader of penny cyclopaedias, desirous to share his knowledge. The usual criticism accuses him of being a pedant, as a compensation for being an autodidact. Raymond Williams has exploded this myth.[32] The truth is that in his writing, as in the story of Tess, the themes of language and school are inextricably mixed. It is at school that one learns the correct language, at university that one is taught to write in the approved style.

For an author who finds himself in Hardy's position, a position of linguistic plurality and contradiction, of potential stylistic violence, there are two solutions: suture or polyphony. Suture, a psychoanalytic concept,[33] means the weaving together at all costs of the various threads of the text into a unified whole — an obsessional activity, a case of paranoid repression. A 'polished' style, as approved by Dr Johnson and his disciples, is the result of suture: all contradictions, all dialectical variations are erased in the perfection of a unified text. The major has eaten up the minor — a situation which is obviously rife with the violence of repression. The other choice, a more difficult one, is to let violence erupt on the surface of the text, to follow the lines of flight it indicates, to let the minor voices engage in their babble/Babel, in other words not to erase the contradictions from the text. To describe this choice, we can borrow Bakhtin's term, 'polyphony'. And this is indeed Hardy's choice: he accepts the violence of an unstable language as an integral part of his style, he lets the different languages within him speak out and contradict one another. This is why the narrator speaks like Tess, but also like Alec and Angel; why he indulges in flights of lyrical fancy, and also speaks the pedantic words of improving knowledge. Hence this impression of instability, of eruptive violence. This is a style which is not as controlled as the academic critic — I am thinking of David Cecil[34] — would wish it. And it is the stylistic equivalent of Tess's position in the novel.

Against the academic critic, we shall maintain that this style, with all its 'defects' (which are only the symptoms of linguistic violence) is particularly apt, that it is faithful to the violent reality of language. If the novel is based on a contradiction (if it is a myth retelling the age-old opposition between Nature and Culture, folklore and history, *aiôn* and *chronos*), and if this narrative contradiction is a metaphor for the instability and violence of language, Hardy's own stylistic contradiction is the best possible reflection of this. Hardy's stylistic gift is that he dares unleash the violence of language, that he does not attempt a mythical solution to the contradiction, but lets it stand and be perceived.

To sum up. Starting from the theme of physical violence in *Tess*, i.e. violence in the strictest sense, I have tried to show that another type of violence is at the centre of the novel: symbolic violence, the preferred locus of which is language. The novel is about the passage from the one to the other — and, *en abyme*, the novel is also about the violence of style: in *Tess* Hardy comes to terms with his own linguistic contradictions. The position of women in *Tess* I have interpreted as the crucial point where physical violence becomes symbolic: Tess is subjected *to* physical violence, she is subjected *by*, i.e. made a subject by, a process of symbolic violence, in which her relation to language plays the essential part. Behind my reading of the novel, there is a rather contentious theory of violence, distinctly continental in flavour.[35] I make no apology for this: it allows me to move from a purely metaphorical conception of the violence of Hardy's language, interpreted in psychological terms as the expression of his 'rage', to a more literal description of the violence of language as constitutive of his style.

Notes

1. *Tess of the d'Urbervilles*, p. 387. All the references are to the Everyman edition (London, 1984).
2. F. E. Hardy, *The Life of Thomas Hardy* (London: Macmillan, 1962) pp. 243–4.

3. It comes from Aeschylus, *Prometheus Bound*, I, 169.
4. *The Return of the Native* (London: Macmillan, 1974), p. 191.
5. The *Life* quotes this 'casual thought', jotted down when Hardy had started writing *Tess*: 'When a married woman who has a lover kills her husband, she does not really wish to kill the husband; she wishes to kill the situation. Of course in Clytaemnestra's case it was not exactly so, since there was the added grievance of Iphigenia, which half justified her', Hardy, *Life*, p. 221.
6. See *Tess*, p. 384.
7. In *A Changed Man*, 1913. See G. Wing, 'Tess and the Romantic Milkmaid', *Review of English Literature*, III, (1962), pp. 22–30.
8. Hardy is a master at this game: cf. the reference to Keelwell's marmalade in the scene of the baby's burial.
9. *Tess*, p. 28.
10. R. Girard, *La violence et le sacré* (Paris: Grasset, 1972).
11. *Tess*, p. 116.
12. C. Levi-Strauss, 'The Structural Study of Myth', in *Structural Anthropology* (New York: Basic, 1963).
13. G. Deleuze and F. Guattari, *Mille Plateaux* (Paris: Minuit, 1980). For the English terms, see the glossary to F. Guattari, *Molecular Revolution* (Harmondsworth: Penguin, 1984).
14. Oxymoron is a favourite trope in the rhetoric of titles: see the title of a Mills and Boon romance, *Forbidden Rapture*, or *Lady Audley's Secret*: she may be a lady, but there is a secret in her life; she is pure, and yet she is a woman.
15. *Tess*, p. 74.
16. Levi-Strauss, 'Structural Study'.
17. The 'metaphysical' nature of the oppositions on which our culture is founded, indeed of the very concept of a binary opposition, is a well-known theme in Derrida. Following F. Jameson (*The Political Unconscious*, Ithaca: Cornell University Press, 1981), we must historicise the concept. The series of antinomies which I analyse determines the ideological closure of Hardy's text. The violence of Hardy's style lies in his attempt at making these antinomies problematic, at treating them as contradictions.
18. I do not claim to be faithful to Greimas's method. My use of his semiotic square is similar to Jameson's, in *Political Unconscious*.
19. See G. Deleuze, *Logique du sens* (Paris: Minuit, 1969), pp. 77–81.
20. *Tess*, pp. 115–16.
21. C. Ginzburg, *I Benandanti* (Turin: Einaudi, 1966). A similar episode can be found in the sleepwalking scene in *Silas Marner*.
22. *Tess*, p. 7.
23. *Tess*, p. 301.
24. On the concept of 'schizoanalysis' see Deleuze and Guattari, *Anti-Oedipus*, passim.
25. See Deleuze and Guattari, *Mille Plateaux*, for a systematic development of this opposition.
26. *Tess*, p. 122.
27. Ibid., p. 76.

28. See Deleuze and Guattari, *Kafka* (Paris: Minuit, 1975), especially pp. 33–45.
29. J. Derrida, *De la grammatologie* (Paris: Minuit, 1967), p. 162 (English translation by Gayatri Chakravorty Spivak *Of Grammatology*, Baltimore: Johns Hopkins University Press, 1976).
30. A. Bammesberger, *English Etymology* (Heidelberg: Carl Winter, 1986), p. 99.
31. F. E. Hardy, *Life*, pp. 32–3.
32. See R. Williams, *The Country and the City* (London: Chatto & Windus, 1973), ch. 18; see also T. Eagleton, *Walter Benjamin* (London; Verso, 1981), p. 129.
33. See J. A. Miller, 'La suture — éléments de la logique du signifiant', *Cahiers pour l'analyse*, 1 (Paris, 1966) (English translation in *Screen*, Winter 1977/8, vol. 18, no. 4). For the use of the concept in the field of political science, see E. Laclau and C. Mouffe, *Hegemony and Socialist Strategy* (London: Verso, 1985).
34. D. Cecil, *Hardy the Novelist* (London: Constable, 1943). Apart from the notorious strictures on Hardy's style and the rather snobbish assessment of his lack of formal education, the book contains many remarkable insights.
35. See the use of the concept 'violence' in the Marxist tradition, for instance in Althusser's distinction between repressive and ideological apparatuses; see his 'Ideology and Ideological State Apparatuses', in *Lenin and Philosophy*, translated by B. Brewster (London: New Left Books, 1977).

2

Ill Wit and Sick Tragedy: *Jude the Obscure*

Christine Brooke-Rose

WHY MUST JUDE SUFFER SO?

In an interesting essay, John Goode analyses Hardy's most controversial character, Sue Bridehead, as an image in Jude's life, whose
function is to open a gap between what she says and the way she
is understood, and he argues that we go seriously wrong in
treating *Jude* 'in terms of a representation which we then find
"incomprehensible", for it is the incomprehensibility that constitutes the novel's effect'.[1]

What is interesting about Goode's essay is that while insisting
that representational readings (sexist, feminist or whatever) are
wrong, he inverts, to do so, the type of representational reading
that blames Sue: in a naturalistic interpretation, he says, we would
question the absurdity of Jude's lack of understanding.

> Sue is driven round the country by prejudice and poverty, stuck
> in Christminster by Jude's obsession, and her children are killed
> by Jude's son whom she has made her own . . . But we
> don't consider it naturalistically because we never ask what is
> happening to Sue, it is Sue happening to Jude. So what matters
> is where this reaction puts her, rather than why it came about.[2]

Or again, J. Hillis Miller takes up Hardy's insistent question
'why does Tess suffer so?', which has led critics to assume that
they must find a cause (and a single one), whereas, although
Hardy's work is over-determined, 'the problem is not that there
are no explanations proposed in the text but that there are too
many . . . incompatible causes . . . There is no "original version",
only an endless sequence of them . . . always recorded from some
previously existing exemplar.'[3] For Hillis Miller is exploring the

26

functioning of two different kinds of repetition, as proposed by Deleuze:[4] the Platonic (representations, or the world as icon) and the Nietzschean (simulacra, or the world as phantasm).

It is this kind of functioning in *Jude the Obscure* that I would like to explore, not so much with reference to Sue vs Jude, nor to repetition, but with reference to the problem of knowledge, in fiction generally, in Hardy, in *Jude*.

'BOOKS AND OTHER IMPEDIMENTA' (I.i)

That Hardy, deprived of university education, became obsessed with the acquisition of knowledge and methodical note-taking for incorporation of 'items' into his novels, is particularly stressed in Gittings' biography,[5] as well as his general conviction that everything could be learnt, even the writing of poetry, by consulting the right books. It is this last aspect which is so savagely treated in *Jude*. That he also became a very well-educated man 'in a way that Dickens, Trollope and James were not', as argued by Rehder,[6] is no doubt true but irrelevant to my purpose. What interests me here is the peculiar intensity and the intense peculiarity of Hardy's use of knowledge in *Jude the Obscure*, not only as narrative theme but as narration itself.

As narrative theme, it has been amply (and, of course, contradictorily) treated and I shall merely summarise my reading. There is the clear equivalence of intellectual knowledge and carnal knowledge, each proving evasive and illusory, each killed by the 'letter' of the epigraph. Knowledge is desire and Christminster is clearly female: 'like a young lover alluding to his mistress' (I.iii); or female fused with Christ: 'my Alma Mater, and I'll be her beloved son, in whom she shall be well pleased' (I.vi); the recurrent image of the wall that keeps him out (e.g. II.ii) is paralleled by Sue's behaviour and by: 'Now that the high window-sill stood between them, so that he could not get at her, she seemed not to mind . . .' (IV.i); and when he has lost both, it is Sue who becomes a ghostly presence in Christminster, replacing that of poets and divines (III.viii). As Rehder puts it: 'The tragedy in Hardy's novels is often the end of a dream. The awakening is a prelude to destruction, as if knowledge were forbidden . . . knowledge comes with the force of a blow.'[7]

But the two types of knowledge are also antagonistic, and Jude is perfectly aware, both during and after the early relationships,

that two women have prevented his studies (I.ix, II.iv, IV.iii). At
the same time the reader is made aware that Jude falls, with varying
degrees of blindness, into every trap, and that his problematic love
for Sue replaces (at least in the narration) his single-minded project
of 'reading most of the night after working all day' (II.ii).

There are also complex polarities between types of knowledge,
first of all and very early (I.v), between knowledge as classics and
knowledge as theology, a tug also incarnated by Sue herself as
'pagan' versus Jude as Christian, with the parallel reversal which
is the basis of the novel's structure. But both these unite against
other knowledge, as when Jude 'reads', as craftsman, 'the number-
less architectural pages around him' (II.ii), and has 'a true illumination; that here in the stone yard was a centre of effort as worthy
as that dignified by the name of scholarly study' — though the
narrator steps in: 'But he lost it under the stress of his old idea'
(II.ii). And after the crash of his dream he discovers for a moment,
though as mere spectator still, 'the real Christminster life' and that
'the town life was a book of humanity' (II.vi). A deal of reading,
but of what might be called 'ordinary' knowledge. It is thus rather
odd to find him opposing Divinity as 'ordinary' knowledge to
classics and a moment later also reducing the classics to 'the
ordinary classical grind': 'It was a new idea . . . A man could
preach and do good without taking double-firsts in the schools of
Christminster or having anything but ordinary knowledge . . . it
would be necessary that he should continue for a time to work at
his trade while reading up Divinity, which he had neglected at
Christminster for the ordinary classical grind' (III.i).

For what, finally, is 'ordinary' knowledge? In Tinker Taylor's
words: 'I always saw there was more to be learnt outside a book
than in' (II.vii). But knowledge, whatever it is of, is always a taking
IN what is OUT, in order to pass it OUT again, in teaching, in
bringing up, in communicating, in living: like money or other
acquisitions, you can't take it with you.

And yet, though Jude has read and experienced much, he does
not die with greater self-knowledge, or even with the deep
knowledge of the other that he thought he had. It is news (event)
rather than knowledge as such that 'comes with the force of a
blow', and his bookish quotation from *Job* as he dies seems
abysmally bathetic and irrelevant, as does that from *Agamemnon*
after the children's death; and Sue's reaction to it is amazingly
condescending in the circumstances:

My poor Jude — how you've missed everything! you more than
I, for I did get you! [he got her too, so she must mean he didn't
to the same full extent] To think that you should know that by
unassisted reading, and yet be in poverty and despair! (VI.ii)

In no novel that I have ever read do words of knowledge seem
to occur quite so frequently. The plot manipulations depend on it
(knowledge as secrecy and revelation), as do all the thematic
elements: knowledge as books ('books and other *impedimenta*' says
the narrator, of Phillotson's baggage in the first chapter, and we
need the knowledge that the Latin plural means baggage, to see
the full irony); knowledge as common sense, as craftsmanship, as
superstition, as misleading ignorance from others; knowledge like
money, as access to knowledge ('to get ready by accumulating
money and knowledge', II.ii); knowledge as self-awareness, as
knowledge of the other, perpetually contradicted, or as fear of the
other's knowledge, or as self-assurance (Phillotson in VI.v, 'they
don't know Sue as I do', or Sue in VI.iii, 'I am convinced I am
right'); as public knowledge of private facts: for their troubles, too,
are partly due to the paradox that their illicit union gets 'known',
so that they have to keep going to where they are 'unknown',
while inversely, the theme of legalistic marriage depends also on
knowledge, or not, of consummation ('if the truth about us had
been known' says Sue on getting a divorce under 'false pretences').
It seems that only Arabella reads life correctly, from her viewpoint
of survival, and she is gifted with quite an animal knowledge: she
can tell, not from 'knowing' Sue but simply from looking at her,
that her marriage had not, and has now, been consummated (V.ii),
and naturally imparts this knowledge to Phillotson later.

'BUT NOBODY DID COME, BECAUSE NOBODY DOES.'
(I.iv)

What about knowledge in narration itself?

When the boy Jude has at last obtained his Latin and Greek
Grammars, and learnt, as his first great shock, that a grammar is
not a simple prescription or rule 'or secret cipher, which, once
known, would enable him by merely applying it, to change at will
all words of his own speech into those of the foreign tongue', the
authorial narrator (after giving us extraneous information about

Grimm's Law and showing that he knew better), ends the chapter:

> Somebody might have come along that way who would have
> asked him his trouble, and might have cheered him by saying
> that his notions were further advanced than those of his gramma-
> rian. But nobody did come, because nobody does, and under
> the crushing recognition of his gigantic error Jude continued to
> wish himself out of the world. (I.iv)

Nobody does, except the authorial narrator, who withholds
knowledge from him. And all his life, Jude will seek 'a secret
cipher' to life, and end up wishing himself and getting himself out
of the world. (For the term 'authorial narrator', see note 21.)

Knowledge circulates incessantly in any narrative, which
depends on it, and the proper questions are how much, what kind
and whether external or internal to the fiction; and, within the
fiction, whether external or internal to a character.

In the nineteenth-century realist novel, especially in its naturalist
version, a vast amount of knowledge about the world was circulated
in various ways, and since the ideology of realism (to show, to
teach, a rich but capturable world) was inhabited by the basic
contradiction of all pedagogy (a plethora of information vs the
need for readability), all sorts of disguises had developed.

Hardy had naturally mastered all these, though he is often
accused of clumsiness, notably with point of view. Taking it rather
as mastery, two modern critics have particularly interested me,
Penny Boumelha and David Lodge, who both treat Hardy as highly
innovative.[8]

Boumelha discusses the 'formal experimentation' with genre and
voice and structures of perception that were explored by the 'New
Woman' novels of the eighties and nineties, but which had already
marked Hardy's earlier career, and were now 'given a significant
contemporaneity by the practices of these lesser-known writers'.[9]
These structures attempted a dissolution of the boundaries between
author and character, as opposed to the 'objective', 'scientific',
authoritative narrator of the naturalistic novel. *The Woodlanders*, she
says, is Hardy's 'most experimental' novel, with a 'continuing
multiplicity of generic elements almost to the end', so that in 'the
crucial figure of Grace Melbury, for whom no coherent personality
. . . is constructed . . . the full play of ambiguities and tensions is
enacted in the shifts and vacancies of her role as narrative centre.

It is not by accident that Grace is also the focus of Hardy's most radical attempt so far to confront the issues of sexuality and marriage in his fiction'. Here two ways of writing emerge, the attempt to give a 'scientific authoritative encompassant that will shape the narrative of Tess Durbeyfield, and the deflected and overtly partial mode of narration that will grant to Sue Bridehead an inaccessibility pushing beyond the emptiness of enigma'.[10] *Jude,* she says later,

> is a novel that threatens to crack open the powerful ideology of realism as a literary mode, and throws into question the whole enterprise of narrative. 'The letter killeth' — and not only Jude . . . Sue is progressively reduced from a challenging articulacy to a tense and painful silence that returns her to the fold of marriage — a conclusion which ironically duplicates the death of Jude. Writing comes increasingly to resemble an instrument of death.[11]

I am not sure that generic mixture as such (by which she means reusing traditional elements from other genres, popular ballads, theatricality etc.) is 'experimental', but the word has become pretty meaningless (and at the time was used of the naturalistic novel it opposed, precisely because that was 'scientific'). As for the 'cracking open' of realism's ideology, it is treated (as the quotation shows) much more thematically, so that 'writing' (and 'experiment'?) as instrument of death is rather a sleight of hand. However, without basically disagreeing with Boumelha, I want to show that it is paradoxically through misuse of traditional elements that a novel so concerned with knowledge should turn out to be in the modern sense, so unknowable.

Inversely, David Lodge has stressed Hardy's modernity by showing how cinematic his treatment of perspective is: aerial shots of diminutive figures on a huge landscape (= the vulnerability of human creatures and the indifference of nature) or the illuminated figure inside observed by the unobserved observer outside (= imperfect understanding and defective communication). Or the 'hypothetical or unspecified observer', a sort of 'second narrator' who 'might have seen', which (though impossible in film which has to show) Lodge argues is like a different camera angle that needs no such explanatory supposition in film. And he adds that what is so original in Hardy is commonplace in film (which must narrate in images only), so that transposition of a Hardy novel into film is difficult.

Here too, I doubt whether this treatment of perspective is all that new. Balzac was doing it in the first half of the century — indeed it could be argued that the cinema inherited all the clichés of the novel except the narrative voice.

Balzac's fascination with visual treatment has been well analysed by Jean Paris and by Le Huenon and Perron,[12] notably for the descriptive aporia it often entails. The knowledge imposed is both postulated and concealed. 'Every reader of Balzac is familiar with those introductory descriptions set into play by an image, a picture, a vision that is immediately indexed as lack of knowledge.'[13] This refers specifically to Balzac's many 'hypothetical observers', and similarly Jean Paris shows that Balzac's use of this device produces indetermination. In fact Poe used it for the ambiguity of the fantastic in 'The Fall of the House of Usher' (1845): 'Perhaps the eye of a scrutinizing observer might have discovered a barely perceptible fissure . . .' In Balzac, this 'veiled indexation of knowledge' results in a shift from descriptive to narrative programme, but also in a reversal of function, because it is still necessary 'to demonstrate that the narrator can effectively take over the function of guarantor' [of knowledge known to him but not to the character].

'But what is the nature of knowledge?' ask Le Huenon and Perron, and reply by quoting Balzac on the *Comédie Humaine*, to the effect that knowledge is moving from effects to causes, and then to principles. 'The customs are the spectacle, the causes are the wings and the machinery. Principles, that's the author.'[14] They comment: 'This, taken literally, postulates a sharp dissociation between the realm of representation and the realm of knowledge.'[15]

Above all, it postulates the place of representation as the place of accident, chance and the subject of knowing as 'principle'. The 'author' will, for instance, interpret an obscure inscription on a house (his technical knowledge), while the idle passer-by (the hypothetical observer) stays at the level of appearance. Where Jameson[16] sees in this ordered visual topos the constitution of the bourgeois subject and narrative strategies that block development, Huenon and Perron refute this and suggest on the contrary another space of knowledge:

These interminable comings and goings are final moments in the constitution of a new space, a new knowledge where the subject cannot find a place; they are the end terms of transformation processes that take archaic spaces of knowledge originally inscribed in the text, redistribute them, and re-present them according to an incoherent and incomprehensible logic.[17]

One might almost be reading about Hardy. Doesn't Sue rearrange the books of the New Testament in the order they were written, which shocks Jude, but makes it 'twice as interesting' (III.iv)? Except that, for Hardy, there were (ultimately) no 'principles'. And therein will lie the contradiction.

'THE SAME WOMANLY CHARACTER' (III.vi)

Hardy, to be sure, achieves his indetermination in other ways, When Balzac uses the hypothetical observer it is to create a blur, a 'veiled indexation of knowledge'. In Hardy it has already become an empty trick, which can even abolish the hypothetical observer:

An hour later his thin form . . . could have been seen walking along the five-mile road to Marygreen. On his face showed the determined purpose that alone sustained him but to which his weakness afforded a sorry foundation . . . Jude crossed the green to the church without observation. (VI.viii)

The external focalisation necessary to a hypothetical observer is contradicted by information only the authorial narrator can know, whereupon the hypothetical observer textually vanishes. Similarly the device of the 'pretended unknown', already a cliché in Balzac, is used for pointless exclusion of the reader who nevertheless knows from immediate context:

[previous paragraph about Sue]
On an afternoon at this time a young girl entered the stone-mason's yard . . . 'That's a nice girl . . . who is she . . . I don't know . . . Why yes' [identification by the craftsman]. Meanwhile the young woman had knocked at the office (II.iv)

Meanwhile a middle-aged man was dreaming a dream of great beauty concerning the writer of the above letter [whom we know to be Sue]. He was Richard Phillotson [whom we already know,

and know to be interested in Sue], who [description and analeptic
information . . .] These were historic notes, written in a bold
womanly hand at his dictation some months before . . . letters
. . . the same womanly character as the historic notes . . . frank
letters signed 'Sue B' . . . written during short absences with
no other thought than their speedy destruction . . . forgotten
doubtless by the writer . . . in one of them . . . the young woman
said . . . (III.vi)

The perspective of the craftsmen is suggested in the first passage,
though there is no particular narrative point in this. The perspective
of the second passage becomes aporetic; who speaks? Both the
authorial narrator and Phillotson know who wrote the letters. Only
the former knows the 'thought', and Phillotson could be said to
guess ('doubtless') the forgetting. There is an uncertain hovering
between the 'pretended unknown', narration in internal focalisation and free indirect discourse (to which I shall return). The
'pretended unknown', frequent still in *Jude*, has become a pointless
trick of pseudo-exclusion of readers for its own sake.

Elsewhere, however, readers are, on the contrary, as in melodrama, let *in on* the terrible traps that are preparing for Jude, and
this with ultra-simplistic shifts of focalisation derived from popular
forms, almost of the 'little-does-he-know' type, usually signalled
by 'Meanwhile Arabella', 'Meanwhile Sue' etc., like cutting in the
cinema, where it is fundamentally a popular technique but also,
as Lodge does not say, authoritarian as to camera angle for
limitation or revelation. Today the trick has become mechanical
and meaningless in soap opera. And what the readers are and are
not told can seem visibly arbitrary. In *Jude*, for instance (to remain
with the more trivial items), we are let in on Arabella's false
dimples (so watch Jude discover them) but not on her false hair,
which has been elided (we discover it with him). Similarly the
frequent voyeuristic or overhearing scenes sometimes tell us
something new (Sue walking close with Phillotson, II.v) and
sometimes not; Jude overhearing Arabella's friends on their 'advice'
to her (I.x) — and even then he only surmises, so that some readers
may feel particularly exasperated at his stupidity, as throughout
his courtship.

Thus, on the level of plot, readers are ostentatiously manipulated,
as Jude is (Hardy said Jude was a 'puppet'), and made to enter a
crudely ironic structure (rather like that of a Punch-and-Judy show

where the children cry 'look out!'), not an identifying one that makes them share the experience.

With other elements of knowledge, however, like knowledge as self-awareness (wisdom), or knowledge of the other (insight), we are on the contrary drawn into an identifying structure, but in a peculiar way, through a similar dialectic of the hidden and the revealed but on a different scale, a dialectic as cockteasing as Jude's 'ever evasive Sue'. And this is achieved through:

(1) a skilful use of dialogue to conceal what it suggests;
(2) a heavy-handed use of narration;
(3) a blurred use of free indirect discourse.

'YOU DON'T KNOW HOW BAD I AM, FROM YOUR POINT OF VIEW' (III.i)

By definition, the most mimetic passages are in direct discourse. Hardy is a master of dramatic form, and *Jude* has perhaps more dialogue than any of his other novels. Dialogue has a revealing/concealing structure since we reveal ourselves through utterance, but only to the limits of what can be articulated. It thus draws us IN and keeps us OUT, guessing. So it is interesting that Sue and Jude come alive chiefly in dialogue, but only when they are talking about the *problems* of their relationship (and of the book): 'You must take me as I am', says Sue, twice, the first time meaning one kind of opposite (non-consummation, V.i), the second time another kind (she is about to leave him, VI.iii); there too she says 'Ah — you don't know my badness!' and he exclaims vehemently 'I do! Every atom and dreg of it! You make me hate Christianity, or mysticism, or whatever it may be called, if it's that which has caused this deterioration in you.' And much earlier she had said 'Only you don't know how bad I am, from your point of view', meaning her paganism, but also perhaps 'The Ishmaelite' (III.i, III.ii), and later she repeats 'I said you didn't know how bad I was', meaning (apparently) what 'people say', that 'I must be cold-natured — sexless' (III.iv).

Not all the dialogue is so 'writerly'. More often it is punctuated by narrator–comment: 'with the perverseness that was part of her' (III.i), 'with a gentle seriousness that did not reveal her mind' (III.vi), 'in the delicate voice of an epicure of the emotions' (III.vii) or her 'tragic contralto' (IV.i). And even here all these perceptions might be Jude's, in free indirect discourse, which is not always clearly distinguished from narration in internal focalisation (see the next section, the point is important to understand Jude). But the viewpoint of Sue, and above all the nature of their relationship, its quality, its texture (what attracts two such different people, apart from loneliness, especially on Sue's side) and its development, is treated much more bizarrely, from regular distancing to total occultation, whereas we are given all the scenes with Arabella straight — a much simpler affair.

'A CHRONICLER OF MOODS AND DEEDS' (V.v)

At their first meeting, Jude and Sue at once go off to see Phillotson, and any talk they might have had on the way is elided. When they arrive Jude's interest shifts at once to Phillotson, then the walk back is distanced by narrative summary in internal focalisation on Jude (II.iv). This is followed by a practical discussion about why Sue has to leave and Jude's fatal suggestion that she should go to Phillotson as pupil–teacher. And this sort of occultation will mark the whole development: desperate dialogue, desperate messages, internal focalisation on Jude, narrator-comment on both, or ellipsis.

We do, of course, have separate access to Sue, but only in dialogue or letters with Phillotson, or in dialogue with Arabella or with Mrs. Edlin, and hardly at all in internal focalisation.

The most remarkable occultation is that of their happiness. The kiss which 'was a turning point in Jude's career', for instance, is elided, then hinted at by a hypothetical observer (who has authorial narrator-knowledge) as he returns from the station ('in his face was a look of exultation not unmixed with recklessness'), then told in summary analepsis: 'An incident had occurred' (IV.iii). And when Sue at last comes to live with Jude they merely have another intense conversation about their situation, then a scene about Arabella, then we switch to Phillotson and Gillingham. The next section starts: 'How Gillingham's doubts were disposed of will most quickly appear by passing over the series of dreary months and incidents that followed the events of the last chapter' (V.i).

The same happens after the consummation, finally achieved through Jude playing on her jealousy and followed, after the normal Victorian ellipsis, by a sad absent-mindedness on Sue's

part and immediate departure, out of guilt, to see Arabella, and a
switch to the arrival of Jude's son. Then:

> The purpose of a chronicler of moods and deeds does not require
> him to express his personal views upon the grave controversy
> above given. That the twain were happy — between their times
> of sadness — was indubitable. And when the unexpected
> apparition of Jude's child in the house had shown itself to be no
> such disturbing event as it had looked . . . (V.v)

The sleight of hand is obvious: the reader's desire is not for the
chronicler's personal views but for the moods and deeds. And
after the incident which makes them decide to leave Aldbrickham
the narration resumes: 'Whither they had gone nobody knew,
chiefly because nobody cared to know. And anyone sufficiently
curious to trace the steps of such an obscure pair might have
discovered . . .' (V.iii).

Nobody knows, chiefly because the author, momentarily hiding
behind 'nobody', does not care to tell us, though as usual the
hypothetical observer does tell us at once, but in summary. And
suddenly we're at the Kennetbridge Fair, in dramatic form again,
but between Sue and Arabella, and Sue has two children of her
own. As Patricia Ingham says in her excellent introduction to the
Oxford edition: 'The joy is looked forward to and back, but it is
never actually there',[18] at least, not for most readers, for whom it
is occasionally evoked, but rarely, and always as 'veiled indexation
of knowledge', as vanishing-point in the narrative technique, the
authorial narrator heavily marking or not marking his ellipses and
sudden shifts.

The reason is the *author's* knowledge: what matters to Hardy is
desire (male), while marriage is death: hence the allowance we
have to make, not for Sue's (and Hardy's?) horror of sex (a Victorian
commonplace no odder than the post-Freudian treatment of any
sex-refusal as abnormal), but for her horror of *legalised* marriage,
three times endorsed separately in comment and clearly a euphemism for the death of desire through familiarity, or knowledge possessed and therefore undesired, since desire is by definition for
something absent. The equally obvious fact that it is sometimes not
so, that some rare people have the ludic 'art' of love, another form
of 'knowledge', does not interest Hardy, or indeed most novelists,
since narrative is based on desire, yet for this of all relationships,

where so much depends on that mysterious quality called companionship (which is what Sue wanted), the imaginative effort should have been made. It is a serious lack, for it pushes the reader further OUT, alienates him from Jude and Sue.

'A VOICE WHISPERED THAT, THOUGH HE DESIRED TO KNOW HER' (II.iv)

Narrator-comment pulls us OUT, as does narration in external focalisation. Narration in internal focalisation gives the viewpoint of the character but wholly as told by the authorial narrator, in summary for instance, or in narrativised discourse, which summarises a character's words (spoken or thought) without giving them.[19] Free indirect discourse or, better named by Ann Banfield, Represented Speech and Thought (here RST or, almost entirely, RT),[20] draws us much further IN, since it gives the character's words or thoughts, but still in narrational sentences (in the third person and past or conditional, where the character would use the first person and present or future), though some deictics remain unchanged (past = now, exclamations, questions, words and tone of the character etc.). This device, which is wholly a literary invention and impossible in film or theatre or non-narrative speech, has fascinated the linguists, and is clearer in French, which uses the imperfect for it as distinct from the narrative aorist, than in English, where that distinction does not exist. Nevertheless it is clearly marked, and was very clearly used, especially for comedy, by Jane Austen. It developed throughout the nineteenth century (Flaubert, Zola), coming to an apotheosis in Forster and Virginia Woolf.[21]

Since then RST (and more especially RT) vanished from much avant-garde writing, though without the manifesto-fuss that was made (rather short-sightedly) against the past tense as *the* mark of traditional fiction. It vanished also, together with separate narrator-comment, within the work of single writers, such as Doris Lessing, who prefers rich variations of direct discourse by characters. It must have been unconsciously felt as belonging, by its very structure, to the ironic mode of writing. And it has now become an extremely blurred narrative cliché of average realist fiction, where it is often used to pass narrative items that could not possibly be going through the character's mind in that form. The distinction is very clear when the knowledge is author-knowledge extraneous to the fiction: information about Roman Britain is passed through Jude's mind in RT in I.viii, but the history of Shaston comes from the authorial narrator in IV.i (transferred from III.vi where it presumably formed part of Phillotson's interests). But when the knowledge is the content of a consciousness the distinction is much less clear. This blurring seems to me to begin with Hardy, and is, together with simple occultation, largely responsible for the indetermination, the 'ambiguities and tensions', the 'shifts and vacancies' (Boumelha) or the 'incomprehensibility that constitutes the novel's effect' (Goode). For Hardy constantly shifts from narrational to RT sentences, and it is often impossible to discern 'who speaks':

> To be sure she was almost an ideality to him still. Perhaps to know her would be to cure himself of this unexpected and unauthorized passion. A voice whispered that, though he desired to know her, he did not desire to be cured. (II.iv)

We start in RT ('To be sure', 'Perhaps'). But does one think to oneself 'a voice whispers'? Does not that voice of conscience also 'represent' narrator-comment? Here it is unimportant, but there are strange moments of aporia with Sue:

> Sue paused patiently beside him, and stole critical looks into his face as, regarding the Virgins, Holy Families, and Saints, it grew reverent and abstracted. When she had thoroughly estimated him at this she would move on and wait for him before a Lely or Reynolds. It was evident that her cousin deeply interested her, as one might be interested in a man puzzling out his way along a labyrinth from which one had oneself escaped. (III.ii)

Evident to whom? Who says or thinks 'her cousin'? Until then we could be either in narration (internal focalisation) or (less likely) in RT (the 'would' as future), then suddenly we veer, not just to narration but to an implied hypothetical observer, followed by narrator-comment. Or:

> . . . to keep him from his jealous thoughts, which she read clearly, as she always did. (IV.i)

But Sue either saw it not at all, or, seeing it, would not allow herself to feel it. (IV.ii)

Grammatically both could be RT. Who says 'as she always did'? Since Sue is rarely treated in internal focalisation, we must assume (as with the first example) that it is narrational, but then it is either untrue, or Sue must be interpreted (elsewhere) as consciously cruel. And in the last example the authorial narrator is explicitly not telling.

One of the rare examples of RT with Sue immediately veers to narrator-comment:

> Meanwhile Sue . . . had gone along to the station, with tears in her eyes for having run back and let him kiss her. Jude ought not to have pretended that he was not her lover, and made her give way to an impulse to act unconventionally, if not wrongly. She was inclined to call it the latter; for Sue's logic was extraordinarily compounded, and seemed . . . (IV.iii)

These various unclarities naturally happen all the time with Jude, who is treated constantly in RT, which critics do not always distinguish from narration in internal focalisation or even from their own comments. In fact it will be easier to show the blurring by quoting one good critic producing just that confusion. Patricia Ingham writes:

> Rather disconcertingly for the reader, the narrator, whose sympathy with Jude has been acute so far, now berates him for 'mundane ambition masquerading in a surplice' and rebukes him for that social unrest, that desire for upward mobility, which from the 1870's had been an explicit reason for Oxford in particular holding back the spread of adult education to the working class in order to protect 'the over-crowded professions'. The narrator's volte-face sets the future pattern. He may condemn Jude sometimes but elsewhere, for instance in Jude's speech to the crowd at Christminster, he will support his attempt to 'reshape' his course and rise into another class . . .[22]

The 'narrator' does not 'berate' Jude for mundane ambition, Jude berates himself, since the passage is in Represented Thought (III.i, opening, 'It was a new idea . . .' partly quoted on p. 28. Nor, *a fortiori*, does he rebuke him for 'that social unrest' and all that follows, since all that follows is the critic's language (outside the text), whereas the text says, much more vaguely, 'a social unrest which had no foundation in the nobler instincts; which was purely an artificial product of civilisation'. Nor, for that matter, does the 'narrator' 'support' Jude during his speech at Christminster, since it is given by Jude in direct discourse, with no narrator-comment but plenty of disapproval from Sue, and irony of event: she keeps saying they ought to find a room first, and Jude's ignoring her leads to their difficulty in finding a room and the boy's disastrous reactions.

Ingham also says first that 'the narrator makes clear from the start the delusory nature of the boy's quest *and*, later, that 'Jude and the narrator are seized with the desirability of the learning that the university offers', and then again (after dealing with the irony of the quotations): 'What Jude only learns of life's cruelty the narrator knows from the start; he is already aware of the ironic irrelevance of the literary text.'

This seems to be having it all ways, and like the previous example, comes from a misreading of narrative techniques, which are much clearer than this reading implies. The 'delusory nature of the boy's quest' refers to his seeing or perhaps not seeing Christminster from Marygreen as a boy, but this is told in internal focalisation and dialogue without narrator-comment, and to say 'the narrator makes clear from the start' is to mistake narration in internal focalisation for comment (obviously the *whole* text is told by the author in a narrative voice, so Ingham's phrase blurs important distinctions). Nor is the 'narrator' at any point seized with the desirability etc., only Jude, and the ghastly irrelevance of the bits of classical knowledge and theological authors he tries to study on his own is not commented on: it can only be *at once* clear to the reader (as opposed to later) from a shared cultural code (knowledge again, but outside the text), which varies in time and space. Ingham's last statement fuses narrator with author.

It is probable that in Hardy the (authorial) 'narrator' only speaks clearly as such when he is giving us information unknown to the characters, and this he does a great deal (he didn't know, he didn't notice, he had an illumination . . . but forgot it, etc.), sometimes heavily and oddly, as when he tells us that Jude (then a boy) 'was the sort of man who was born to ache a good deal before the fall of the curtain upon his unnecessary life should signify that all was well with him again' (I.ii); sometimes wrongly, as when he says that 'Sue did not for a moment, either now or later, suspect what troubles had resulted to him [Phillotson] from letting her go' (IV.vi — 'later'? she obviously learns it eventually); or dogmatically: 'He did not at that time see that mediaevalism was as dead as a fern leaf in a lump of coal . . .' (II.ii — which is the author's view). All the internal focalisation on Jude, however, hovers between narration (authorial viewpoint) and RT (character's viewpoint). And much of the ambiguity lies here.

'OR IS IT THE ARTIFICIAL SYSTEM OF THINGS?' (IV.iii)

John Goode quotes Jude asking what Goode takes 'to be the fundamental ideological question posed by the novel' and found unforgivable by the critics who cannot take Sue:

> What I can't understand in you is your extraordinary blindness now to your old logic. Is it peculiar to you, or is it common to woman? Is a woman a thinking unit at all, or a fraction always wanting its integer? (VI.iii)

> If this question [Goode continues] is asked in the novel it is surely naïve to ask it of the novel. What is more important is that this question should be asked; it poses for Sue only one of two possibilities — that the nature of her blindness to her own logic must be explained either by her 'peculiarity' or by her belonging to womanhood. Either way, she is committed to being an image, and it is this that pervades the novel. Nobody ever confronts Jude with the choice between being a man or being peculiar. The essential thing is that Sue must be available to understanding. We might want to deduce that Hardy feels the same way as Jude at this point, but I think to do so would go both against the consistency of the novel and against Hardy's whole career as a writer . . . [his theme being woman as the object of male understanding].[23]

The point is excellent, but I am not so sure of his last arguments for the author not sharing Jude's feelings. Jude had already expressed a similar view long before, in ambiguous RT, then in direct discourse to himself, when he reflects on two women blocking his aspirations: '"Is it," he said, "that the women are to blame; or is it the artificial system of things, under which the normal sex-impulses are turned into devilish domestic gins . . ."' (IV.iii), while a few paragraphs later it is unambiguously the author who says 'for Sue's logic was extraordinarily compounded . . .'. The 'artificial system of things' is, of course, made by men, but neither Jude nor the authorial narrator seems aware of that. Elsewhere Jude exclaims that he is not against her, 'taking her hand, and surprised at her introducing personal feeling into mere argument' (III.iv), and this is narration not RT, and, of course, a gender image, though Jude himself takes her arguments personally all the time. Moreover, Jude's own blindness to his 'old logic' (for instance, his own past belief in legalistic marriage, which allowed him to sleep with Arabella and then be horrified to learn of her bigamous remarriage 'why the devil didn't you tell me last night?' III.ix); or his total unawareness that his speechifying was as much the cause of the tragedy as were Sue's careless answers to the boy, whereas it is Sue's awareness of this (her long habit of apparently neurotic self-reproach) that destroys her:

> 'Why did you do it, Sue?'
> 'I can't tell. It was that I wanted to be truthful. And yet I wasn't truthful, for with a false delicacy I told him too obscurely. Why was I half wiser than my fellow-women? and not entirely wiser! Why didn't I tell him pleasant untruths, instead of half realities! It was my want of self-control, so that I could neither conceal things nor reveal them!' (VI.ii)

As always. But if her self-imposed penance seems excessive, at least she is given to know that it is for this 'half' wisdom, and whatever the readers feel about her description of it they must surely know during the scene with the boy (and think 'look out!') that the boy is being wholly misled. Jude, however, talks here of 'our peculiar case', and his only apparent self-reproach is that he 'seduced' her, and 'spoilt one of the highest and purest loves that ever existed between man and woman' (VI.iii). This shows a very limited self-awareness, for it is no more than the simplistic Victorian dualism of purity vs sex, and his own remarriage and self-imposed penance of death seem far blinder than hers. Thus Sue, whose complex inner feelings are occulted throughout, turns out, in dialogue, to be more self-aware than he is, while the gender images of Jude, despite constant internal focalisation, are left for some readers to see and some not to see. Sue must be pin-pointed for Jude as image of guilt and blindness.

Lance Butler[25] has argued that Hardy is one of the rare writers who does not have a 'world-view', whereas for most literary texts we do a 'doublethink' and 'make allowances' for cosmological orders that are 'frankly ludicrous' (e.g. Dante, Dickens's innocent children, Eliot's providential endings). He takes the endings of the six major novels and shows a clear progression from various compromises (there is a providential structure) to *Jude* where Hardy finally achieves 'an ending that isn't false'. Since the novels are minutely planned and orchestrated, the paradox is that the order imposed 'implies that there is no final order . . . that in this rich patterned universe, there is no ultimate meaning. Whatever happens in Hardy's major fiction, however much he manipulates and controls it, he finally finds out how to prevent it from falling into a contrived moral or supernatural order.'[25]

But we are not told how, apart from the endings, which are summarised. This leaves us with one highly reductive content (the absence of plan), which could also be said of Voltaire's *Essais sur les moeurs* (and Jude twice accuses Sue of being Voltairean); and it sems to me in the 'how', in the meaning producing differentials of language, that the difficulties arise. Butler says that Hardy has received too much formal attention, so that his supposed 'faults' have excluded him from the company of the great. I had the opposite impression: that traditional attention had been thematic and formal attention superficial (often falling back on the famous descriptions) and that Hardy is now being revalued in many exciting ways, while Boumelha's formal study turns the 'faults' into high experiment and Lodge's turns them into anticipations of film. I have tried to go further and point up, within the 'experiment', a basic contradiction that in no way belittles Hardy (as deconstruction is not demolition) but seems deeper than that of careful structure revealing absence of structure.

For the attempt to blur the gap between authorial narrator's discourse and characters' discourse is already traceable in *Daniel Deronda* twenty years earlier, together with an attempt, more radical than anything in Hardy, to disrupt the determinism of sequence and plot (origin), and these will not fully flourish until) Virginia Woolf (see Gillian Beer[26]). Hardy is part of that struggle, but his endings, like those of Eliot, still 'exceed the book's terms' or 'strive structurally for a unity its perceptions will not fully permit' (Beer on Eliot), if for inverse reasons: a clinging to providential structure/a rejection of providential structure. And I see little difference between 'making allowances' for Dickens's innocent children and doing so for (among other things) a concept of tragedy that depends so heavily on organised stupidity, that is, on limitation (a secular version of a theological stance, the orthodox Augustinian one), while the characters blame institutions and faintly hope for change (a Pelagian stance, whose secular version was liberal socialism). I agree with Lance Butler about the 'doublethink' we bring to literature (though that is part of the pleasure, unless we read only for our own period truth), but I do not agree that Hardy is as exempt as he claims or that he 'speaks to us today, as Shakespeare does and Beckett does, because he faces the ultimate penury of the world'.[27]

For Shakespeare wrote plays, and Beckett wrote either plays or novels mostly in what Bakhtin calls 'free *direct* discourse' (one voice, but wholly dialogical, undeterminable).[28] Hardy's indeterminacy seems addressed (more like Shakespeare's than Beckett's) to different readers — which is why I have been using the plural rather than the unified subject implied by THE reader of theory:[29] readers whose relation with the text may be submissive and coerced, readers whose relation with it may be subversive or conflicting or resisting. This may well explain his universal appeal despite the 'allowances' we make, which can thus be regarded as internal to the period fiction, like the 'allowance' we make for, say, the divine right of kings in Shakespeare. Formally, however, I suggest that Hardy's *poetic* indeterminacy, the feeling of a meaningless chasm behind the very precision, comes from his handling of direct discourse, while the *pointless* indeterminacy and compensating pinpointing come from his handling of traditionally narrative devices, which he has, if anything, weakened rather than enriched, and which have largely vanished except as fatigued stereotypes. They may of course return, if the present philosophy of 'ultimate penury' (should we survive it) is succeeded by another period of firm beliefs, as Voltaire (and the concomitant eighteenth-century games with narrative authority) was succeeded by Victorian faith and its crises. But then, like the faith and authoritarian certainties, they would surely return in a refreshed and more energetic form.

Sentimentality, says Butler, 'is not simply an error of taste but the inevitable product of a world-view in which man comes into the world trailing clouds of glory'.[30] I wholly agree, but would add: the blurred and empty use of old ironic devices is not simply an error of taste but the inevitable result of a world-view in which, however 'not false' one's endings, someone controls things, but indifferently and unfairly. A doublethink world-view. Hardy stands between the two centuries a great transitional figure.

For the treatment of knowledge, in narrational terms, wraps up all the fundamental ideological questions, telling us, like the cinema, too much when we would rather not know and, like the cinema, blurring the very origin of knowledge when we want to know 'who speaks' (or why that camera angle). This, so stated, can be interpreted as highly modern, but it can also be said to mean that, in the practice of reading, the narration still mimes God.

For example, if Jude's quotations are 'ironic' because incomplete, he may or may not know this, and the readers depend on outside knowledge, a cultural code. On the other hand, Jude doesn't know that the epigraphs frame his story. Or *does* he? He quotes that of the book at Sue: 'Sue, Sue, we are acting by the letter, and "the letter killeth"' (VI.viii). Is Jude, after all, a dialogical character carrying on a 'secret polemic' with his author or any other defining entity? In whom he loses faith.

But no. The quotation is 'ordinary' knowledge, available to authors and characters and readers alike, and he quotes it only about their legalistic marriages, not about the deathly and lifely power of language to say the opposite of what it says. We are still too much in traditional, ironic, monological modes, however indeterminate, the author manipulating the very indeterminacy before our eyes: now you see it, now you don't. There is Christminster, there it maybe isn't. There is knowledge, there it isn't. There is desire, there it isn't. There is the voice that utters, there it isn't, it was only Jude, the obscure.

Notes

1. John Goode, 'Sue Bridehead and the New Woman', in Mary Jacobus (ed.), *Women Writing and Writing about Women* (London: Helen Croom; New York: Barnes & Noble, 1979), p. 108.
2. Ibid., p. 104.
3. J. Hillis Miller, *Fiction and Repetition — Seven English Novels* (Harvard University Press, 1982), pp. 140–1.

4. Gilles Deleuze, *Logique du sens* (Paris: Minuit, 1969).
5. Robert Gittings, *Young Thomas Hardy* (London: Heinemann, 1975).
6. R. M. Rehder, 'The Form of Hardy's Novels', in Lance St. John Butler (ed.), *Thomas Hardy After Fifty Years* (London: Macmillan, 1977), pp. 13–27.
7. Ibid., p. 24.
8. Penny Boumelha, *Thomas Hardy and Women — Sexual Ideology and Narrative Form* (Sussex: Harvester Press; New York: Barnes & Noble, 1982). David Lodge, 'Thomas Hardy as a Cinematic Novelist', in Butler (ed.), *Thomas Hardy After Fifty Years*, pp. 78–89.
9. Boumelha, *Hardy and Women*, p. 93.
10. Ibid., p. 114.
11. Ibid., p. 146.
12. Jean Paris, *Balzac* (Paris: Balland, 1986). Roland Le Huenon and Paul Perron, 'Reflections on Balzacian Models of Representation', *Poetics Today*, vol. 5 (1984) no. 4, pp. 711–28.
13. Huenon and Perron, 'Reflections', p. 716.
14. Honoré de Balzac, *Lettres à Mme Hanska*, vol. I (Paris: Les Bibliophiles de l'Originale, 1967), p. 270.
15. Huenon and Perron, p. 722.
16. Frederic Jameson, 'Balzac et le problème du sujet', in R. Le Huenon and P. Perron (eds), *Le roman de Balzac* (Montreal: Didier, 1980), p. 69.
17. Huenon and Perron, 'Reflections', p. 728.
18. Patricia Ingham (ed.), Introduction to *Jude the Obscure* (Oxford University Press, 1985), p. xx.
19. Genette (1972) analyses these types of discourse as ways of varying Distance (under Mood), the most distant being 'narrativised discourse', the least 'direct discourse' (the character's words). In 1983, p. 38, he summarises McHale (1978) who proposes 7 degrees of distance to his 5.
20. Ann Banfield, *Unspeakable Sentences — Narration and Representation in the Language of Fiction* (London: Routledge & Kegan Paul, 1982).
21. Free Indirect Discourse has been discussed by critics for many decades now, but always as a 'mixed' discourse, part character's voice and part narrator's. Banfield, with linguistic arguments that have not convinced literary critics, follows on Hamburger (1957, transl. 1973) and refutes the notion of a narrator, except for dramatised narrators, and insists on one voice only in RST. Her theory has proved as controversial as Hamburger's. Genette does not accept it (see also McHale 1978, 1983, and bibliography there). I cannot enter into this controversy here, or into any controversy about the theoretical status of narrator as opposed to author (excellently discussed by F. K. Stanzel, 1984, Ch. 1 and 3) but for my present purpose I have used Stanzel's term 'authorial narrator' (but 'narration', 'narrational sentences', 'narrator-comment' etc. as peculiarly apt for Hardy, whose 'narrative rhythm', unlike that of James or Flaubert, fluctuates between 'authorial narration' and 'figural narration', but has not yet achieved the modern phenomenon of 'narrateur flottant' or 'viewless viewpoint' (Ricardou, Barth, see Stanzel, 1984, p. 64). The term 'authorial narrator'

should help me emphasise the points I shall be making.
22. Ingham, Introduction to *Jude*, pp. xiii–xiv.
23. Goode, *Sue Bridehead*, p. 103.
24. Lance St. John Butler, 'How It Is for Thomas Hardy', in Butler (ed.), *Thomas Hardy After Fifty Years*, pp. 116–25.
25. Ibid., p. 125.
26. Gillian Beer, 'Beyond Determinism — George Eliot and Virginia Woolf', in Jacobus (ed.), *Women Writing*, pp. 80–99.
27. Butler, 'How It Is for Hardy', p. 119.
28. Mikhail Bakhtin, *Marxism and the Philosophy of Language*, published under the name V. N. Voloshinov (1929); translated by L. L. Matejka and I. R. Tibunik, under that name (New York: Seminar Press, 1973).
29. See Mary Louise Pratt, 'Ideology and Speech Act Theory', *Poetics Today*, vol. 7 (1986) no. 1, pp. 59–72.
30. Butler, 'How It Is for Hardy', p. 118.

Further Reading

Barthes, Roland, *S/Z* (Paris: Seuil, 1970; translated by Richard Miller, *S/Z*, New York: Hill & Wang, 1974).
Genette, Gérard, 'Discours du récit', in *Figures III* (Paris: Seuil, 1972).
Genette, Gérard, *Nouveau discours du récit* (Paris: Seuil, 1983).
Hamburger, Käte, *Die Logik der Dichtung* (Stuttgart: Ernst Klett Verlag, 1957; translated by Marilyn J. Rose, Indiana University Press, 1973).
McHale, Brian, 'Free Indirect Discourse: A Survey of Recent Accounts', *Poetics and Theory of Literature*, vol. 3 (1978) no. 2, pp. 249–87.
McHale, Brian, 'Unspeakable Sentences, Unnatural Acts — Linguistics and Poetics Revisited', *Poetics Today*, vol. 4 (1983) no. 1, pp. 17–45.
Stanzel, F. K., Theorie des Erzahlens (Gottingen: Vandenhoeck & Ruprecht; translated by Charlotte Goedsche, *A Theory of Narrative*, Cambridge University Press, 1984).

3

Provisional Narratives: Hardy's Final Trilogy

Patricia Ingham

The Well-Beloved is and is not Hardy's last novel. No manuscript exists, but the serial version, *The Pursuit of the Well-Beloved, A Sketch of a Temperament*[1] was printed weekly in *The Illustrated London News* from 1 October to 17 December 1892. In book form there was published in March 1897 *The Well-Beloved, A Sketch of a Temperament,*[2] a text usually taken as definitive and yet regarded simultaneously as a 'variant' of 1892. By this sleight-of-hand a date 1892 is attached to the work and *Jude the Obscure* (book version 1895) is somewhat confusedly given the status of the last novel that Hardy wrote. The canon then ends with a bang. But the three works are both linked and discrete. *The Well-Beloved*, though closely linked with *The Pursuit*, has major differences from it in plot, character and narratorial stance, giving it practical claims to be regarded as the last work of fiction. Theoretical claims I shall turn to later. *Jude*, while overtly different, shares a common matrix with the other two and is particularly close to *The Pursuit*. These facts about the texts and their ambiguous chronology encourage the reader to regard them as a trilogy. Such a reading potentiates the understanding of Hardy's last work as a 'feminist' novelist and suggests that he did not abandon novel-writing only because of critical hostility to the immensely successful *Jude* but because he had so far unravelled the traditional fictional processes of 'classic realism'[3] towards the poetry that he published for the rest of his life. In 1912, possibly re-writing history, he was able to see poems already written before 1871 'dissolving . . . into prose' in his first published novel, *Desperate Remedies*.[4] Conversely his last novels examined together show narrative dissolving into poetry. His descriptions of *Jude* in the 1895 Preface as a 'series of seemings' and of *The Well-Beloved* in the 1912 Preface as 'subjective' echo the phrases he applies repeatedly and passionately to the poems as 'fugitive impressions',[5] 'impressions of the moment',[6] 'unadjusted impressions', for which he claims value[7] with their 'sense of disconnection'.[8] Between 1897 and 1912 his retrospective account of his vision as lying at 'the indifference point between rationality and irrationality'[9] becomes more attractive to him and in the *General Preface* to the novels and poems published in 1912 he speaks of consistency as 'objectless'.[10] This passion complements the irritation always evoked by those who sought 'mathematical consistency'[11] in his narratives. What I wish to show is that already the last three novels have become what his imaginative works were declared to be, '*seemings*, provisional representations only'.[12] Since they have a common matrix, reading them as a metatext can reveal transpositions everywhere within relating to all aspects of the fiction. Every discourse speaks of provisionality. One might characterise this provisional quality of the trilogy in linguistic terms: characterisation is conditional on the intersection of discourses and so exclamatory only; plots are subjunctive as well as indicative; and the handling of gender shows a reversal of subject and object. This language enacts the profound uncertainties and conflicts in Hardy's final account of women and their relationship to men. It is the only language that could express them.

Taking the two versions of *The Well-Beloved* back into the canon from which they are often displaced (by critics who ignore them) depends on some displacement of *Jude* itself, or rather of Sue Bridehead. *The Well-Beloved* is marginalised because of *Jude* and Jude himself is often marginalised by critics for Sue. The final title of the volume edition (replacing the earlier 'The Simpletons', 'Hearts Insurgent' and 'The Recalcitrants') attempts to deflect attention towards the male protagonist. But critics undeterred reclaim her as 'more complex', more 'significant'[13] than 'the title character', while Jacobus[14] rightly appropriates male territory by writing of 'Sue the Obscure', where obscurity is critical limelight.

The obscurity of Sue is a suitable focus of contradiction from which to begin a re-examination of the three novels and to develop a new perspective. What rivets attention on Sue is the fact that her motives present 'one lovely conundrum', her actions a mass of inconsistencies. In the 1912 edition she negotiates alternately an idealised romantic relationship with Jude and a position of authorised sexual tormentor. She plays him with a coquetry so volatile that it draws his hostility to a point where he sees her frequently as merciless. She accepts him verbally as a lover but allows possession only under duress; makes a worldly marriage but claims not to have known what marriage really meant. Thus critics who centralise her and chart in detail her inconsistency do so in order to solve the conundrum, resolve the contradictions if only by blanket statements of her 'profound and representative problems',[15] 'the gap between what she thinks and what she does, between belief and behaviour'.[16] A mathematical equation is sought, a formula that will equal all the sum of her inconsistencies. Formulas offered include the suggestions that coherence is achieved by seeing her and Arabella as 'inverse parallels in their failure to realize the ideal of Mill';[17] or by recognising that 'because of Hardy's change of subject, there is an imbalance in the narrative technique never compensated for despite revision'.[18] Even Goode, who comes closest to a full account of Sue, is to an extent reductive in describing her precisely as a combination of 'image' and 'logic'.[19] These attempts fail even mathematically; there remains always a surplus. Each represents one more grid over intractable material. And if the reader moves back into the marginalised hinterland of textual revision before 1912 more linear or diachronic inconsistencies can be found here as in other areas of the text. The Sue of the earliest draft of the manuscript has a simplicity captured by her 'bright eyes and tender voice' when she encounters Jude. She develops more self-awareness and sophistication in a later version when these are replaced by the assertion that she is 'the one affined soul that Jude had ever met' (p. 122).[20] In a pristine account she 'half unconsciously' expects him to kiss her as a cousin might, but by later changes her more worldly view of how this might be interpreted leads her to expect him (urbanely) not to (p. 137). Just so, in a first draft it 'does not occur' to her to regard him in the way that outsiders might think she does (as a lover) but the later alternative says that it *has* occurred to her (p. 163). The 'tender reflective voice' she possesses at first later becomes the tormentingly 'delicate voice of an epicure in emotions' (p. 180). Her uncriticised 'natural elusiveness' is replaced by the more questionable 'elusiveness of her curious double nature' (p. 219). This move from simplicity to some manipulativeness is early; later revisions undo the picture somewhat. In the hallowed 1912 edition a mild sexual warmth is introduced: where earlier she was 'cold' she is now less specifically a 'fay, or sprite' (p. 372); an earlier vague kiss becomes 'close and long' (p. 227); and she actually at last utters to Jude words not possible in previous incarnations — 'I do love you' (p. 280). These versions plainly defy attempts to provide formulas for coherence. Yet inconsistencies in the printed text of 1912 seem merely a natural extension of them: moments with their own temporary validity but resistant to the notion of logical coherence. This latter description would fit Hardy's own complex of emotional and intellectual attitudes to women in his later life. Even his uncompromising support for women's suffrage is expressed with a chill menace when he writes to the suffragette leader, Helen Ward, in 1908:

> Though I hold . . . that women are entitled to the vote as a matter of justice if they want it, I think the action of men therein should be permissive only, not cooperative. I feel by no means sure that the majority of those who clamour for it realize what it may bring in its train: if they did three-fourths of them would be silent. I refer to such results as the probable break-up of the present marriage-system, the present social rules of other sorts, religious codes, legal arrangements on property, &c (through men's self-protective countermoves.) I do not myself consider that this would be necessarily a bad thing (I should not have written 'Jude the Obscure' if I did), but I deem it better that women should take the step unstimulated from outside. So, if they should be terrified at consequences, they will not be able to say to men: 'You ought not to have helped bring upon us what we did not foresee'. (*Letters*, 3.360)[21]

Such a move as that made above to examination of textual revisions is not at present critically acceptable. Though tempting to many, it is usually made in equivocal parenthesis. For though the author we know is, critically speaking, dead when the narrator takes over, he does not die until he has made all the changes which create finally that synchronic slice, the last revised version as the author intended it. A practising editor of Hardy, however, is faced by, say, the following passage in the manuscript of *Jude*. Jude says to Mrs Edlin as he lies dying:

> When men of a later age look back upon the barbarism, cruelty, and superstition of the times in which we have the unhappiness to live, it will appear more clearly to them than it does to us that the irksomeness of life is less owing to its natural conditions, though they are bad enough, than to those artificial compulsions

arranged for our well being, which have no root in the nature
of things! (MS, p. 427)

This piece written in the original black ink was not cancelled by
the green/blue pencil used for bowdlerisings; yet it appears in no
printed text in Hardy's lifetime. How are we to calculate authorial
intention with material like this? By a popular analogy with
Saussurean linguistic theory it can be assumed that the synchronic
approach with its spurious precision should prevail. But linguistics
has moved in the last 20 years to a perspective that integrates
synchronic with linear or diachronic approaches in the description
of language. I suggest that the same should be done with texts.
Since the critical interest of revisions is evident and their status a
theoretical embarrassment, an analogy with present-day linguistics
might be made. A critical assumption could be that the implied
author 'Hardy' 'dies' when he takes up the black-ink pen in 1893,
not when he adds the last revision to the Mellstock edition in the
1920s. The defence for this is that it is a logical extension of the
implied author/narrator split and a natural elaboration of the idea
of narratorial unreliability. The revisions then belong to the narrator
as firmly as does the passage in *Villette* where Lucy Snowe pictures
in detail for the reader her happy life after leaving Bretton, only to
cancel the picture by revealing that she did not lead it (ch. 4). The
alternative to my suggestion about the status of revisions is
continuing casuistry in their use by critics. If it is rejected, then
the 1892 serial version of *The Well-Beloved* must be classified as an
interesting curiosity, not a separate novel, a view not supported
by critical intuition nor even by commonsense recognition of the
major differences of plot between 1892 and 1897. Pearston,[22] for
instance, ruthlessly marries twice, once bigamously, Pierston only
once as an act of kindness to an aging and impoverished woman;
Pearston attempts seduction and suicide, Pierston neither. These
are but crude differences representative of many others discussed
later. In my account *The Pursuit* stands reclaimed from the revision
hinterland as a separate novel and *The Well-Beloved* as Hardy's last.
These two and *Jude* can now be regarded as interlocking treatments
of Hardy's obsessive concern with the relationship between the
sexes. This is seen differently in each of the three and within all
the novels contradictions create unease and fragmentation.

The Pursuit shows, like *The Well-Beloved*, in the story of three
generations of women loved by the sculptor Jocelyn Pearston

(Pierston), who pursues a migrating 'well-beloved', three Sue characters: the romantic ingenuous girl who loves him, Avice Caro the first, the knowing coquette who marries another man, Avice the second, and a virginal creature forced into loveless marriage and sexual relations with him, Avice the third. This lends a curious significance to the novel's epigraph, 'One shape of many names'. It has a general relevance to the earlier names of those said to have embodied the well-beloved. But in relation to the Caro women of one name it represents a partially successful attempt at appropriating them as unitary woman despite their differences. The conflict between signifier and signified that the quotation itself involves is emphasised by its context in Shelley's *Revolt of Islam* where it is the forces of evil that take many shapes:

> Thus evil triumphed, and the Spirit of evil
> One Power of many shapes which none may know,
> One Shape of many names . . .
>
> (I.27)

The hostility towards women which paradoxically runs through three texts that overtly elevate them begins here.

Both *The Pursuit* and *The Well-Beloved* centrally appear simpler than *Jude* in the presentation of women: they show the many-women-in-one seen in Sue in obviously analytic form in the three separate girls. Yet even broadly viewed they have a dimension lacking in *Jude*: through their kinship with each other the three Avices manifest another confusing aspect of individual identity, that which is assumed to be inherited. The personal dilemma created by the constraints of inherited identity is poignantly expressed in Hardy's poem *The Pedigree*, when a man tracing his ancestry is forced to realise:

> That every heave and coil and move I made
> Within my brain, and in my mood and speech,
>   Was in the glass portrayed
> As long forestalled by their so making it;
> The first of them, the primest fuglemen of my line,
> Being fogged in far antiqueness past surmise and reason's reach.

In *The Pursuit* and *The Well-Beloved* the problem is at first the male onlooker's: for Pearston/Pierston the Avices are the same and not the same. This is momentarily crystallised for him when, standing with the second Avice, he sees her daughter for the first time:

> Pearston stood as in a dream. It was the very girl, in all essential particulars, and without the absence of a single charm, who had kissed him forty years before. When he turned his head from the window his eyes fell again upon the old Avice at his side. Before but the relic of the Well-Beloved, she had now become its empty shrine. Warm friendship, indeed, he felt for her; but whatever that might have done towards the instauration of a former dream was now hopelessly barred by the rivalry of the thing itself in the guise of a lineal successor.
>
> (*Ill. L. News*, 1892, p. 273)[23]

He resolves his problem about their identity by a violent decision that they are the same. This makes inherited personality into a burden for the female inheritors, Avice the second and third. It is Pearston's identification of them with his first Avice that leads to his attempt at marriage with the second and his bigamous marriage to the unwilling third.

So the bizarre story of the sculptor's pursuit of the well-beloved in the three Avices shows an extreme insistence on the unitary nature of women. Time is generally regarded as the unifying thread of a single personality. What Pearston insists on is, ironically, the opposite: that it creates for the three Avices a single not a triple identity. The women only partly resist this by their individuality; to some extent they succumb to his claim. This crude attempt to appropriate gives way to a more complex one in *Jude* where a single woman is manifestly (as I have shown above) so contradictory that no critical reading of her as unitary will hold. The same is true of the narrator's formulas and Jude's; they fail completely. As a signifier she is inconstant and the text enacts the struggles of all accounts of her to recreate stability. Her existence or rather presence in the novel is evoked, like Christminster's, by 'unadjusted impressions' of the males involved: those of the narrator, Jude's, and to a lesser extent Phillotson's. Each impression is in fact conditional on how at that point all the fictional processes intersect. The narrator's 'own unadjusted impressions' read back into the so-far marginalised hinterland of the manuscript from which they are only rescued by editorial assistance. Others still occur within the printed text. For instance, brooding on her guilty reaction to the children's death, he produces a new reading of the past:

Vague and quaint imaginings had haunted Sue in the days when
her intellect scintillated like a star, that the world resembled a
stanza or melody composed in a dream; it was wonderfully
excellent to the half-aroused intelligence, but hopelessly absurd
at the full waking; that the First Cause worked automatically like
a somnambulist, and not reflectively like a sage; that at the
framing of the terrestrial conditions there seemed never to
have been contemplated such a development of emotional
perceptiveness among the creatures subject to those conditions
as that reached by thinking and educated humanity. But affliction
makes opposing forces loom anthropomorphous; and those ideas
were exchanged for a sense of Jude and herself fleeing from a
persecutor. (p. 361)

This edits both present and past, presenting Sue as someone who
can be captured by a simple linear formula; someone who has
done nothing but progress in a describable way from A to B. To
accept this as definitive is like accepting the phrase 'slydynge of
corage' as definitive of Chaucer's Criseyde. Both are the truth of a
moment only, contradicted by the truth of other moments. Such a
contradiction is found, for instance, in Sue's own account of her
early dealings with Jude in the days when, according to the
narrator, she was all intellect that 'scintillated like a star':

When I first knew you I merely wanted you to love me . . . That
inborn craving which undermines some women's morals almost
more than unbridled passion — the craving to attract and
captivate, regardless of the injury it may do the man — was in
me. (p. 372)

Similarly, Jude's attempts to pin down the woman as signifier lead
him into assertions that are themselves contradictory. He sees her
coldness at different times as sexual frigidity, cold-heartedness that
makes her not worth a man's love, or glorious chastity: 'I seduced
you . . . You were a distinct type — a refined creature, intended
by Nature to be left intact. But I couldn't leave you alone!' (p. 362).
These unexpected words reveal in this period of uncertainty the
absence of a role for the male feminist: fumbling to find one, Jude
paradoxically adopts a Ruskinian viewpoint. But soon he is equally
vehement that Sue is 'not worth a man's love'(p. 411). These
formulaic assessments do not cumulatively contribute to a coherent

creation of the 'subject' Sue. Along with other evocations, they destroy that coherence, although she herself accepts most of them. These and many more contradictions do not, like the conventional nineteenth-century novel, create a particular subject as heroine; conflicting 'subjects' replace each other. Some on accepted lines, others not: Jude and the narrator all present these uncertainties, struggling with old and new images. What a woman signifies was unclear to Hardy as to many others (male and female) in the 1890s.

An unremarked phrase in the 1895 Preface where Hardy refers to *Jude* as 'a series of seemings' is relevant here: the assertion that 'the permanence or transitoriness' of these seemings is 'not of the first moment' (pp. xxxv–xxxvi). This constitutes a recognition that the second novel in the trilogy entirely discards continuity in time as the thread to unify character, rather than ironising the idea of it as cohesive as happens in the other two works. Readings of the female subject Sue are instead lent transient authority by their temporary place at the end of the reading process but as this moves on definition fades. They become, as Hardy wrote of certain poems in 1920, 'exclamations in fact'.[24] The conflicting readings, emotionally as well as logically inconsistent, are barely held in tension by narrative strained to limits at the opposite extreme from 'classic realism'. By comparison, Hardy's poem 'The Chosen' concerning 'a woman for whom great gods might strive!' and her five predecessors is a thin example of the poetic apostrophe or exclamation on many-women-in-one:

> All the five women, clear come back,
> I saw in her — with her made one . . .
>
> A various womanhood in blend —
> Not one, but all combined.

This captures only the idea of 'woman' as unitary not, as the novel does, the struggle between that and the idea of woman as non-unitary that takes place within the liberal-minded male. Fragmentation rather than integration of human character is the necessary implication of this conflict.

Chronologically *Jude* gives way to *The Well-Beloved* with 'Sue' again overtly transposed into three personalities. The surface of the text still asserts Pierston's control of their identity as of many other women's under the well-beloved, but the third Avice breaks free of appropriation by eloping with her lover before a forced marriage to the elderly Pierston can take place. Marcia has already much earlier in the novel freed herself from the imposition of signifying only the well-beloved. Both women have a new autonomy unknown to any previous Marcia/Avice/Sue figure. Avice resists appropriation even by her chosen husband Leverre from whom in the final chapter she is seen in unexplained flight. The movement between the three novels from a triple to a multiple–single to a triple female identity is under my perspective of the metatext to be read as the conflicting Sue figures are read: alternatives signifying only 'at this point — so'. They do not sequentially cancel each other out; no spurious authority should be given to the final Avices, or we are back with the synchronic slice.

There is nothing in the male protagonists to match the problematising of female identity but the events described above do involve alternative demarcations to the limits of their characters within the three novels, suggesting uncertainties that fragment the stereotypical males of Victorian fiction. Central identifications can be made: Pearston/Pierston the artist hero-figure aspires like Jude the stonemason hero-figure to an elusive sexual ideal. But provisionality prevails here too, preventing a sense of clear-cut limits between different images of men. That Pearston/Pierston is in some sense Jude remains clear, but Pearston at 60 marrying the twenty-year-old Avice becomes in the second novel the exploitative Phillotson marrying the girl Sue. In a scene anticipating that where Sue jumps from the marital bedroom window Pearston enters his wife's room:

> When he moved forward his light awoke her; she started up as if from a troublous dream, and regarded him with something in her open eyes and large pupils that was not unlike dread. It was so unmistakable that Pearston felt half paralysed, coming, as it did, after thoughts not too assuring . . . All of a sudden he felt that he had no moral right to go further. He had no business there. (*Ill. L. News.*, p. 711)

But Pearston does not simply split into two distinct individuals in *Jude*; the ruthlessness (unremarked by the narrator) which allows him to blackmail the third Avice into marriage through her sick mother is shared by both men in the second novel. True, it is Phillotson who is obviously ruthless in first marrying and later accepting the half-demented Sue back to his bed knowing she finds him physically repugnant; but Jude unobtrusively initiates a worse blackmail in 'Nature's own marriage' by using the threat of returning to Arabella to force Sue into sexual relations. It is the inevitable consequence of dealing with a figure so ambiguous as Sue that both Jude and the male narrator should find themselves in difficulties. They try to find a role for the feminist male, and like others before and after fail, in part through the duality of old and new attitudes that they embody and in part because of similar ambivalence in the woman they have to deal with. The change in demarcation between the man in *The Pursuit* and the men in *Jude* appears a simplification but because of the overlap between Jude and Phillotson it is not so.

Pierston in the final novel represents the coming together of Jude and Phillotson into a single figure again: he still plays the romantic side of Jude to the first Avice though as the elderly lover of the third Avice he is less ruthless than Pearston was. Limits between men are drawn approximately on the same lines in *The Well-Beloved* as in *The Pursuit*, but the essential nature of Jocelyn (a name of male or female shape) in the last novel is different. He can induce neither the young Marcia nor the last Avice to marry him.

So to an extent the transpositions of female figures are matched by the male, though masculine subjectivity presents simpler forms of inconsistency than the feminine. The poetic force of these provisional male alternatives is, however, brought out strikingly by comparison with a poem, 'So Various', printed in 1928. Lacking the resources of such narrative as the final trilogy, it expresses the complexities of identity only numerically:

> Now . . . All these specimens of man,
> So various in their pith and plan,
> Curious to say
> Were *one* man. Yea,
> I was all they.

The introduction of provisionality into Victorian novels has been much discussed in relation specifically to endings. From *Villette* onwards, instead of closure which in its classic form explains and reassures, open-endedness spasmodically and variously increases in the direction of twentieth-century experiments. For this reason, despite its dubious critical status discussed above, *The Pursuit* has long been regarded in some sense as the provider of an alternative ending to *The Well-Beloved*. Pearston attempts suicide to end his marriage to the third Avice and wakes from a subsequent illness to find his real wife Marcia, once Juno, now become the Witch of Endor. This contrasts with Pearston still unmarried in the final chapter who accommodates to the mundane and marries the aging Marcia out of kindness. Only by reading the two novels as separate can these episodes be accepted as examples of open-endedness; otherwise that of *The Pursuit* is cancelled. With the trilogy as metatext the death of Jude (a Pearston/Pierston figure) provides a third option which leaves Arabella/Marcia free.

Hillis Miller,[25] in an essay offering many new insights, has even interpreted the two 'versions' as opening up four endings by including the possibilities raised in *The Pursuit* of Pearston disappearing to America or succeeding in his suicide attempt. But he is wrong here: these are not alternative endings such as *Villette*, *Great Expectations* or *The French Lieutenant's Woman* offer. They are already explicitly ruled out before the story comes to an end. The other options truly left open beside the overt endings are what may follow Pearston's hysterical laughter when he recognises the decrepit Marcia: 'O — no, no! I — I — it is too, too droll — this ending to my would-be romantic history!' (*Ill.L.News*, p. 775). The uncertainty of what this will lead to is increased by the immediately following 'Ho — ho — ho!' from the narrator himself which closes the novel. This is disconcerting immediately, retrospectively and predictively from one who has constantly seen events with detachment. Such endings are critically allowable as relevant, of course, only under the altered critical status I propose for early variants. And overlooked in the last novel in the trilogy, *The Well-Beloved* is the rift in closure represented by a prospective addition to the chain of like/unlike events that Hillis Miller identifies as comparable with the multiplot novel: the sudden appearance in the last chapter of the third Avice running away from her apparently much-loved husband Henri Leverre. This episode begins another unfinished and open-ended story as the young couple are left 'to adjust their differences in their own way' (p. 193). The final phrase reverberates with ironic possibilities, given the Caro inheritance. The absence of closure in *Jude* is present not only in the prospects for Arabella and Vilbert but also in Arabella's final misreading of the past and prediction for the future. No more unreliable commentator could be found except perhaps Lockwood in *Wuthering Heights*. All three novels refuse to resolve definitively the relationships between the sexes: taken together they offer mockingly different options. They isolate the reader in doubt where tradition had reassured him with certainty. He must write his own text.

Concentration on openness of endings has meant a failure to recognise an equally important aspect of the final trilogy: provisionality of plot. Hillis Miller's suggested alternative endings, for instance, are rather to be construed as alternative plots frustrated before the novel ends, not left open. They are two of many; openness goes further back into the texts than a stress on endings suggests. It makes evident the fact that all accounts are interim and it reveals the potential of all events to take another course or courses.

A sense of the openness or uncertainty of narrative seems to be Hardy's from an early date. In the Preface to *The Trumpet Major* (1880):

> Those who have attempted to construct a coherent narrative of past times from the fragmentary information furnished by survivors, are aware of the difficulty of ascertaining the true sequence of events indiscriminately recalled.[26]

His grasp of the fictional nature of history leads naturally to an understanding of the precarious nature of fictional narrative. A tendency in the direction of provisional plots can be seen in 1871 when he produces alternative outlines for a short story. In Plot 1 he suggests: ' — Girl goes to be schoolmistress: leaves her village lover: loves a school-master: he meets old lady in cathedral: she proposes.' But side by side with this in Plot 2 we read:

> Violinist in country town: poorish: is going to marry neighbouring village girl (school-mistress) or one of same town: loses his finger: hopeless case: strolls into cathedral or abbey: old lady meets him there . . . she proposes to him . . . they marry privately: go away to her house. Another man, a school-master, who has long secretly loved the school-mistress now hopes to make way with her.[27]

This sounds like an illustration of what the Preface to the *Trumpet Major* describes: the original subject of the story (the girl) is displaced by a new one, the violinist whose object she becomes. Similarly the school-master is displaced as the husband of the old lady by the intrusive violinist. The contrast is disconcerting: is this the same story? Where is the reader to draw the limits between the same story and a different one? This is a question which the trilogy also poses.

The same process is seen at the end of Hardy's career when he collaborated with Florence Henniker in writing the story 'The Spectre of the Real' (earlier 'The Desire'). According to his biographer, who draws on the evidence of letters written in 1893: 'He provided an initial outline and suggested a number of alternative directions which the narrative might take, especially at the very end.'[28] As late as 1926 it is recorded in *The Life* that he wrote to a friend with reference to a proposed dramatisation of *Jude*:

> Of the outlines I sent you which suggested themselves to me many years ago, I thought the one I called (I think) '4th scheme' most feasible.
>
> Would not Arabella be the villain of the piece? — or Jude's personal constitution? — so far as there is any villain more than blind Chance.[29]

In fact *Jude* itself is an expansion of the process of the production of alternative plots by Hardy in drafts and letters. It is one of the alternative plots in *The Pursuit* that developed into a novel before *The Well-Beloved* was written. It derives from Pearston's disastrous marriage with Marcia. This is the germ that burgeons into a lengthy and detailed narrative displacing all other major elements of plot. After marrying Pearston for mainly economic reasons Marcia like Arabella quarrels bitterly with her husband and leaves him to go to the other side of the world with close relatives. As Arabella damages Jude's books Marcia smashes one of Pearston's statuettes. The two partners in the 1892 marriage see general implications in their own mistake:

> A legal marriage it was, but not a true marriage. In the night they heard sardonic voices and laughter in the wind at the ludicrous facility afforded them by events for taking a step in two days which they could not retrace in a lifetime, despite their mutual desire as the two persons solely concerned.
>
> (*Ill. L. News*, p. 481)

Marcia articulates fully the generalisation about this 'ludicrous facility':

> Was there ever anything more absurd in history . . . than that grey-headed legislators from time immemorial should have gravely based inflexible laws upon the ridiculous dream of young people that a transient mutual desire for each other was going to last for ever! (*Ill. L. News*, p. 481)

In *Jude* this bitter condemnation of marriage expands to become a constant accompaniment to events. It is recurrently rehearsed by Sue, Jude and the narrator. Hardy, not always his own best interpreter, later described the marriage laws as 'the tragic machinery of the tale'. The general drift of the story on the domestic side, he said in 1912, tended to show that '. . . in Diderot's words, the civil law should be only the enunciation of the law of nature' (p. xxxvii). This simplistic description is modified and complicated in the text itself where the characters' construct, 'Nature's own marriage', as opposed to legal marriage, disintegrates in the experiences of Sue and Jude who are supposed to embody it. This chilling and bitter account is an amplification of *The Pursuit*'s assumption of a true marriage remote from that which entraps Pearston and Marcia. Their legal and 'untrue' marriage disappears altogether in *The Well-Beloved* in a fashion reminiscent of the 1871 short story plots. The provisional nature of narrative again subverts the reader's trust in a single reality: events, like people, can take many shapes.

This comparison of narrative line in the trilogy shows change not as a method of subtle adjustment but as the law of a world where all is chance. The provisionality of narrative is amplified still further by what I have characterised in Hillis Miller's material as alternative plots: in the last three novels 'ghost' plots shadow real ones. Pearston *might have* disappeared, *might have* committed suicide, but does neither. These ghost plots represent the subjunctive mood of non-fact alongside the actual events which involve the indicative mood of fact. They emphasise again the fact that any story is one of many possible alternatives that chance plucks into reality. Gillian Beer, though not recognising this generalisation about the subjunctive, speaks briefly of 'optative' plots in Hardy, seeing them as frustrated happy endings.[30] But not all 'subjunctive' plots are optative and even with those that are, distinctions have to be drawn. Pearston's failed suicide and cancelled disappearance in *The Pursuit* are optative on his part but not on that of the narrator. Nor does the text strain forward with his desire to accomplish these events, willed but undesired. It does so with his unfulfilled hope of marrying the second Avice which is both willed and desired. His desperate plans bespeak necessity, his marriage plans volition.

But other frustrated or subjunctive plots are not optative at all, rather they are contingent. They say not 'if only' but 'what if' and evoke the potential of all sequences of events to take another course through the labyrinth. There is in both *The Pursuit* and *The Well-Beloved* the pivotal episode in which Jocelyn is doubtful about deserting the first Avice and marrying Marcia and consults his friend Somers. The friend's advice is to marry Avice 'if anybody'. If he had taken the advice it would have been a route to a different (and possibly incestuous) outcome, for it would have made him father to Avice the second. But Somer's advice is ignored and this lurid plot remains non-fact. However, the story is drawn back later to a similar line of narrative development when it is suggested that he is about to marry the second Avice and so unwittingly become stepfather to Avice the third, who represents his final obsession. Twice the shadow of Pearston's potential incest is strongly evoked, only to vanish. It underlines the already incestuous overtones of his love for mother, daughter and grand-daughter. Similarly the possibility of the chaste well-beloved, Avice, becoming impure is raised in *The Pursuit* in a carefully introduced confession from the second Avice Caro of the shifting object of her erotic desire. Besides being secretly married when Pearston woos her she has already transferred her affection to a soldier and has 'loved' fifteen men before (of whom Pearston was briefly one). 'What if the ideal woman were as promiscuous as a man?' asks the text before this thread is concealed rather than broken. The epiphany remains a disturbing minor element in *The Pursuit*; is perhaps dimly referred to in Sue's multiple lovers in *Jude*; and only brought to prominence through the occurrence of related elements in *The Well-Beloved*. In 1892 the narrator toys with the possibilities of incest or female promiscuity by the raising of these episodes. He creates a dark hinterland at odds with the continual assertion of the sexual purity of both sexes. 'The plot' repeatedly bifurcates into the actual (and indicative) and alongside it the desirable or possible (and subjunctive). Hardy, typically indignant at the charge of having breached conventional moral standards, particularly when he had done so, wrote in 1897:

> That a fanciful, tragi-comic half allegorical tale of a poor visionary pursuing a Vision should be stigmatized as sexual and disgusting is I think a piece of mendacity hard to beat in the annals of the press. (*Letters*, 2.154)

As with *Jude*, the hostile reviewers were more exact than he about the handling of sexual matters measured by the prevailing standards.

The subjunctive plots of *The Pursuit* are of two kinds, optative and contingent; one kind deriving from Pearston striving after the ever-shifting well-beloved; the other from the narrator aware always of possible alternative sequences of events, conventionally shocking. They run alongside an already ambiguous actual plot discussed later. In *Jude* a narrowing occurs and subjunctive plots are all optative. The text is haunted by 'if only . . .', overridingly from Jude, aspiring to a shifting elusive well-beloved and to a Christminster which is the creature of his imagination only. But for the detached narrator of *The Pursuit* is substituted the neurotically involved teller of Jude's tale. Already by his title he has claimed it as Jude's own, though it is equally or perhaps more Sue's. And what is optative for Jude is so for him too, despite his partial understanding of how fictional women are conventionally appropriated to signify limited meanings and despite his partial rejection of these limits. At one point in the novel Jude and Sue try to dismiss 'a too strenuously forward view' (p. 303); this the narrator cannot do. He strives forward willing Jude's dreams to come true and lamenting their frustration. When the boy Jude discovers that there is no simple code for translating Greek and Latin the narrator invokes another more desirable world in a past subjunctive that always captures in English the frustation of desire or hope:

> Somebody might have come along that way who would have asked him his trouble, and might have cheered him by saying that his notions were further advanced than those of his grammarian. But nobody did come because nobody does. (p. 27)

Like the vast web of subjunctive plots underlying *Little Dorrit* (or

Nobody's Fault) these frustrated optative plots recur at crucial points in Jude's life: his ardent plan for self-instruction is first aborted by 'the unvoiced call of woman to man' in the person of Arabella who holds him 'against his intention — almost against his will' (p. 37). He has a glimpse of his dreamt-of future briefly: 'as by the light of a falling lamp one might momentarily see an inscription on a wall before being enshrouded in darkness' (p. 39). Sexuality as the death of other higher aspirations and the world they might involve extends even to his relationship with Sue, and charges that sequence of actual events with more complex frustrations than appear at first. The course of events in relation to both women is determined by 'conjunctive orders from headquarters, unconsciously received by unfortunate men when the last intention of their lives is to be occupied with the feminine' (p. 36). In his pursuit of Sue, frustrated optatives, of course, occur. When she leaves her husband to live with him everything progresses on the assumption that they are to be lovers, but at the last moment on their way to a hotel she makes it clear that they are not. This subjunctive plot is one in which Jude and Phillotson participate; only Sue's equivocation prevents them from realising its unreality until Jude is enmeshed. The pathos of his frustration which these plots evoke represents a traditional view of the havoc wrought by the sexuality of women. They also contain a hostile view of the New Woman at odds with much of what the text asserts about Sue.

The pattern of verbal mood of plot in *The Well-Beloved* is different again. As in *The Pursuit* the narrator is still detached in relation to optative plots and intrigued particularly by those contingent ones which involve potential incest that may be optative on his part. But some of the previously actual plots now move into the realm of non-fact and become like several in *Jude*, frustrated optatives. Pearston's attempts to marry Marcia and the third Avice are both examples. So, seen against *The Pursuit*, what the last novel shows is earlier fact now become non-fact; the two worlds are separated by only a hair's breadth as *Jude* constantly makes clear, and now the reader sees that the line can be and has been crossed. These plots are not a *combination* of 'the gratuitous and the inevitable'; *only* the gratuitous is inevitable and its form is provisional and by implication endlessly variable.

These changes in plot between the two texts involve changes in the handling of gender roles, implicit also in the transposition of characters. There is no need to argue the centrality to *Jude* of legal and physical relationships between the sexes, but there is for the other two novels, so often regarded as fantasies remote from legalities or the flesh. This is a grossly inaccurate description of *The Pursuit* and is reductive of *The Well-Beloved*; both subjects are central to them. In fact the very issue over which Sue, Jude and the narrator attack the marriage laws is one specifically raised by Marcia in the earlier 1892 novel: that a 'legal' marriage is different from a 'true' one and (in all circumstances?) is based on a 'ridiculous dream . . . that a transient mutual desire . . . was going to last for ever!' (*Ill. L. News*, p. 481). This same point is made about the marriages watched by Sue and Jude as well as Jude's union to Arabella. On that the narrator comments:

> And so, standing before the aforesaid officiator, the two swore that at every other time of their lives till death took them, they would assuredly believe, feel, and desire precisely as they had believed, felt, and desired during the few preceding weeks. What was as remarkable as the undertaking itself was the fact that nobody seemed at all surprised at what they swore. (p. 56)

But *The Pursuit*, that delicate fantasy, according to some modern accounts, goes much further than *Jude* in its unconventional handling of the legalities of marriage. In a contemporary view it was outrageous: Pearston accepts his wife Marcia's argument from analogy that separate hemispheres equal divorce and 20 years later decides to marry the second Avice. Though a common law presumption of a spouse's death after seven years of absence existed until 1938, there remained also a legal requirement that each case be determined on its own facts, with reference to such matters as whether the person had been heard of by those likely to hear of her and whether due enquiries had been made. Pearston concerns himself with none of these and yet is furious to discover that such a marriage as he proposes would be bigamous on Avice's part. Before he finally succeeds in committing bigamy with the next Avice he does follow up a possible clue to his legal wife's whereabouts in an overheard conversation:

> Pearston was instantly struck with the perception that these facts . . . were in accord with the history of his long-lost wife, Marcia. To be sure they did not go far; and he hardly thought that she would be likely to hunt him up after more than thirty years of separation. (*Ill. L. News*, p. 642)

And when he sees no more of the talkers he is 'not deeply concerned'. The report is that she has gone back to the Isle of Slingers. His search there is desultory, his conclusion casual:

> Nothing had been heard of any such lady, the nearest approach to a visit of the kind being that made by a woman whom a flyman had driven over the island in search of a family now dead. As this lady did not answer to the description . . . Pearston concluded he had got to the bottom of the matter in considering it a casual correspondence only. (*Ill. L. News*, p. 642)

His concern is with whether she will reappear, not whether she is alive. His doubts about marrying have no reference to possible bigamy; his torments are to do with his age.

Pearston's high-handed way with legality again emerges when, after his marriage to the third Avice, he discovers her love for Leverre. He writes magisterially to Somers:

> My marriage with Avice is valid if I have a reasonable belief in my first wife's death. Now, what man's belief is fixed, and who shall enter into my mind and say what my belief is at any particular time? The moment I have a reasonable belief that Marcia lives Avice is not my wife . . . I have only therefore to assume that belief and disappear, and she is free.
>
> (*Ill. L. News*, p. 774)

This takes the case against legal marriage much further than *Jude*. Its source is somewhat laconically explained by the narrator who describes Pearston as a man 'whose pursuits had taught him to regard impressions and sentiments as more cogent than legal rights' (*Ill. L. News*, p. 741). His advanced attitude to the law, however, is combined with a high degree of sexism. The character of Jude in the next novel shows that feature splintered and questioned but not eradicated. It is *The Well-Beloved* which, ironically, though it removes all traces of bigamy, completely overthrows conventional images of male and female roles.

To understand fully this pattern of change in the handling of gender roles through the trilogy it is necessary to be clear that both *The Pursuit* and *The Well-Beloved* are dealing with sexuality. Their

loud insistence that Pearston/Pierston's love is spiritual and platonic, that 'it was not the flesh' cannot be accepted at face value.
It is an insistence made all the more emphatic and high-flown in
The Well-Beloved. Already in *The Pursuit* the stress is there: 'Essentially she was perhaps of no tangible substance; a spirit, a dream,
a frenzy, a conception, an aroma, an epitomized sex, a light of the
eye, a parting of the lips' (*Ill. L. News*, p. 426). In 1897 it becomes
extravagant, reducing carnal love to the sterility of a classical
allusion: 'Sometimes at night he dreamt that she was "the wile-
weaving daughter of high Zeus" in person, bent on tormenting
him for his sins against her beauty in his art — the implacable
Aphrodite herself' (p. 34).[31] But descriptions of the well-beloved's
embodiments are all too tangible and constantly subvert such
grand claims by their physicality. She is always seen as flesh even
when Pearston/Pierston is only viewing prospective candidates for
the role. One such is the 'young lady of the house' at Lady
Channelcliffe's party who 'appeared to more advantage that night
than she had ever done before — in a sky-blue dress, which had
nothing between it and the fair skin of her neck, lending her an
unusually soft and sylph-like aspect' (p. 71). Similarly with the
possible Nichola Pine-Avon he is first struck by how her 'black
velvets and silks . . . finely set off the exceeding fairness of her
neck and shoulders, which, though unwhitened artificially, were
without a speck or blemish of the least degree' (p. 74). This
close scrutiny of her skin has a detail lacking in his subsequent
assessment of her intellectual gifts: 'she held also sound rather
than current opinions on the plastic arts, and was the first
intellectual woman he had seen there that night' (p. 74). It is the
back not the brain that interests him. He hardly gets close enough
intellectually to any of the women to find out what they are really
like. Indeed with the laundress Avice he recognises a social and
intellectual inferior and focusses his attention on things like her
'shapely pink arms' which 'though slight, were plump enough to
show dimples at the elbows, and were set off by her purple cotton
print' (p. 102). Marcia with her 'fine figure' and imperiousness
becomes the well-beloved on the basis of appearance and proximity:
'The Beloved was again embodied; she filled every fibre and curve
of this woman's form' (p. 48). With all this, the link he makes
between women and his interest in beauty for his art's sake sounds
like protesting too much; the more it is emphasised the less
conviction it carries.

There are too oblique but significant references to sexual awareness or arousal in both novels. He is disappointed at the lack of a
matching 'consciousness' in the second Avice who when alone at
night with him in his London house concentrates all her attention
on a troublesome mouse: 'Her lack of all consciousness of him, the
aspect of the deserted kitchen, the cold grate, impressed him with
a deeper sense of loneliness than he had ever felt before' (p. 128).
He wants her to recognise 'a danger in their propinquity'. There
is, too, arousal implicit in the scene where Pearston/Pierston, after
sheltering from the storm with Marcia under a boat, walks on with
his steadying arm around her waist:

> Somewhere about this time . . . he became conscious of a
> sensation which, in its incipient and unrecognized form, had
> lurked within him from some unnoticed moment when he was
> sitting close to his new friend under the lerret. Though a young
> man, he was too old a hand not to know what this was, and felt
> alarmed — even dismayed. (pp. 45–6)

Since he is thinking 'how soft and warm the lady was in her fur
covering, as he held her so tightly' the conclusion that this means
'a possible migration of the Well-Beloved' becomes a euphemism.
Especially as further reflection on her 'fine figure' and then
contemplation of the clothes she gives him at the inn for drying
bring him to 'adore' her (p. 47) and complete the migration. The
meaning of the Avices' surname plays a part here. It has, like the
epigraph, more significance than at first appears. *Caro* is, according
to Hardy, an 'imitation of a local name' modified to connect it with
the Italian word for 'dear'.[32] So much for the surface. It is also, as
he fails to point out, the masculine not the expected feminine form
of the word and a Latin word meaning 'flesh'. As the savagely
hostile reviewer of *The Well-Beloved* in *The World* (24 March 1897)
puts it: '*Caro, carnis* is the noun with the declension of which Mr.
Hardy is perpetually and everlastingly preoccupied in his new
book' (p. 13).

So all three novels are centrally concerned with legal and physical
relations between the sexes; and the handling of gender is different
in each. In *The Pursuit* Pearston for all his advanced views on
marriage is sexism incarnate: women are merely present as the
objects of his desire. He is subject of the narrative sentence and
manipulates two women, Marcia and the third Avice, into wretched

marriages. He appropriates them physically by this bond and intellectually (along with many others) by incorporating them into his fantasy of the well-beloved. Women are categorised always and only as being either the well-beloved or not the well-beloved. They exist in no other relation for he creates their identity as he creates a common identity for three separate and distinct Avices; and as he sees fit he erases their identity just as Angel Clare erases that of Tess. He dehumanises them by equating them with his sculptures. The narrator remains uncommitted in this recital.

In *Jude*, as my account of Jude and Phillotson shows, the nature and roles of men are brought into question. There are conflicting versions of Jude: at one moment a Pearston assuming that male desire is paramount, at another the traditional male led astray by women, or an advanced thinker about women, or an equal with them in love and suffering. Similarly Sue is alternatively an autonomous New Woman or a neurotic, sexually liberated or frigid, or a brain-washed victim of patriarchy and religious superstition. The attempt to find a new balance between the intelligent and liberal-minded woman and her male counterpart results in an enactment of confusion over sexual identity and the struggle between them. Roles of subject and object are interchanged. Old signifiers struggle with new and the narrator is drawn into the conflict of uncertainties.

In *The Well-Beloved* this changes. The narrator is now detached and assured. The sexual objects Marcia and Avice become subjects by asserting their autonomy: Marcia leaves Pierston and Avice also elopes before he can complete their marriage. Pierston becomes the object they act upon until the last chapter when out of pity he marries Marcia (now in a wheel-chair). He then occupies himself with 'a scheme for the closing of the old natural fountains in the Street of Wells, because of their possible contamination' (p. 193). The drying up of erotic and artistic impulses comically imaged here as a job of work has often been noticed. *The Well-Beloved* goes further. The brief moment in a deleted passage in the manuscript of *Jude* when he sees in Sue 'the rough material called himself done into another sex' (p. 149) is transposed into a scene in which the moon seems to Pierston like 'his wraith in a changed sex' (p. 148). But in this version equality vanishes and the male becomes a worshipper bowing his knee to the female divinity. The confession of the second Avice that she too chases the well-beloved now falls into place. Her pursuit is the equal of Pierston's but carried on with a matter-of-factness and sprightliness that makes his claim to connection with Aphrodite seem pretentious. And the hint that though male desire for change may have dried up, the female's has not, occurs in the very belated incident showing that the third Avice has quickly tired of Leverre.

In this changed treatment of the sexes the narrator's detachment takes on a ludic force. Subjects becomes objects, objects subjects, women dislike monogamy as much as men and survive longer as sexual beings. The change from the 1892 text to 1897 is mimicked by the change of title. *The Pursuit of the Well-Beloved* with Pearston as pursuer and women as pursued gives way to *The Well-Beloved*, a simple comic assertion of their supremacy. If this is a fantasy it is not a delicate dream. It does not 'solve' the problems evoked by *Jude* since it shifts the focus of attention from conflicting versions of the protagonists to plot and narratorial stance. It handles those problems on a different level and resolves them only by a *tour de force*. Throughout his earlier novels Hardy had shown an ambivalence in his treatment of women and their relationships to men which have often led to contradictory descriptions: he is, for instance, 'humane and enlightened';[33] or, to take the other extreme, he is essentially 'manipulative, even faintly sadistic' in his narrative stance.[34] Some critics[35] recognise and describe the contradiction. This fault-line perceived by such critics produces in the last three novels an earthquake in which women, their partners and their story fragment under the intense pressure of contradiction and the language of prose fragments into poetry.

Notes

1. Hereafter *The Pursuit*.
2. Hereafter *The Well-Beloved*.
3. C. Belsey, 'Constructing the Subject: Deconstructing the Text', in J. Newton and D. Rosenfelt (eds), *Feminist Criticism and Social Change*, (New York: Methuen, 1985), pp. 45ff.
4. H. Orel, *Thomas Hardy's Personal Writings* (London: Macmillan, 1967), p. 4.
5. Ibid., p. 53.
6. Ibid., p. 49.
7. Ibid., p. 39.
8. Ibid., p. 43.
9. F. E. Hardy, *The Later Years of Thomas Hardy, 1892–1928* (London: Macmillan, 1930), p. 90.

10. Orel, *Personal Writings*, p. 49.
11. Hardy, *Later Years*, p. 54.
12. Ibid., p. 175.
13. R. B. Heilman, 'Hardy's Sue Bridehead', *Nineteenth Century Fiction*, vol. 20 (1966), p. 307.
14. M. Jacobus, 'Sue the Obscure', *Essays in Criticism*, vol. 25 (1975), pp. 304–28.
15. Heilman, 'Hardy's Sue Bridehead', p. 307.
16. Jacobus, 'Sue the Obscure', p. 325.
17. W. J. Hyde, 'Theoretic and Practical Unconventionality in *Jude the Obscure*', *Nineteenth Century Fiction*, vol. 20 (1965), pp. 155–64: p. 156.
18. E. Langland, 'A Perspective of One's Own: Thomas Hardy and the Elusive Sue Bridehead', *Studies in the Novel* (1980), pp. 12–28: p. 25.
19. J. Goode, 'Sue Bridehead and the New Woman', in Mary Jacobus (ed.), *Women Writing and Writing about Women* (London: Helen Croom; New York: Barnes & Noble, 1979), pp. 100–13: pp. 103–5.
20. References are to my World's Classics edition of *Jude* (1985).
21. R. L. Purdy and M. Millgate (eds), *The Collected Letters of Thomas Hardy*, (Oxford: Oxford University Press 1978–).
22. Pearston is the hero's name in *The Pursuit*. I use it to distinguish him from Pierston of *The Well-Beloved*.
23. Quotations from *The Pursuit* are taken from the only full version in print: *Illustrated London News* from 1 October to 17 December, 1892.
24. Hardy, *Later Years*, p. 217.
25. J. Hillis Miller, *Fiction and Repetition* (Oxford: Basil Blackwell, 1982), pp. 147–75.
26. Orel, *Personal Writings*, p. 14.
27. F. B. Pinion (ed.), *Old Mrs. Chundle and Other Stories* (London: Macmillan, 1977), p. 117.
28. M. Millgate, *Thomas Hardy, a Biography* (Oxford: Oxford University Press 1982).
28. Hardy, *Later Years*, p. 249.
30. G. Beer, *Darwin's Plots* (London: Routledge & Kegan Paul, 1983), pp. 239–40.
31. Quotations from *The Well-Beloved* are taken from the New Wessex edition by J. Hillis Miller (London: 1975).
32. Hardy, *Later Years*, p. 60.
33. K. Rogers, 'Women in Thomas Hardy', *Centennial Review*, vol. 19 (1975) no. 4, pp. 249–58: p. 257.
34. J. B. Wittenberg, 'Thomas Hardy's First Novel: Women and the Quest for Autonomy', *Colby Library Quarterly*, vol. 18 (1982) no. 1, pp. 47–54: p. 54.
35. For example, P. Boumelha, *Thomas Hardy and Women: Sexual Ideology and Narrative Form* (Brighton: Harvester Press, 1982).

4

She, to Him

Howard Jacobson

'Why don't you come to the class I'm giving this morning', Camilla asked me, 'on *Our Exploits at West Poley*?'

'*Our* what?'

'*Our Exploits at West Poley*. It's a children's story that Hardy wrote for an American magazine called *The Household*, a publication "Devoted", in its own words, "to the Interests of the American Housewife".'

I gave a little cough at the word Housewife to show that I was through with all that, 'And it's a children's story, you say?'

Camilla could hear me winding up my little *jeu d'esprit*. 'Yes, yes, I know,' she said. 'All his stories are children's stories. But this one has a special interest, because where all the others are meant to be for adults and aren't, this one isn't meant to be for adults but is.'

'You mean it's about virility?' I wondered. If I sounded whimsical it was only because I didn't want to sound desperate. Virility, after all, was the very subject I'd travelled far to Castle Boterel to talk about. Why else had *I* set out for Lyonnesse?

Camilla narrowed her eyes at me. She'd clearly had a lot of experience of dealing with people who thought she was fanciful when she was most serious. She seemed sombre, impenetrable. 'It's a story about caves and potholes,' she said. 'It's about going underground. When a novelist who always has more of himself concealed than an iceberg decides, literally, on a subterranean action, then one has no choice but to lower oneself down with him. The plot centres, by the way, on the damming of rivers.'

If Camilla was prepared to go all the way with Thomas Hardy, I was prepared to go all the way with Camilla. I narrowed my eyes in return. I seemed suddenly to know more than I'd ever known I'd known about the significance of damming rivers. But I was still innocently curious about one thing. 'How come I've never heard of this story?' I asked. A note of scepticism struck me as sensible, just in case Camilla was having me on.

'It was lost for years,' she said. 'Some scholar has just recently dug it up.'

Given what Camilla did to the word scholar I was mightily relieved I wasn't one.

The above being a work of fiction, I felt it was permissible for me to take some minor liberties with chronology — *Our Exploits at West Poley* was in fact 'dug up' in 1952 — in much the same spirit as I believed it wasn't necessary to name the scholar who did the digging. Serious students of Thomas Hardy would know at once, of course, that it was Richard L. Purdy, while less punctilious readers might be presumed to be grateful for being spared the bibliographical inessentials.

The last thing I wanted was to spoil anybody's fun. *Peeping Tom* is a love story after all, and followers of love stories are notoriously more particular than lovers are themselves as to what properly constitutes the discourse of romance. Too much Purdy and God knows how many readers I might have lost. I can confess now, though, *inter nos*, that what was uppermost in my mind as I unzipped my hero from his sleeping-bag, breakfasted him, washed him and prepared him for Camilla's morning lecture, was Richard L. Purdy's introduction to that first publication in book form, in an edition limited to 1050 copies, of *Our Exploits at West Poley*. Distinct above the beatings of Barney's heart within, and the crashing of the wandering western sea without, I could hear Purdy:

> *Our Exploits at West Poley* is only the story of two boys and a cave, but the familiar touches of the Wessex novels are not wanting . . . the rural life and characters, though very lightly sketched, are simple and timeless . . . The figure of the Man who had Failed is a kind of chorus, oddly out of place but oddly characteristic . . .

Faced with such 'onlys', such 'oddly thisses' and 'oddly thats' — tokens of a blank inability, or an even blanker refusal, to engage with the material unearthed — a fellow enquirer might grow apoplectic, or shave his head, or take to crime. I wrote *Peeping Tom*. The chapter which follows that wherein Camilla invites Barney to her class — she runs her own Alternative Centre for Thomas Hardy Studies — might fairly be read as an alternative

Introduction to the children's tale for so long buried in the pages of *The Household*.

Our Exploits at West Poley concerns two cousins with deceptively uncharged names — Steve, tall, masterful and headstrong and not near the Author's conscience, and Leonard, delicate, nervous and acquiescent and the I that grows to tell the tale — who go exploring in the Mendip Caves and accidentally discover that they are able to alter the course of the stream that runs through the local parish, diverting it from West to East Poley and back again, and thus influencing the domestic and commercial well-being of the parishioners in each. The story affects a gently homiletic air, not exactly that of mere precept, but a healthy tone, as Hardy himself put it, suitable to intelligent youth of both sexes, alternating action with comments on the difficulty of discriminating between one community's rights and deserts and another's, and pressing the superior claims of discretion over adventure. In the background but never far away hovers the mythic figure of the Man who had Failed, enabled (and indeed ennobled) by that very failure (he had failed through want of energy and not want of sense) to make the wisest decisions and speak the truest words. 'Quiet perseverance in clearly defined courses is, as a rule,' he tells Steve who needs to be told, 'better than the erratic exploits that may do much harm.'

'Okay,' said Camilla to her class. 'What's this story really about?'

It always makes a melancholy spectacle, adults penned in children's tiny desks, straining their eyes towards a teacher just as they did a half a lifetime before, still without any answers to someone else's questions. And the matrons who sat in rows before Camilla this morning — all members of a vigorous local women's group — were especially touching. Tyrannical instructresses in their own homes, empresses and undisputed law-givers there in all matters great and small, they were cramped and even cowed here, mere vassals in the grip of another's imperious will. Worse for them, too, they had been set the conundrum most bewildering and insulting to the domestic and maternal mind: they had been asked to consider the possibility that a thing was not the thing it said it was but another thing entirely. Motherhood is necessarily inimical to philosophy; the close proximity of a baby fills a mother's head with the inescapable poignancy of the real, and long after the baby has grown up and gone she is still fiercely protective of hard facts and actualities. And so they were angry with Camilla who didn't look as if she had ever kept a child or a kitchen clean, and their anger made them wilfully obtuse, wedded them to their obtuseness, bound them in an intense ideological attachment to it. 'It's just a story,' they said. 'It's about two little boys who go into a cave and get up to mischief. Little boys are like that, you know.'

'Go on,' said Camilla. 'What else is it about?'

'It's about why boys should learn to look before they leap, and to leave things as they find them.'

'Yes, go on,' said Camilla.

'It's about not altering what already works. Not being too ambitious. Not letting other little boys have too much influence over you.'

'Go on,' said Camilla.

'It's about why you shouldn't make comparisons. Why you shouldn't go into caves. Why you should listen to the advice of your elders.'

'Yes, yes, so what is it *really* about?' asked Camilla. She seemed to imply that they were on the brink of it now and needed to make only one more little leap of the mind.

But she had wearied them. She searched the rows of closed faces in vain. I was sitting at the back, lying low and keeping quiet, but I felt that even I had let her down.

'Let me give you a clue,' she said. 'Thomas Hardy was forty-three when he wrote this story, which means that he had been married for almost ten years. He was becoming famous and meeting other women. And as we know, not a woman could alight from an omnibus in sight of Thomas Hardy without suggesting to him another turn that his life might take.' Camilla looked hard at me as she said this, but whether I was meant to see myself as Hardy or the girl getting off the omnibus I couldn't decide. But there was terror in it for me either way.

'And here we find him writing,' she went on 'ostensibly for children, about the damming and diversion of streams, about the small obstacles which hold back the mighty roll of the seas, about the excitement of watching the water change direction, about the havoc it causes, and about the final inadvisability, for

spurious parishional reasons, of altering the directional flow of
a single solitary drop.' She paused and smiled — what a
marvellous public smile she had — at an image that had formed
itself in her mind. 'Let me put it another way. The climax of
this story is reached when the two pre-pubescent males find
themselves lost and drowning in the cave, itself screened and
fringed by bushes, with nothing to help them but a small supply
of inadequate guttering candles,' She threw back her head and
laughed one of those ravening piratical laughs of hers. 'Now tell
me that you don't know what's going on in West Poley,' she
dared us all.

There were still pockets of resistance to her, but the small
guttering candle lit a common recognition amongst the women.
There were some smiles, there was even some laughter, and
more than one curious face swung around to see how I was
taking all this, alone and masculine on the back row. They
needn't have bothered. It wasn't necessary. I had already
sputtered and gone out.

Camilla was now at the blackboard, with an assortment of
coloured chalks between her fingers, drawing a picture. In her
free hand she held a copy of *Our Exploits* and she consulted it
as she spoke and drew as if it were an instruction manual. 'You
will remember,' she told us, 'that the reason the boys play with
the water in the first place is because they want to turn it out of
their way so that they can get to that delightful recess in the
crystallised stone work of the cave which is shaped like the apse
of a Gothic church.' We watched as Camilla carefully drew the
apse of a Gothic church. 'It is Steve, the headstrong one, who
almost pays for his impetuosity with his life, who is most
delighted by this beautiful glistening niche. "How tantalising!"
he says. "If it were not for this trickling riband of water, we
could get over and climb into that arched nook, and sit there
like kings on a crystal throne!" And what is it that Leonard says
in reply? "Perhaps it would not look so wonderful if we got
close to it." The soul of Thomas Hardy is distilled into the line —
that is all you need to know to understand the bitter dejection
of his wives.' Camilla's chalk squeaked on the blackboard. Pink
dust flew like sparks from under her fingers. 'Because what is
that niche that Leonard fears to approach, that beckons so
alluringly to one and threatens so much anti-climax to the other,
and is finally blown up with dynamite and sealed for ever? What

is it that is described as having the colour of flesh, ornamentations
resembing the skin of geese after plucking, or the wattles of
turkeys' — on to the board went the wattles of turkeys – and is
decorated withal with water crystals — what is it if it isn't this?'

Camilla stayed where she was for another half minute, engrossed in the minutiae of art, then, with a theatrical flourish, she
tossed the chalks into their tin and strode from the blackboard,
allowing us all to admire the giant yawning vulva which she
had sketched with such faithful attention to texture and tincture
from its early origins as the apse of a mediaeval church. *Our
Exploits at West Poley* she tossed to me, high over the heads of
the intervening women. It landed open on my desk. 'I think
you'll agree that I've stuck . . . to the text,' she said.

Well, she was a shock tactician. They would never have
granted her tenure at most English universities. But she knew
how to send a current through me. Her drawing galvanised me.
I sat at my desk with my hair erect and light coming out of my
fingers. If I needed further proof that my ties with Thomas
Hardy were not familic, then here it was; not I, nor anybody
else for that matter, could be connected to him through *that*
channel — not I, nor anybody else living or dead, could claim
kinship with him via *that* organ of transmission, enblazoned on
the blackboard in shocking technicolor pink . . .

Is it any wonder that I am consumed by loss? Do you think I
don't know how unlikely it is that I will ever again find a woman
who will do for me what Camilla did?

The ladies, naturally, were not as carried away by Camilla's
demonstration as I was. I wasn't paying them an awful lot of
attention but I had the impression that they were thawing out a
bit. And I do remember that one of their number actually found
the courage to applaud. But of this I am confident: they'd
recognize aggressive misogynistic timidity when they next saw
it, and they'd know what they were reading about when they
next came across the crystallized wattles of turkeys in a so-called
children's book.

'You can now see the significance of the role of the Man who
had Failed,' Camilla concluded. 'The Failure he proudly wears,
like a badge, is a failure, in Hardy's words, of energy. He is a
not uncommon figure in Hardy's works. He represents the
superior moral worth of enervation. He is the apotheosis of
impotence. What a humiliation it must have been for Emma

Hardy to have lived with a man who yearned every day of their
life together to channel his stream into another bed but lacked
the force to do so and called his inertia sagacity. A faithless
husband is a shame to a wife but a husband who is ineffectively
adulterous, who wants but lacks the courage to take, dishonours
her ineradicably. After Emma's death Thomas Hardy found
amongst her papers a mass of diary entries gathered together
under the title, "What I think of my Husband". You won't be
surprised to learn that he destroyed them. His remorse for his
wife is famous, but it wasn't strong enough to allow her to have
her say. People have often speculated as to the contents of those
diaries. It isn't necessary. *I* know what she wrote. *I* know what
She thought of her Husband.'

'Later that day,' my hero confides, having afforded himself the
breathing space of a subchapter, 'I took the step of deciding to
stay in Castle Boterel.'
Quaint of him to suppose it was ever in his power to make a
decision either way. Susceptible men don't escape places such as
Castle Boterel. Hardy didn't. And it was merely a woman who
could ride who trammelled him. My hero is doubly snared; he is
caught by a woman who can read.
There is nothing unusual, of course, in literature pandering to
romance. Aphrodite has always been the patron Goddess of
reading matter. Heloise and Abelard, Francesca de Rimini and
Paolo, Camilla Marteline and Barney Fugleman — they are all
palpitating victims of the Book. Except that in the case of the last
pair it is not so much a shared enthusiasm that lights the torch as
a common disinclination, an interchange of disapprobation. Camilla
Marteline and Barney Fugleman fall in love excoriating Thomas
Hardy. They tear at his flesh with as much self-forgetful industry
as they rend each other's. It would be hard to say which of the
three is ultimately pared most nearly to the bone. And since
we accept such violence as an inevitable, a necessary, even a
complementary component of passion, we must be similarly large-
mind about its place in interpretation and exegesis. No greater
love for the strenuous discipline of literary criticism hath anyone,
than Barney and Camilla with their teeth bared.
It's for her pamphleteering prose, before he knew her face or
name, that Barney fell for Camilla in the first place. The pamphlet
in question, entitled *Hardy's Jaunt With Mrs Henniker* — the subtitle,

The Duffer in the Puffer, might or might not be Barney's invention —
returns to wound him along after Camilla has decamped. Searching
through her papers he finds an early rude form of it, sans footnotes,
sans acknowledgements, sans decorum, in which condition, I feel
sure, Camilla herself would not at all object to its reappearing.

HARDY'S JAUNT WITH MRS HENNIKER

or

THE DUFFER IN THE PUFFER

'I wired a room for us at the Temperance Hotel,' Jude told Sue
Bridehead, after he'd given up his job and she'd given up her
husband, and they were together at last on the 18.52 train from
Melchester, due in at Aldbrickham at 21.59.
  'One?'
  'Yes — one.'
  Sue bent her forehead against the corner of the compartment.
'O Jude! I thought you might do it — but I didn't mean *that*!'
  'So what, for fuck's sake, *did* you mean?' Hardy decided
against letting him reply. (It was an unnecessary scruple in the
event — the book got him into trouble anyway.)
  'Well!' was all Jude was allowed to say instead. But he did get
to say it twice. 'Well!' he said again. And then he stared,
stultified, at the opposite and presumably vacant seat.
  Sue drew away from him and looked out into the darkness.
Whatever she saw it couldn't have been the hill, unless the train
was well off course, where the gibbet of their common ancestor
had stood. It wasn't often that they did anything without the
gibbet symbolically looming up behind them. So this journey at
least had the merit of variety.
  'I resolved to trust you to set my wishes above your gratification,' she reproached him. 'Don't be a greedy boy.'
  This stultified him once more. But his response — 'This is a
queer elopement!' — showed admirable restraint. He might have
been forgiven, in the circumstances and with his history, pulling
the communication cord there and then.

So might, in another verson of a strikingly similar story, Florence Henniker, the apparently emancipated and promising society woman with whom, at the very time that he was writing *Jude*, Hardy took an abortive train trip of the heart to Winchester, and who, whatever it was she'd promised or that Hardy thought she'd promised, found herself, like Sue Bridehead, having to explain the whys and the wherefores of non-delivery in that perfect setting for disappointment, that place from which everything seems possible but nothing much happens in, a railway carriage. The metaphor of the train as an inexorable engine of non-consummation had been a favourite of Hardy's long before he'd failed himself to run away in one with Mrs Henniker. Stephen Smith and Elfride Swancourt, fleeing Castle Boterel (the lucky blighters), have their passions rocked and cooled on the Plymouth to Paddington express some twenty years in advance — and when the trains were that much slower — of Jude and Hardy having theirs. This might seem another intriguing example of the faculty of prophecy in novelists, their uncanny knack of being able to describe in their early fiction what they are going to do in their later lives; but in fact it's no more than rudimentary self-knowledge. One has a pretty good idea at thirteen, let alone at thirty, what sort of fool one's going to be; one might as well get in first with the fable and steal a march on fate. That's the only advantage over it one is ever going to enjoy.

But even if Hardy had been a dab hand at queer elopements all his life, the connection between Jude's with Sue and his own with Florence Henniker doesn't look fortuitous. He's been hurt by a woman's prevarication afresh, and Jude made to look an oaf is a reproach to Mrs Henniker, a prick, if ever there was one, to her Christian conscience; just as the sepulchral humour of the scene is a go at putting a brave face on mortification.

And why not? Mistaking the intentions of the other sex is never much fun, and all the evidence suggests that Hardy mistook Mrs Henniker's, eyeball to eyeball in that compartment, on a scale. Part of the trouble, of course, was class. By which I don't mean that Hardy couldn't afford to travel first. Florence Henniker was the daughter of an aristocrat; and the daughters in the Hardy family were not always dead certain whose they were. That in itself didn't stand in the way of friendship and needn't have been a bar to romance; but a woman at home in society, accomplished in all the conversational arts, of which

flirtation — especially literary flirtation — would of necessity
have been one, such a woman could not have supposed, merely
because she sent a fifty-three-year-old novelist photographs of
herself in average *décolletage* and translations, done in her own
hand, of only moderately doubtful French poets, that she was
thereby embarking upon a desperate passion. The point is not
that she was unaware of the way things worked in Dorset; what
she could never have known was that the novelist fell in love
with every woman he met, fell in love with her instantly and
irremediably and on the spot, and all the more ardently if her
spot was at some remove from his, that's to say on the far side
of a busy street or on the opposite bank of a wide swirling river,
espied from the top of turning omnibuses or through the
windows of fast moving trains. As long as she was walking in
the opposite direction or was too far away from him to catch, he
needed no further encouragement. He left home and changed
his life for her, imaginatively, there and then. Which was a lot
of fun for Mrs Hardy. Fifty years on he would remember in fine
detail the features of a girl who had flitted past him while he
was in a florist's and he would ache for the happiness with her
that he'd missed. But if it was distance that did the trick, if he
sought the contrivance of some impediment or barrier, it didn't
have to be material. Glass was good. Class was better.

So Florence Henniker, sister of the Viceroy of Ireland, daughter
of literary Lord Houghton, who entertained famously and owned
a notorious collection of erotica — erotica! who collected erotica
in Puddletown? — Mrs Henniker could be construed as leading
Hardy on just by being alive.

As for being alive where he could *see* her — that was nothing
short of coquetry. And she piled it on. She smiled at him and
shook his hand. They conversed and corresponded. He wrote
to her about church architecture and she, throwing prudence to
the wind, replied. She accompanied him to the theatre to see
Ibsen — Ibsen! And finally she agreed to take a train with him
to Winchester. It must have felt to him like a betrothal.

No wonder he was disappointed. Men far less susceptible
might have pinned their hopes on Winchester. It's not only for
convenience and privacy that Henry James's most intensely
adulterous couple go off to plight their infidelity in Gloucester.
There's something in the air of cathedral cities.

Just as there's something in the movement of a railway

carriage, which was where, alas, it was all decided, long before they got to Winchester. No. No. She shook her head. She was sorry. She wasn't as free a thinker as he thought she was. She hadn't meant *that*.

'Well!' he might have been excused exclaiming, in the circumstances and given his history. 'Well! This is a queer elopement!'

But it's unlikely that he would have enjoyed himself with her in Winchester whatever she'd said. He was, above all things else, the poet of the disappointment of the actual moment. A successful afternoon with Mrs Henniker would have left his creative sensibility in ruins. You can't throw yourself into writing *Life's Little Ironies* or *Time's Laughing-stocks*, if you've got a warm aristocrat snuggled into your shoulder. Those whom the Muses love must go without. *Ecce signum!* —

> And we were left alone
>   As Love's own pair;
> Yet never the love-light shone
>   Between us there!
> But that which chilled the breath
>   Of afternoon,
> And palsied unto death
>   The pane-fly's tune

— he got the thing he wanted after all.

But since they were in town, not doing what he thought they were going to do and therefore doing something even better, he had the opportunity to take her to look at the milestone where, impelled by a force which seemed to overrule their will, Angel Clare and 'Liza-lu had stopped, turned, waited in paralysed suspense, and seen the black flag signifying Tess's successful execution move slowly up the mast. Florence Henniker, as an admirer of his prose, would not have needed pressing to see such a distinguished landmark. And Hardy himself was never loth to imagine or re-imagine the hanging of a woman — particularly, perhaps, in these circumstances, one whose death made it possible for Angel Clare to get a second bite of the cherry and toddle off up the hill hand in hand with with 'Liza-Lu, as he, Thomas Hardy, was not destined to toddle off anywhere with Mrs Henniker. Which is not to say that Mrs Hardy was the only obstacle, any more than it is to say that he would have taken active steps to remove her if she were. A wife is an absolutely essential possession to those pathological romancers who see a shimmering new future in every woman they meet but are congenitally parsimonious with their seed. She saves them from their own timidity. She serves as a bulkhead against which they can knock their skulls, a moral impediment in the name of which they can curse the fates, and thus she confers a tragic grandeur on a small disability. It's difficult to imagine Hardy taking the chance of laying a single part of himself on any woman, let alone as current speculation would have it, being careless, or giving enough, to get Tryphena Sparks with child. As for Florence Henniker, think of it like this: if he had really hoped to hear her call him hers, he would surely have chosen a different place to hear her call him hers in — he had known all his life to expect nothing good from public transport.

Barney has reasons other than dispassionate literary ones — unnecessary to go into here — for finding Camilla's case persuasive. But he is speaking in a general and impersonal way, and is certainly not anticipating contradiction, when he says, 'Camilla's argument had the unmistakable ring of truth: it was witty and acerbic and misanthropic and disdainful. And if you can't trust acerbity and wit backed up by misanthropy and disdain, what can you trust?'

Acerbity and wit, misanthropy and disdain — those are, it almost goes without saying, a young man's words. Only ever intermittently young herself, and never verdant as only a man can be verdant, Camilla would certainly have employed a less flashy vocabulary of cynicism to describe the quality of her own thoughts. A plain little word like experience might well have done her, as a substitute for Barney's mouthful of milk teeth. It being always understood that the experience she had in mind benefited specifically from being a woman's.

I do myself happen to think that there is such a thing as a woman's intelligence, proceeding from a woman's experience. There is nothing mystical about this. We need not invoke genetics or biology or even role sociology. It is simply something which derives from the sensation of not being a man, yet of listening to men at their most urgent and confidential, and of coming to know them at their most profligate or grudging. Thus the idea that a man might be parsimonious with his seed, and that this might be a moral and intellectual condition which will show, first and last, in the very rhythms of his speech and art, is one most likely to be in the gift of someone who has suffered, as it were at first hand, the infinite varieties of non-delivery. What Barney likes to see as Camilla's brilliance is often, for her, a matter of seasoned and sombre reflection on the dishonesties which prevail between the sexes. It is Camilla, ultimately, who does the leaving; not Barney. And her decision to go is entirely consonant with all that she has offered to know about Thomas Hardy and all that she has offered to understand about the bitterness of being either one of his wives.

In this way I see her as a more tragic figure than the man she walks out on. More serious and philosophical than him, and therefore more certain of the limits of romantic rapture. Not unlike Thomas Hardy himself, you might say, except that Camilla would argue that it was expectancy itself that flickered forever in the Max Gate grate, amid the ashes of so much else; and that it was precisely that expectancy which broke the spirit first of one, then of the other co-occupant of that cold house.

'Look at his face', Camilla one day orders Barney, showing him a collection of photographs of Hardy ripped from the frontispieces of old novels, 'what do you see in it?'

Not knowing what to look for, Barney does his best in the circumstances. He mentions what we all see: the drooping moustaches, the weary eyes, the general sag of disappointment.

'Fancy dress,' Camilla tells him. 'Mere muscular imposturings. You're just describing the man's idea of himself.'

I like Camilla for that; for reminding us that one man might *choose* to look sad and sorry, as another might affect an air of indifference or scorn. But she hasn't finished. 'What you should be asking yourself,' she goes on, 'is what the disappointment and the moustaches are there for. What are they hiding?'

Hiding? Barney knows better than to protest that they need not — need they? — be hiding anything. The language of concealment has a special frisson in relation to Hardy. The novels are ingeniously constructed hidey holes. The poems shiver with quarter promises of half-confessions. Mere letters and apparently plain biographical data are not what they would seem. So why not also the moustaches?

Led to look where he would never of his own accord have thought of finding secrets, Barney notices — 'The lip?'

Of course the lip. That's the one real and uncontrolled feature on his face. The reason why of all the others. The soft, moist, plump, vulnerable vermilion lower lip. Can you imagine what it must have been like for him, having that as a permanent flashing beacon of his uncertain maleness? Not surprising, is it, that he duplicated its expression — 'significant flexuousness' he called it — on every one of those less than decisive heroes of his. Look, look, even in his eighties it's still there, making a liar out of the tragic philosopher, a hot little protrusion of wet flesh, full of blood and girlish expectancy. So picture it in the heyday of his long delayed and long extended adolescence, while he waited and waited for his virility: how it must have glowed and throbbed, as fresh and as sweet as the skin behind a cherub's knee, as palpitating and as erubescent as a virgin's closest secret.

It's presumably only because Barney is still untutored in the ways of understanding men and women, whether they are writers or not, that Camilla slips in 'significant flexuousness', to remind him that a discussion of the face must of necessity also be a discussion of the prose. She is not unaccustomed to the charge of fantasticalness. And she is not unfamiliar with that half-understanding of things which would argue for the rights of the arbitrary and the contingent, as if what we think and write, and what etches itself upon our features, are matters of mere hazard. Does not Richard L. Purdy see *Our Exploits at West Poley* as 'only' a story, 'simple and timeless'? When prose itself is held to be no clue to the prose, how much the more contentious the lip.

No one knows better than Camilla how difficult it is to argue on the side of seriousness.

Note

Peeping Tom was published by Chatto & Windus, the Hogarth Press, in 1984.

5

Hardy's Fictional Process and his Emotional Life

Michael Rabiger

Because a biographer does not work from facts alone, but also from an unavoidably personal response, each tends to see a subject differently. To Robert Gittings[1] Hardy had the naïve craftiness of the French peasant and a secretive, poetic genius behind which lay a warped sexual identity and a meanness of spirit towards his wives. Michael Millgate's Hardy[2] on the contrary is honest and true, faithful to his obligations, uncomplaining, and discreet rather than secretive.

Reviewers have said that after these two lengthy biographies we should neither expect nor need another for a long time to come. Actually, what we have seen in these new accounts (not to mention *The Collected Letters* and *The Life and Work of Thomas Hardy*) is a huge increase in Hardy's accessibility as a man. Such enlarged and differing perspectives send one back to the literature in excitement and perplexity, especially as both biographies confirm the reader's intuition that Hardy makes an almost documentary connection between his private life and his fiction.

But where, since 1982 when Millgate's superb *Biography* appeared, is the discussion one might expect? Most scholars seem to have averted their attention from these new Hardys and their contradictory implications. Though Hardy's richest and most committed creation, *Tess*, has sustained an uproar of debate and reinterpretation for a century, most scholars appear indifferent to changes in perception of its author, as if Hardy's life remains too ordinary to be worth associating with his work. Yet it seems to me that uncovering more about Hardy's life simply highlights how much of his artistic process remains to be defined and appreciated.

The new biographical information reiterates how often and closely Hardy dramatised episodes in his personal life. My interest has been to search Hardy's large output for any common denominators in theme, character and life-originals that might reveal

88

underlying methods in his habitual conversion of life into art. Any defined method, if at all correct, should indicate more clearly what his most meaningful experiences were, and perhaps what might be missing from the present biographical record. Of course one must seek the essential Hardy more through his works than in what he wrote about himself, for, as Havelock Ellis says of fiction, 'Every artist writes his own autobiography.'[3] This is wonderfully ironic applied to Hardy, who ghosted *The Life* specifically to overturn the popular image of himself established by his fiction. But *The Life* is an old man's book that skilfully papers over the cracks. Its omissions and distortions, particularly in his early life, send one back to his works in a frustrated search for what is missing.

Obviously one should not read fiction as transcribed autobiography. However, the sequence — where it can be established — of Hardy's large body of work is in itself a telling record of how his imagination and ideas evolved. Because he uses stock figures, and sometimes follows favourite patterns of adaptation, a consistent approach is possible to help interpret his underlying emotional life. By focussing upon the repetition of particular roles, themes and situations developing through the works, an archetype keeps obtruding, much in the way that archetypes have been discerned from their variations in Arthurian romance. The strength of this archetype, its endurance and consistency with known facts, suggest that some unresolved and deeply painful experience stands as a motivating source at the core of Hardy's work. My purpose here is to propose on a very modest scale how deeply Hardy's fictional process was fuelled by his archetype, and to briefly demonstrate how it provides a constant by which to assess some of the nature and development of Hardy's inner life.

While Hardy left only fragmentary evidence of his working methods and thus a great deal is open to conjecture, there can be little doubt over his esteem for the authenticity of the real. Of this, Millgate says:

Hardy's plots may be invented or borrowed, but much of his richest narrative material is re-worked more or less directly from the life. If he never tells a wholly autobiographical story, the texture of his work is nevertheless thick with remembered experience and observation, and with family and local traditions possessed so absolutely by the imagination as to be indistinguishable from memory itself.[4]

The implications of an 1860s note that Millgate calls 'eloquent of [Hardy's] conception of working through imitation to originality' should not, however, be confined to Hardy's youthful period of self-education. He never revised his early opinion that the 'Same sitn from experience may be sung in sevl forms',[5] adapting from actuality not through any lack of imagination, but out of wonderment at the enormous and fertile ambiguity of the real. Apologising rather satirically in the April 1896 Preface for misrepresenting Rhoda Brook in 'The Withered Arm' as throwing off the incubus at night when in life it had happened in daylight, Hardy asked readers to forgive the way that 'our imperfect memories insensibly formalise the fresh originality of living fact — from whose shape they slowly depart, as machine made castings depart by degrees from the sharp-work of the mould'.

Millgate comments that 'for Hardy "living fact" had an integrity to which fiction could offer, at best, a poor approximation'.[6] Though this is undoubtedly true, the formalisation to which Hardy alludes is less the degradation inseparable from reproduction than it is the much misunderstood expressionism of his artistic process itself. Distortions arising when his tales depart from their factual origins really signify the intensity and nature of Hardy's poetic insight rather than any abandonment of intrinsic truth.

If we are to understand the underpinning to Hardy's fictional and autobiographical world, we must concern ourselves with the spirit of Hardy's representation, as well as with the sources of his borrowed plots and 'living fact'.

Hardy was also quite able to absorb a favourite artwork into the general texture of his personal experience, and in his writing was equally likely to explore its hold on him. He adapted in a wide variety of ways, openly using Gottfried von Strassburg's *Tristan* as a source for *The Queen of Cornwall* (1923), and less openly adapting other works in the making of his own. Hardy's career in literature even began from adaptation, by cannibalising his unpublished first novel,[7] and feeding it in bite-size pieces back to the literary establishment that had rejected it. Rather more shadowy was his plagiarism from the *Quarterly Review*[8] for *A Laodicean*, and again from a history of the Napoleonic wars[9] to fill out *The Trumpet Major*. The latter was doubly unfortunate as its author had himself plagiarised it from elsewhere.

There is also a literary indebtedness in some Hardy works which he must, through preserving names and situations, have been ready to acknowledge, though he seems to have gone unchallenged. The first was the early work, *A Pair of Blue Eyes* (1873), which was initiated from the characters in Jane Austen's *Emma*.[10] Probably begun at Weymouth in summer 1871, he first gave it the rather recriminatory title, *A Winning Tongue Had He*, suggesting that the tale was first conceived as a ballad treatment focussing upon Knight. The novel developed by making extensive use of Hardy's visits to Emma Gifford in Cornwall. Apparently as a tribute to her, he took some of the names, characters and central relationships from Austen's novel and rearranged them around this Emma of his own, assigning other roles to friends and family from his small circle of intimates.

Of Austen's six main characters Hardy takes four; that is, the heroine, her father Mr Woodhouse, their neighbour Mr Knightley, and her protégée, Harriet Smith. In Hardy's version, Emma Woodhouse is recast as Elfride, the isolated daughter of a snobbish rural parson. Austen's self-centred Mr Woodhouse reappears as the autocratic Parson Swancourt, while her gentleman farmer Mr Knightley is reincarnated through the literary reviewer Henry Knight. Rather enterprisingly, Hardy puts the lower class Harriet Smith through a sex change to become Stephen Smith, the girlishly handsome architect of humble parentage.

Hardy's version is piloted into foreign waters by very different characters and the author's utterly different outlook.[11] Where Austen's novel focusses on strong-willed Emma trying to steer the weaker Harriet for her own good, and later learning from her mistakes, Hardy's transcreation subjects Austen's characters to a series of traumatic displacements in which the disadvantaged are consumed by the strong. The displacement of a weaker man by a stronger in a competition for a woman is the heart of the archetype I want to demonstrate, and emerges first and unequivocally in *A Pair of Blue Eyes*.

Stephen Smith, by extolling his mentor's superiority, unwittingly ensures that Elfride's emotions will migrate to the other man when he enters her life. Elfride, seeing Knight as more worldly and established, dumps Stephen, who realises bitterly that he has been displaced by the only man he truly admires. Then Knight, who has virtually no women in his life, drops Elfride because his virginal ego cannot accept she has kissed another man. The reader is made to discover, along with Stephen, that Knight, unlike his chivalrous prototype, is a hollow man, a literary mandarin whose pronouncements conceal the prudery and dishevelment at the centre of his life. By the time Knight returns from his flight abroad — like Angel Clare, in a more liberal frame of mind — Elfride has in turn dumped him and made an advantageous marriage to Lord Luxellian. She, dying prematurely, is, however, dumped by life itself, and in a contrived ending, Hardy makes the two former friends, Knight and Stephen, stand united again through loss at her graveside. By thus discarding its heroine the novel shows her to be an outworn catalyst and reveals its primary concern to be with the rupture of friendship between the two men.

Most of Hardy's life-models are easily distinguished: the architect Stephen, developed out of the illegitimate Harriet Smith, reflects the premaritally conceived Hardy himself; Stephen's parents, a stonemason father and a servant mother, evoke Hardy's own parents; Parson Swancourt, derived from Mr Woodhouse, is a composite of Emma Gifford's parson brother-in-law and her unpalatable father; the reviewer Henry Knight reflects Hardy's own mentor, the classics scholar and reviewer Horace Moule. One should note that, as the owner of the 'winning tongue', Knight suffers a transformation from Austen's Mr Knightley that is nothing less than scathing. Elfride, the Emma Woodhouse figure, embodies Emma Gifford's blue eyes, equestrian skills, romantic Cornish setting and aspirations to be a writer.

For a literary tribute, however, the book strikes some oddly discordant notes, depicting Elfride as very young and inexperienced, which Emma was definitely not, and by naming her Elfride yoking her behaviour to that of a murdering, twice-married Dorset queen. Equally incongruous, if he has Emma Gifford in mind, is the critical, even censorious attitude Hardy takes towards his heroine over her abandonment of Stephen. That Hardy should associate the woman he was going to marry with such behaviour is hard to understand until, as will be shown, she too proves to be a composite — in appearance modelled after Emma Gifford, but in her actions of rejection incorporating those of quite another and much younger woman with whom Hardy was angry.

There is a shift in point of view that further indicates an autobiographical thrust. *Blue Eyes* does not attempt to play out Austen's relationships from the manipulating Emma's point of

view, but instead focusses our perceptions through the manipulated figure of Harriet Smith. For Stephen more often than Elfride is
the novel's point-of-view character, even though his pale personality and lowly antecedents lead to his undoing. Again, this is hard to
reconcile with the novel's roots in Hardy's Cornish experiences,
where his prospects were rising and we are supposed to believe
he was well over the threshold of romance. Instead, *Blue Eyes* is
about losers and deliberately told from the stance of the most
victimised character. Its tone is sometimes cynical and embittered,
yet, dealing as it does with the themes of female impressionability,
male friendship, class barriers, and sexual eclipse, it departs only
moderately from Austen's model. But Hardy's *tone* could hardly
be more different, and I shall argue that it reflects powerful,
unexorcised feelings arising out of events concluded before he ever
arrived in Cornwall.

That Hardy was a man of powerful feelings is undeniable, for
all his lifelong stance of neutrality. Yet nowhere can one read of
him *acting* upon his passions, nor even of his once being candid
about them — not in his letters, not in surviving notebooks, not
in Emma's diary, not in anyone's memoirs. This type of imprisoning
silence and passivity so often causes excruciating pain in his best-
loved characters that one must surely discard the conventional
labelling of it as a dramatic device. Rather, it attests to a lifelong
emotional straitjacket confining Hardy himself, one that made
writing, and writing a displaced personal commentary, a daily
necessity. Hardy's writing is not just a place where, like other
sincere artists, he confronts and organises the dominant forces in
his life; it is the *only* place. To comprehend this isolation fully
means understanding at a stroke why local people thought he
withheld himself from them, why he was so dependent on the
women who knew him from domestic life, why his wives felt so
excluded from his real existence, and also why we at this remove
can feel instinctively protective of him.

Thus writing was not simply a discharge of feeling, but a bid to
validate his own emotions through arousing the sympathies of a
readership, both general and particular. *A Pair of Blue Eyes*, like
much that he wrote, should be read as a fictionalised address —
in part victimised, in part indignant, in part candidly confessional —
written with specific readers in mind. One such was Emma, seldom
closer than a hundred miles during all their lengthy courtship.
Another was Horace Moule, the master surpassed by his pupil,

surely being castigated through the portrait of Knight. A third
person, a young woman who jilted or rejected Hardy, is consistently
his most important reader, and we shall come to her.

If Hardy saw himself as he describes Stephen Smith — an
adapter lacking in originality[12] — it did not deter him from using
the same method and even the same novel as quarry for the next
and vastly more successful *Far From the Madding Crowd* (1874). Here
he makes use of characters and relationships from *Emma* previously
overlooked. He again acknowledges his literary debt by retaining
similarities in his characters, their names, professions and places.
Highbury is reflected in Weatherbury; Enscombe in Norcombe;
Frank Churchill in Frank Troy; and Miss Taylor in the Taylor
sisters. Two of the suitors are farmers of widely differing means,
and both books contain scenes set on a farm with ecclesiastical
associations.

Austen's clandestine lovers reappear: Frank Churchill, whose
sin in *Emma* is to flirt with the heroine while engaged to Jane
Fairfax, is expanded in *Madding Crowd* into Frank Troy, whose
amoral charm ensnares Bathsheba and her property. Like Frank
Churchill, Frank Troy has a prior liaison concealed, and, predictably,
the pregnant Fanny Robin suffers a magnified fate. Following
Austen's pattern, Hardy makes Troy's heart, like Churchill's,
belong ultimately to the concealed, wronged woman from his past.
Farmer Martin's patient and ultimately rewarded love for Harriet
Smith is faithfully paralleled in Farmer Oak's for Bathsheba, but
though the heroine's name is this time biblical rather than historical,
Hardy has again picked a name associated with infidelity and
betrayal.

Significantly, Hardy returns to the same love triangle from *A
Pair of Blue Eyes*. Once more a fickle woman is courted by a young,
lower class man who is displaced by a socially superior elder,
likewise sexually repressed. A new development is the arrival of
the sexually adept and aggressive third contender, Sergeant Troy.
The character of Bathsheba now incorporates elements of both
Emma Woodhouse and Harriet Smith. Just as Hardy extends
Bathsheba's impetuosity and intrusiveness beyond Austen's
model, so he heightens Boldwood's potential, developing his initial
imbalance into obsessiveness, insanity and self-annihilation.

Bathsheba, learning the cost of her impulsiveness and unfettered
sexuality, and recognising how seriously she underestimated her
own vulnerability, is greatly chastened at the end. Implicit is a

close scrutiny of how she handled the power derived from her beauty and material inheritance. In fact, Hardy is critical and even disparaging towards both Bathsheba and Elfride for too lightly exercising their power of sexual choice. This judgement befalls far too many of Hardy's heroines for it to be a dramatic convenience: rather, he appears to be repeatedly revisiting some block in his personal life.

An underlying drive to render private account is most readily established by returning briefly to Knight and Boldwood, each suggested by Austen's courtly and wise Mr Knightley. Henry Knight is unmistakably developed from Hardy's experience of Horace Moule[13] and though Moule's tutoring and friendship did so much to raise Hardy's sights to becoming a writer, this and other portrayals suggest that his influence was not wholly benign. Despite this ambiguity, or maybe because of it, the role he played influenced Hardy's work immeasurably.

The outlines of Moule's character are fairly well known: a talented and ambivalent Victorian parson's son, he was almost certainly a homosexual trying to conform to a heterosexual style of life.[14] His career as a university student, teacher and reviewer was dogged by inconsistency, failures and terrible bouts of drinking that led to delirium tremens. One must believe that his private miseries were as extreme as the refuge he periodically sought. In 1873, four months after *Blue Eyes* was published, and supposedly after a 'governess of sterling character' broke off her engagement to him,[15] Moule cut his throat in his Cambridge rooms.

Hardy was, I believe, much more deeply distressed than might appear. Though a friend's suicide always causes guilt, Hardy's writing shows he felt more deeply implicated. Not only had his once affectionate relationship with Moule recently contained rivalry and bitterness, but he had expressed it trenchantly through the portrait of Knight. Moule's disturbed and equivocating initial reaction to the novel is glimpsed in a letter worthy of Henry Knight himself. Though superficially jocular and warm, Moule uses a condescension not found in other surviving correspondence, lancing away at Hardy's vulnerabilities: 'You understand the *woman* infinitely better than the *lady* & how gloriously you have idealised here and there, as far as I have got. Your slips of taste, every now and then, I ought to say pointblank at once, are *Tinsleyan*.'[16] Hardy, seemingly, must be reminded not only of his lower class limitations, but that his publisher drops his aitches.

Soon after, when Moule must have read the remainder, the two met for a long talk in Cambridge, where Moule was now a Poor Law Inspector. By this time, Moule's engagement — if it existed — had failed. Hardy waited half a century before alluding to his last meeting with Moule. In 'Standing By the Mantelpiece (H.M.M., 1873)' the speaker, evidently Moule, says:

> Let me make clear, before one of us dies,
> My mind to yours, just now embittered so.
>
> Since you agreed, unurged and full-advised,
> And let warmth grow without discouragement,
> Why do you bear you now as if surprised,
> When what has come was clearly consequent?

The person addressed has been variously identified, but is most probably Hardy himself. The poem's 1873 confrontation, foreshadowing the speaker's death, centres upon a third person, presumably a woman, who is the subject of jealousy and bitterness. Read thus the poem parallels the confrontation between Stephen and Knight in which Knight berates Stephen for keeping silent about his engagement to Elfride.

Five weeks after the Cambridge meeting, Moule published a generous and approving review of *Blue Eyes* in the *Saturday Review*. The implication is that Moule had accepted a degree of responsibility for whatever had clouded their relationship, and either in recompense or to demonstrate goodwill, wrote a magnanimous review that only protests at the priggishness of Knight. Six weeks after, and for possibly unrelated reasons, he took his own life.

The impact upon Hardy can be assessed from seeing how differently Boldwood is handled compared with his predecessor Knight. Both are older, socially superior and emotionally unstable. Unlike Austen's Mr Knightley, both intrude between the younger man and his beloved. Boldwood replicates Knight's pattern of obsession and loss, becoming dominated by a dream in which the idealised younger woman assuages his loneliness, and losing his bid to possess her. Like Knight, he does so because of his inexperience and unease with women. But while Knight fails and simply returns in tragi-comic defeat to bachelorhood, Boldwood's failure, written after Moule's death, leads through rising frustration to insane jealousy. He kills his rival Troy, and then attempts to kill himself. Hardy attributes this violence to the effect of emotional turmoil on a radically unstable personality, and thus Boldwood, unlike the worldly and sanctimonious Knight, is relieved of responsibility.

Both novels depict similar events and explore similar aspects of the same troubled personality, but the changes of characterisation are telling: while Knight is hypocritical, pompous and patronising towards the younger man who had so admired him, Boldwood is by contrast honourable, isolated and repressed, someone for whom the reader feels exasperation and pity. Stephen's disenchantment with Knight had been a baptism of fire which enabled him to grow up, while Oak's feeling for Boldwood remains fixed at a high level of compassion and respect. At the end, it is Boldwood's legacy which makes him prosperous.

To draw the older man in the triangle more sympathetically without making Oak any less of a victim than Stephen, the woman must be held correspondingly more accountable. It is fascinating to consider that Bathsheba's bold and active personality may thus be the result of Hardy's search for those womanly qualities which could, without evil intention, make so much misery for the two displaced men, Oak and Boldwood.

If one searches Hardy's work more widely for the older man role, one discovers nothing less than a cavalcade of these haunted, alienated and often misogynistic figures. Surveying the novels alone, we find Manston, Knight, Boldwood, Lord Mountclere, Sir Blount Constantine, Henchard, Fitzpiers, Phillotson and Pierston — each counterpoised against a young man competing for a woman. There is a vast range of ideas and human experience generated from the tension and rivalry between these figures, whose range of relationships all appear to explore aspects of Hardy's unresolvable relationship with Moule.

Thus for Hardy writing fiction was not a substitute for living, but an adjunct and an extension to it — a necessary completion process by which he might either travel deeper into underexplored territory or, as Millgate puts it, venture down 'a road not taken'.[17] In the early years of his marriage, while keeping his distance from the Dorchester area, he appears to have tried withdrawing from active emotional life in order to sift and express what had so far taken place. If he intended investigating the past only, he soon found himself dealing with the pressures of the present: *The Hand*

of Ethelberta (1876), for instance, uses a female protagonist to delve
into the dilemma of a member of the servant class masquerading
as an upper class storyteller, while *The Return of the Native* (1878)
dramatises the internal conflict in a married man whose loyalties
are divided by a rivalry between wife and mother.

Hardy seems to have started each novel with a plot framework,
often borrowed. Into this he placed characters modelled upon
individuals with a private emotional importance to him. In *Blue
Eyes* and *Madding Crowd* he had cast his own actors in Jane Austen's
roles, but their individuality made them take such idiosyncratic
directions that Hardy effectively created a new novel. In modern
drama composition, allowing players to influence or redirect a text
is common in experimental and improvisational work. A director
will forgo the (often arid) security of the premeditated script and,
using charismatic actors, give them their head in a skeletal script.
By encouraging the actors' initiative, by shaping and editing
their improvisations, the director taps the individuality and life
experience of each while still pursuing the original thematic
intentions. In his films, Ingmar Bergman has long followed this
procedure, using actors who in reality populate his private life.

Actually the process is almost certainly very old. Being actor-
centred rather than text-centred, and found today in both the
theatre and the cinema, it probably revives the collaborative
way drama was developed before directors and writers became
common. Though Hardy predates modern practices, he was the
child of folk-musicians and professional renovators who made no
distinction between art and living. Having a faculty for recalling
distant events and personalities, and even a taste for the rural
theatrical tradition, Hardy seems to have envisaged play performances in his mind's eye, writing down what he saw.

This emerging pattern, where Hardy develops the cross-fertili-
sing potential of a repertory cast, a text and reinterpretive aims, is
further visible in *The Mayor of Casterbridge* (1886), *Tess of the
d'Urbervilles* (1891), and *Jude the Obscure* (1896). But it is in *Tess* that
his drive to fictionalise around emotionally loaded figures from his
past is at its most haunting. In an essay, '*Tess* and St. Tryphena',[18]
I have outlined how strikingly both the novel's plot and heroine
resemble those of a Breton mystery play depicting the life of
an unfairly victimised princess. Titled 'King Arthur and Saint
Tryphena', the folk-play is on the fringe of Arthurian tradition,
and being Breton, embodies the medieval magic kingdom setting

that pervades *Tess*. The Breton Tryphena was an historical figure, and in Brittany there is a shrine to her. Guidebooks describe her as the patron saint of women with unsatisfactory husbands,[19] and describe the cult of lying in her open stone coffin overnight by supplicants wanting to acquire superior qualities.[20] This seems certainly where Hardy got the singular idea for Angel laying Tess in the abbot's coffin at night. A copy of the play was in the British Museum library at the time Hardy was much in the reading room and beginning *Tess*. This was also a time when his cousin Tryphena, the cousin with whom he had been romantically linked in his youth, was dangerously ill, although she remained in contact with her Puddletown relatives. She died while the novel was in progress, and its tone of personal and elegaic loss is, in my opinion, the outpouring of Hardy's complicated sense of bereavement.

While *Tess of the d'Urbervilles* is a literary prism reflecting a multitude of literary influences, the 1979 essay by Clarke and Wasserman, 'Tess and Iseult',[21] draws a significant link between aspects of *Tess* and parallel episodes in Gottfried von Strassburg's *Tristan*. The authors argue that this derivation explains how Tess's baby came to be called Sorrow (from *triste*) and how Hardy has the temerity to equip Angel with a harp (Tristan is a harper). The essay proposes that Izz Huett's name is a metamorphosis of the name Iseult, and that she and Tess are the two Iseults to Angel's Tristan. Hardy earlier considered, instead of the name Tess, calling his heroine Sue — a name close to the French pronunciation of 'Iseult' and one that Millgate notes is unaccountably meaningful to Hardy.[22]

Hardy's use of *Tristan* proves to be much more pervasive. Consider the novel centring upon Jude Fawley, that other divided figure in Hardy's fiction whom D. H. Lawrence called Tess's inverse. Here again the traditional outline is carried forward by a Victorian cast. A striking parallel is where Phillotson lets Sue go to join Jude, which closely follows Gottfried's scene between King Mark and Iseult. Much later Hardy directly retold Gottfried's version in *The Queen of Cornwall*, making Iseult instead of Tristan the centre of the tragedy. Of his play he wrote a trifle defensively, 'There are so many versions of the famous romance that I felt free to adapt it to my purpose in any way — as, in fact, the Greek dramatists did in their plays . . .'[23] Though he claimed that Arthurian legends began interesting him from 1870 when he and Emma visited Tintagel, it is significant that out of the wealth of tales available, he concentrates overwhelmingly on the one that echoes his personal background, redeploying its central situation over and over again.

A selective summary of Gottfried's *Tristan* will by now sound rather familiar: the love-child Tristan becomes the dispossessed young man who unwittingly interests his uncle and patron King Mark in the distant princess Iseult. Tristan, in love with her himself, must impotently watch as his beloved becomes the wife of his benefactor. Iseult, in love with Tristan, maintains a clandestine and adulterous relationship until the betrayed King, discovering their secret, magnanimously sets them free to love as they will. But the guilt and conflict they suffer over their disloyalty ensure they do not find happiness.

The first part of the story recalls *A Pair of Blue Eyes*, and the more complete version, *Jude the Obscure*. In fact, variations with many resolutions run like a connecting thread throughout Hardy's fiction. The Tristan figure is generally younger and less socially established, while the king figure is usually older but always in a stronger social position. As Hardy ages, he identifies increasingly with the older man. Working chronologically, one discovers the legendary love triangle, sometimes involving cousins, in a long list of works: In *Desperate Remedies* (1871) Cytherea loves architect Edward Springrove but is pursued by Manston, to whom she is attracted when she thinks Springrove has abandoned her; Fancy Day in *Under the Greenwood Tree* (1872) is engaged to Dick Dewy but secretly attracted by the attention of the new vicar; Elfride of *A Pair of Blue Eyes* (1873) migrates from Stephen Smith to 'Cousin Henry', the older Henry Knight, but she ends up marrying a different man; Bathsheba in *Far from the Madding Crowd* (1874) likewise graduates from teasing the young Farmer Oak, to the older gentleman farmer Boldwood, but moves on to a third contender; in *The Hand of Ethelberta* (1876), the heroine is pursued by the timid musician Christopher Julian and in the end marries Lord Mountclere, after rejecting Neigh and Ladywell; Thomasin's first interest in *The Return of the Native* (1878) is her cousin Clym, but she marries the publican Wildeve.

Short stories also make use of the triangle: Emmeline of 'The Duchess of Hamptonshire' (1878) is caught between the romantic young curate and her father's choice of an older, farming aristocrat; Lizzy Newberry in 'The Distracted Preacher' (1879) is courted by the curate who suspects she is having an affair with her cousin;

the non-conformist Paula Power in *A Laodicean* (1881), vacillates between the young architect Somerset and the reformed alcoholic aristocrat, William de Stancy.

From the early 1880s Hardy increasingly portrays marriage as something forced, uphappy or even violent. The heroine in 'The Honourable Laura' (1881), who is secretly married to her dour cousin James, responds to the winning tongue of the singer Smittozzi. When confronted by her husband, Smittozzi tries to kill him, recalling the violent destructiveness of Boldwood. In 'What the Shepherd Saw' (1881), Harriet is wooed by her cousin Fred, who is killed by her jealous husband, the duke. Another jealous aristocrat is Sir Blount Constantine, the husband of Viviette in *Two on a Tower* (1882). In his prolonged absence she falls in love with the younger Swithin St Cleeve. Margery in 'The Romantic Adventures of a Milkmaid' (1883) has an artisan fiancé Jim, but is attracted to the mysteriously sick and suicidal Baron.

'A Mere Interlude' (1885) presents Baptista Trewthen as an Iseult set to depart by sea to marry her father's marriage choice, the middle-aged shopkeeper Heddegan. Instead she resumes an old love affair with the young schoolmaster. With its Cornish geography and use of a sea passage, Hardy mischievously lays a clue by giving Baptista's landlady Mrs. Wace the name of the medieval Arthurian author.

In *The Mayor of Casterbridge* (1886) Hardy makes a breakthrough in empathising with the older figure. King Mark's role is taken by Mike, as his wife Susan calls Henchard, a dispossessed labourer who rises to be Casterbridge's king. Tristan, the singer of sad songs, is Farfrae, who enchants the town's inhabitants by singing of a lost homeland. His two Iseults are Lucetta and Elizabeth Jane. Lucetta, once involved with Henchard, rejects the mayor for the younger man, just as Iseult prefers Tristan over Mark. It is interesting, as Hardy faced his inevitable replacement by younger writers, to see that before Henchard becomes a king figure he starts as a Tristan, having an unwanted wife Susan as his Iseult, and later acquiring a second, Lucetta Le *Sue*ur. By hard work and self-denial Henchard ascends to Casterbridge's throne, a king who must by Hardy's natural law inevitably be challenged and deposed by the Tristan figure of Farfrae.

From about 1886 the woman in the triangle is more often unhappily married. As in the Tristan legend where Iseult's marriage is arranged by her father, Baptista's had been so arranged, and so is Grace Melbury's in *The Woodlanders* (1887). First promised to her childhood companion Giles to atone for a wrong, her father raises his ambitions for her to the philandering scholar Fitzpiers. The theme, of a woman being persuaded to marry against her will and missing her true love, is played out again in 'The Waiting Supper' (1888): Christine Everard loves Nicholas Long but instead must marry the squire's nephew, who is cruel to her. In spite of opportunities later, she and Nicholas never make it to the altar. And again, in 'The Melancholy Hussar' (1889), Hardy makes Phyllis Grove, engaged to the negligent older Humphrey Gould, fall in love with the homesick young foreigner Matthaus Tina, whose execution she must witness.

Betty in 'The First Countess of Wessex' (1889) is forced to marry the older Stephen Reynard but falls in love with Charles Phelipson. When she puts her two lovers to the extreme test, Hardy makes her discover the older man to be the one who truly loves her. In *Tess* (1891) too, it is the quality of men's love which is responsible for the tragedy. The heroine is attracted to the wandering harpist Angel, but instead gets Cousin Alec, and suffers for the incompleteness of each man's love. In *Jude* (1896) the primary triangle is the teacher Sue, her stonemason cousin Jude, and Jude's former mentor Phillotson. Here it is Jude's sexuality and Sue's inability to commit herself which bear out the family incapacity for marriage. In *The Well-Beloved* (1897), Ann Avice is courted by her social superior Pierston, all the while married to her cousin Isaac. In a later incarnation of the same affair, Pierston loses the third Avice, a governess, to the teacher Henri Leverre. Here the drama is replayed from King Mark's vantage, and it is Pierston's fatal idealisation which places him at ever greater distances from the woman in the one family with whom he belongs.

Eventually, beginning in 1916, Hardy dramatised the legend itself, releasing his play for mummers *The Queen of Cornwall* in 1923. In it a dark-haired Iseult who has married her lover's patron King Mark, longs for Tristan who, in a fit of despair, has gone to Brittany and married a fair-haired surrogate.

Nearly always the woman's choice in the triangle is between alternative men having antithetical qualities. The woman has usually risen through her wits and a superior education, while the men are divided by class, age and values. Each Iseult has her husband in name and her husband in Nature. Each Tristan is shackled to one woman and in love with the other. Each of the lovers must try to balance social and intellectual commitments against the needs of the heart. Each King Mark must face overthrow by a Nature bent implacably upon renewing her players.

Hardy finds endless creative possibility in these dialectical tensions, but almost without exception it is hesitation or unwise sexual choice that shapes each tragic character's destiny. What is truly fascinating is that even a tale for children must reiterate the same obsessive theme. In 'Our Exploits at West Poley' (1893) two boys clandestinely switch the course of a stream between neighbouring villages, which then become rivals for the precious supply. One can hardly fail to note the symbolism here, or its parallel in *The Well-Beloved*, when Pierston's sexual life is finished and he closes up the ancient wells. Especially striking is the boys' solution one September to the pressure of irreconcilable claims, watched as in everything by The Man who has Failed. To pre-empt all further choice they detonate a subterranean explosion that favours West Poley with water and forever denies it to East Poley. An east–west polarity has a profoundly personal significance for Hardy and is expressed in the poem 'The Wind's Prophecy'. It dramatises Hardy's fateful journey in 1870 — away from a dark woman in the east towards a fair woman in the west who is undoubtedly Emma. Considered in this light, the entombing September explosion, in which west wins over east, is revealed as a violent and disquieting metaphor for Hardy's September 1874 marriage to Emma.

Thus among Hardy's many characters and many themes, one love triangle surfaces repeatedly and potently for more than fifty years. If indeed 'Every artist writes his own autobiography', and if anything important is missing from *The Life*, this must surely be a key.

Who were the real-life protagonists? The men are clear: one, usually representing aspects of Hardy, faces a rival originating in Horace Moule. The dark woman left in the east is surely Tryphena Sparks, the woman whose death is mentioned in the preface to *Jude*, and the cousin named in the poem 'Thoughts of Phena' as his 'lost prize'. *The Life* says he began the poem just days before her death in 1890 in what he called 'a curious instance of sympathetic telepathy'.[24] As so often, the distancing intended by the word 'curious' is the very reverse of what was true. His numbed, disoriented reaction can be found expressed through the artist Pierston in the scene in *The Well-Beloved* when the sculptor learns of Avice Caro's death. Pierston reads the letter from home at a society party obviously drawn from the one Hardy attended in 1890, two days before Tryphena's death. Probably that same year Hardy copied this quotation from Havelock Ellis's 1890 book, *The New Spirit*:

> Heine never mentioned her name: it was not till after his death that the form standing behind this Maria, Zuleima, Evelina of so many sweet, strange, or melancholy songs, was known to be that of his cousin, Amalie Heine.[25]

Traces of the cousin standing behind Thomas Hardy were claimed twenty years ago by Lois Deacon in *Providence and Mr. Hardy*. The book's critics were quicker to seize upon its highly visible faults than to grant the significance of this figure to Hardy's work, which in my opinion goes far beyond regret and nostalgia. Hardy raises up her image in so many composite incarnations that its power to fuel his imagination seems unlimited. For instance, as the child of baptists, who went to non-conformist schools and rose through teaching to become a headmistress, Tryphena is seen in the schoolmistress Baptista Trewthen. Born in March by a mill, she is Ella Marchmill,[26] whose address, number and names of children correspond with Tryphena's. The succession of village girls who rise through education, such as Ethelberta, Grace Melbury, Bathsheba and Tess, all bear her imprint, as do the schoolmistresses Fancy Day and Sue Bridehead. All leave home to return changed, as Tryphena did. All in some way reflect biographical details of Tryphena's life, and some even her appearance and home. Paula Power's alter ego Charlotte de Stancy, for instance, walks homeward to Myrtle Villa along a route suspiciously like the journey from Higher Bockhampton to the villa that replaced the Sparks' cottage in Puddletown. Suspicion turns into conviction when one learns that the ajacent property was named Myrtle Cottage.[27]

From the beginning of his career, Hardy is a poet inhabiting a poet's complex, personally symbolised world, and signifying the imprint upon his heart of everything, even the associations of local geography. Many apparently minor details of Hardy's broad terrain of Wessex are actually found near Bockhampton, so Hardy's Wessex may first have evolved less as an organising device than as a necessary enlargement to mask the archetype's tellingly localised origins.

If indeed the older man of the archetype represents aspects of Moule, the younger man aspects of Hardy and the vacillating woman aspects of Tryphena Sparks, it follows that the rejections by Bathsheba and Elfride (both of whose names reflect treachery and double marriage) probably indicate a hurt inflicted upon Hardy by Tryphena near the time of writing. The triangular situation we have traced usually depicts the woman taking an initiative in the man's absence or powerlessness. In the major fiction alone, there is a veritable procession of these displaced men — Springrove, Dick Dewy, Stephen, Gabriel Oak, Christopher Julian, George Somerset, Swithin St Cleeve, Giles Winterborne, Angel Clare and Jude — each seeing his beloved pass into the sphere of a more established man who offers the lure of status and financial stability. Given what we know about Hardy's use of the real, it seems unlikely that this repetition is without a personal origin.

The short story 'The Lady Penelope' shows that as late as 1889 Moule and Tryphena continue to appear in Hardy's dramas, but offers a sharply different interpretation of the same events. Adapted from *Hutchins History of Dorset*, it was written when Hardy's family — and surely Hardy himself — knew that Tryphena was dangerously ill. Published two months before her death, it is ostensibly an historical retelling, but read as an autobiographical analogue its message is terribly direct: the vivacious heroine marries Sir George Drenghard, because her first love Sir William Hervy is abroad. Drenghard, a Casterbridge man, soon dies from hard drinking. Hervy still being absent, she then marries Sir John Gale and is very unhappy. She is at last visited by Sir William Hervy who still loves her. Gale then dies, but her relationship with Hervy is mired in suspicion over the cause of Gale's death. Eventually, after Penelope's death, he discovers that she was faithful and faultless all along, and remorsefully he leaves the country, never to return.

The historical originals, as Kristin Brady points out,[28] had lived so long ago that disguising their names was unnecessary. Indeed, Hardy does not disguise them; he minimally alters them to recreate yet again his personal history: in Hervy's (Hardy's) absence Penelope (Tryphena) accedes to the most comfortably established suitor, a hard-drinking Dorchester man (Moule) who drinks himself to death. Because Hervy is absent (Hardy with Emma), she marries the second suitor, whose name Hardy amended from Gage to Gale. Tryphena indeed married a Charles Gale in 1877, a man

thought poorly of by two of his own children and who was said
to have made her unhappy. In Hardy's wishful tale, Gale too dies,
leaving Hervy and Penelope to face the doomed task of reviving
their love and trust.

The tale is surely a poignantly transparent analogue for Hardy's
aborted love affair with his cousin. If she read it, as she is said to
have read all his work, she would understand that he assumed
responsibility for the failure of their love affair, and absolved her
of all blame.

But blame for what? The truth seems to be that some time
between Tryphena leaving Puddletown school under a cloud in
January 1868, and her reappearance at teacher's college in January
1870, Hardy had introduced her to Moule, just as a decade earlier
he had introduced his sister Mary. Where and how this happened
is not clear, but she was probably taken to meet him much as Jude
proudly presents Sue to Phillotson. Evidently the two, both
teachers, saw enough of each other to establish an independent
relationship which may at first have been professional. Moule's
interest deepened to the point of considering marriage, but he was
probably unaware that she and Hardy considered themselves
engaged. Hardy was deeply hurt and angered at the manner in
which his cousin's interests had migrated, blaming first Moule for
having a winning tongue, later Tryphena for being flighty, then
later still invoking a whole range of social and personal causes,
including finally his own neglect and inattention.

There are more indications that this scenario is likely to be true
in Hardy's raw story outlines dating from 1871, and published as
'Plots for Five Unpublished Short Stories',[29]

Plot 1

(a) Girl goes to be school-mistress: leaves her village lover:
loves a school-master: he meets old lady in cathedral: she
proposes.

(b) Violinist in country town: is going to marry neighbouring
village girl (school-mistress) or one of same town: loses his finger:
hopeless case: strolls into cathedral or abbey: old lady meets him
there, day after day: she proposes to him. Another man, a
school-master who has long secretly loved the school-mistress
now hopes to make way with her . . .

Plot 2

A girl whose parents wish her to marry A begs to be allowed to marry B, her (secret) lover. They are surprised, as they know nothing of him.

After much entreaty from her they agree to her wishes. Engagement announced etc.

The wedding day draws near. Unpleasant traits in her betrothed reveal themselves and at the same time that worthy qualities reveal themselves in A, the rejected one. She suspects that [B] drinks.

The ambiguity of this quadrille — the village violinist (Hardy), the schoolmaster (Moule), the schoolmistress (Tryphena) and the old lady (Emma) — would probably in real life have been resolved as banally as any other emotional tangle between acquaintances had not Moule's suicide and Hardy's retreat into marriage transfixed the remaining players in a play with no conclusion. Though even while writing *Far from the Madding Crowd* Hardy seems not to have felt directly responsible for Moule's death, he was plagued with feelings of self-recrimination. Thereafter in his writing he began pushing the figures in the overlapping triangles toward roles of increasing mythical, representational stature. Partly this was in quest of a more satisfying universality of meaning, and partly as a conventional vehicle for his working novelist's stock of social and philosophical ideas.

The feelings of self-recrimination persisted: offered first to Moule's memory, they were next extended to Tryphena, whose death released a work of legendary proportion. After *Tess* Hardy concluded his major fiction by recreating in *Jude* something much closer to a biographical account of his life prior to marrying Emma, while in *The Well-Beloved* he subjected his own character and emotional life to a devastatingly ironic analysis.

These last novels are the funeral pyre for the actors of his youth, indeed for his youth itself. Hardy shaved off his beard and entered almost lightheartedly upon his new incarnation as a poet. His sense of guilt, never very far away, returned in full force with Emma's death in 1912. As with the deaths of Moule and Tryphena, her departure released the full compass of his creativity.

Notes

1. Robert Gittings, *Young Thomas Hardy* (Boston: Little, Brown, 1975); *Thomas Hardy's Later Years* (Boston: Little, Brown, 1978).
2. Michael Millgate, *Thomas Hardy: A Biography* (New York: Random House, 1982).
3. Henry Havelock Ellis, *The New Spirit* (London, 1890), p. 185.
4. Millgate, *Biography*, p. 201.
5. Millgate, *Biography*, p. 89: 'Lyrical Meth Find a situn from expce. Turn to Lycs for a form of expressn that has been used for a quite difft situn. Use it (Same sitn from experience may be sung in sevl forms.)'.
6. Millgate, *Biography*, p. 362.
7. 'The Poor Man and the Lady' 1867–8.
8. Millgate, *Biography*, p. 227n.
9. Ibid.
10. Desmond Hawkins, *Hardy Novelist and Poet* (Newton Abbot, Devon: David & Charles, 1976).
11. See Millgate, *Biography*, pp. 278–9 for discussion of *Woodlanders* and Hardy's use of his characters to propel a story and take hold of it; see pp. 346–8 regarding *Jude*.
12. 'His brain had extraordinary receptive powers, and no great creativeness. Quickly acquiring any kind of knowledge he saw around him, and having a plastic adaptability more common in woman than in man, he changed colour like a chameleon as the society he found himself in assumed a higher and more artificial tone. He had not many original ideas, and yet there was scarcely an idea to which, under proper training, he could not have added a respective co-ordinate.' (Ch. 10)
13. Millgate, *Biography*, p. 295, links Horace Moule with both Knight and Angel Clare.
14. See Michael Rabiger, 'The Hoffman Papers Discovered', *Thomas Hardy Yearbook*, No. 10 (1981), pp. 13–16.
15. Letter, Mary A. Blyth, *Times*, 13 March 1969.
16. Letter quoted in part in Millgate, *Biography* pp. 150–1.
17. Millgate, *Biography*, p. 201.
18. Norman Page (ed.), *Thomas Hardy Annual No. 3* (London: Macmillan, 1985), p. 54.
19. S. Baring Gould, *Brittany* (London: Methuen, 1925), p. 46.
20. Francis M. Gostling, *The Bretons at Home* (London: Methuen, 1909), p. 137.
21. S. L. Clark and Julian N. Wasserman, 'Tess and Iseult', *Thomas Hardy Society Review* (1979), pp. 160–3.
22. Millgate, *Biography*, p. 353.
23. Purdy and Millgate, *The Collected Letters of Thomas Hardy*, vol. VI, p. 221.
24. *The Life* (London: Macmillan, 1965), p. 224.
25. Henry Havelock Ellis, *The New Spirit* (London: W. Scott, 1892), p. 75.
26. Ella Marchmill surely incorporates aspects of Florence Henniker, as Millgate points out in *Biography*, p. 342.

27. Myrtle is also the present Stephen Smith gives Elfride, its presence triggering the discovery by Knight of her double-dealing in love.
28. Kristin Brady, *The Short Stories of Thomas Hardy* (New York: St Martin's Press, 1982), p. 88.
29. Quotations edited from Evelyn Hardy, 'Plots for Five Unpublished Short Stories', *London Magazine* II (November 1958), pp. 33–6.

6
Prosopopoeia in Hardy and Stevens

J. Hillis Miller

In a remarkable essay on the critical theory of Michael Riffaterre,[1] Paul de Man moves towards the conclusion that prosopopoeia, the ascription of a name, a face or a voice to the absent, the inanimate or the dead, is the fundamental trope of lyric poetry. Prosopopoeia is more essential to poetry, de Man argues, even than metaphor. Without prosopopoeia no poetry, though prosopopoeia is, for him, fictive, without ontological ground. A mountain does not have a face, but though the poet can expunge metaphor from his language, see things 'with the hottest fire of sight', as Wallace Stevens says, 'without evasion by a single metaphor',[2] he cannot avoid those personifications that are woven into the interal fabric of our language, like 'face of a mountain', 'headland', 'eye of a storm'. This essay explores the consequences of this fact about poetic language through discussion of two poems, Thomas Hardy's 'The Pedigree' and Wallace Stevens's 'Not Ideas about the Thing but the Thing Itself', along with ancillary passages about prosopopoeia in a pamphlet by Immanuel Kant and in Hardy's book of short stories, *A Group of Noble Dames*.

First the passage from Kant's 'Of an Overlordly Tone Recently Adopted in Philosophy', to identify what is at stake in the trope of prosopopoeia:

The veiled goddess before which we on both sides bend our knees is the moral law in us in its invulnerable majesty. We clearly perceive its voice, and we understand very clearly its commandments. But in hearing it we doubt whether it comes from man and whether it originates from the all-powerfulness of his very own reason, or whether it emanates from some other being, whose nature is unknown to man and who speaks to him through his own proper reason. At bottom we would perhaps do better to exempt ourselves entirely from this research, for it is simply speculative, and what (objectively) devolves upon us to do remains the same, let one found it on one or the other principle. The only difference is that the didactic procedure of leading the moral law in us back to distinct concepts according to a logical method is alone properly *philosophical*, whereas the procedure consisting in personifying this law and in making of the reason that morally commands a veiled Isis (even when we attribute no other properties to it than those the first method discovers in it) is an *aesthetic* manner of representing (*eine ästhetische Vorstellungsart*) exactly the same object. It is indeed permitted to rely on this manner, since one has already started by leading the principles back to their pure state, in order to give life to this idea thanks to a sensible, though only analogical, presentation (*Darstellung*), not however without always running some risk of falling into an exalted vision, which is the death of all philosophy.[3]

For Kant, the personification of the moral law as a veiled Isis is merely 'an *aesthetic* manner of representing' something beyond all figuration and especially beyond personification. The moral law is not a person. It is permitted to use such personifications as long as we begin with the naked concept and as long as we understand that the personification is a merely sensible, analogical and aesthetic presentation of something that is unavailable to the senses, not able to be grasped by any trope, and invisible behind the veil of all aesthetic representations. To take the prosopopoeia literally is an exalted vision that is the death of all philosophy because it is a mode of idolatry. Such idolatory takes the merely analogical figure, that gives life to a concept, as a breakthrough, beyond the veil, to a direct confrontation with the moral law. Such idolatry would give the merely aesthetic priority over philosophy, rather than the other way around. Such an idolatrous exaltation would claim insight through the veil, whereas Kant defines the human situation as the necessity of remaining in doubt, not about the categorial claim on us of the moral law, but about the source of the moral law. Of that source we can know nothing except that it speaks authoritatively, with absolute sovereignty. The moral law is an 'unknown X', not a thing, nor a thought, nor a word, especially not a person, but not nothing either.

I mean to argue here, against Kant, that the prosopopoeia is not added to something that has the clarity of philosophical reason

and has been already taken back to first principles. The personification of the moral law as a veiled goddess is fundamental, original,
there from the beginning. It cannot be erased or suspended by
a return to clear, philosophical, reasonable, non-figurative first
principles. The demand made on us by the moral law is always
made through the veil of personification. The same thing may be
said of the claims made on us by lyric poetry and by works of
fiction. Prosopopoeia is not adventitious in them but essential.

Paragraphs at the end of the first story in Thomas Hardy's *A
Group of Noble Dames* introduce the topic of prosopopoeia. The
issue of prosopopoeia is already folded within the frame story.
This frame story is introduced only at the end of the first story
proper. As Kathy Psomiades observes in a brilliant unpublished
essay on *A Group of Noble Dames*, in this case the frame is framed
by what it frames. In these paragraphs the frame-story narrator
draws a parallel between the bringing to life of the stuffed birds,
'deformed butterflies, fossil ox-horns, prehistoric dung-mixens'[4] in
the provincial museum where the male members of an antiquarian
club tell their stories about dead women, and, on the other hand,
the bringing to life of the dead noble dames in the act of
story-telling. Both these events are prosopopoeias in the strictest
dictionary sense. They give life to the absent, the inanimate, the
dead. Here is the passage:

> As the members waited they grew chilly, although it was only
> autumn, and a fire was lighted, which threw a cheerful shine
> upon the varnished skulls, urns, penates, tesserae, costumes,
> coats of mail, weapons, and missals, animated the fossilized
> ichthyosaurus and iguanodon; while the dead eyes of the stuffed
> birds — those never-absent familiars in such collections, though
> murdered to extinction out-of-doors — flashed as they had
> flashed to the rising sun above the neighbouring moors on the
> fatal morning when the trigger was pulled which ended their
> little flight . . . Many, indeed, were the legends and traditions
> of gentle and noble dames, renowned in times past in that part
> of England, whose actions and passions were now, but for men's
> memories, buried under the brief inscription on a tomb or an
> entry of dates in a dry pedigree. (pp. 49–50)

As the firelight animates the stuffed birds and animals in the
museum, so the memorial story-telling of *A Group of Noble Dames*

brings the dead women back to life, animates them, lets them speak again. What is problematic about this act of personification is most fully developed in the Preface to *A Group of Noble Dames*. It is presented by way of the image of the pedigree. The opening of the Preface of *A Group of Noble Dames* is an extraordinary affirmation of the power of prosopopoeia to raise the dead. This power of resurrection is like falling in love with a statue and giving it a voice, a face, a personality. This is, in fact, what the heroine of 'Barbara of the House of Grebe' does. At the same time, however, Hardy at least implicitly recognises that the act of prosopopoeia is fictive, illusory, mystified, as deluded as falling in love with a statue. The personalities that are raised from the dead were never there as such nor can they in any way be verified to have been there. Here is Hardy's account of this process. It is the process of 'reading' 'the pedigrees of our county families'. Such pedigrees are rudimentary, iconic poems. They mix words and the diagrammatic or ideographic feature of 'family trees':

The pedigree of our county families, arranged in diagrams on the pages of county histories, mostly appear at first sight to be as barren of any touch of nature as a table of logarithms. But given a clue — the faintest tradition of what went on behind the scenes, and this dryness as of dust may be transformed into a palpitating drama. More, the careful comparison of dates alone — that of birth with marriage, of marriage with death, of one marriage, birth, or death with a kindred marriage, birth, or death — will often effect the same transformation, and anybody practised in raising images from such genealogies finds himself unconsciously filling into the framework the motives, passions, and personal qualities which would appear to be the single explanation possible of some extraordinary conjunction in times, events, and personages that occasionally marks these reticent family records.

Out of such pedigrees and supplementary material most of the following stories have arisen and taken shape. (p. vii)

In this extraordinary passage, each story is seen as rising like a ghost from the dry bones and dust of the schematic pedigree on the page. Or rather, first the personalities arise, spontaneously, 'unconsciously', as Hardy says, as the only possible explanation of a given conjunction of times, the dry facts of marriage, birth and death. Then the story is written down. The story is figuratively another pedigree, in the sense that it is black marks on the page from which the reader raises the personalities and the story that were originally suggested to Hardy by the diagrammatic pedigrees, as dead on the page as a table of logarithms. Hardy does not say that what is raised was what was really there, but that 'the motives, passions, and personal qualities . . . would appear to be the single explanation possible of some extraordinary conjunction'. What Hardy says is rather like what Sigmund Freud says about 'constructions in analysis'.[5] The analyst's construction ('You had a passion for Frau X', or whatever) is the only possible explanation of the patient's memories and symptoms, but there is no way whatsoever to verify that construction. In this sense, it is fictive, like all prosopopoeias, like, for example, my ascription of an interiority or selfhood like my own to the faces of those loved ones around me.

If Hardy's framing in the Preface and in the frame story describes the fiction of prosopopoeia as the source of the stories, the stories themselves in *A Group of Noble Dames* are about the devastating effects of the same process. An example is Barbara's infatuation with a face, which becomes, after her husband's death, infatuation with his statue. When she is cured of that infatuation by her cruel second husband, her insane laughter is like the laughter of Jocelyn Pierston in the original version of Hardy's *The Well-Beloved*. Both Barbara and Jocelyn suffer the madness of insight into the fact that personification is fictive. It is not that Barbara has loved a statue, but that her first husband was in a sense also a statue. She did not love him. She loved his face and figure and raised a suppositious personality on that iconic basis. The mutilation of the face first of the real husband and then of his statue shows her this fact and leads to her mad laughter. Insight into the power of prosopopoeia is intolerable. No human being can live with it. Barbara, in 'Barbara of the House of Grebe', shifts immediately to an infatuation with a displaced substitute for the substitute, that is, with her second husband, who replaces the statue of her first husband, that replaces the first husband himself. Barbara clings to Uplandtowers, her second husband, bears him baby after baby, in a frenzy of sexual bonding. It is no wonder the male club members who hear the physician tell this story conspicuously misunderstand it and make absurd comments on it in the paragraphs that end the story. The listener or reader too cannot look the meaning of this story in the face. We return spontaneously to that ascription of a personality not only to the people around us but even to inanimate things, as in my figure of looking the truth in the face.

I turn now to Hardy's poem, 'The Pedigree'. This poem has rarely been anthologised or interpreted. It is an example of the many extraordinary poems the reader may find more or less buried in the splendid abundance of Hardy's poetry. 'The Pedigree' makes a series of transformative equivalences from stanza to stanza. These are in fact the same set of equivalences on which Hardy's novel, *The Well-Beloved*, is based, or rather, they are the symmetrical narcissistic image of those equivalences. The novel is in the poem as mirror image. Here, first, is the passage from *The Well-Beloved* on which 'The Pedigree' might be said to be a commentary, or vice versa. Both texts echo Shelley's fragment, 'To the Moon', in which the moon is 'ever changing, like a joyless eye / That finds no object worth its constancy':

> He was subject to gigantic fantasies still. In spite of himself, the sight of the new moon, as representing one, who, by her so-called inconstancy, acted up to his own idea of a migratory Well-Beloved, made him feel as if his wraith in a changed sex had suddenly looked over the horizon at him. In a crowd secretly, or in solitude boldly, he had often bowed the knee three times to this sisterly divinity on her first appearance monthly, and directed a kiss toward her shining shape.[6]

Here is 'The Pedigree'. The same motifs are present as in the passage from *The Well-Beloved*, but in the case of the poem, the meaning emerges from the superimposition of its successive stanzas.

The Pedigree

I

I bent in the deep of night
Over a pedigree the chronicler gave
As mine; and as I bent there, half-unrobed,
The uncurtained panes of my window-square let in the watery
light
Of the moon in its old age:
And green-rheumed clouds were hurrying past where mute and
cold it globed
Like a drifting dolphin's eye seen through a lapping wave.

II

So, scanning my sire-sown tree,
And the hieroglyphs of this spouse tied to that,
With offspring mapped below in lineage,
Till the tangles troubled me,
The branches seemed to twist into a seared and cynic face
Which winked and tokened towards the window like a Mage
Enchanting me to gaze again thereat.

III

It was a mirror now,
And in a long perspective I could trace
Of my begetters, dwindling backward each past each
All with the kindred look
Whose names had since been inked down in their place
On the recorder's book,
Generation and generation of my mien, and build, and brow.

IV

And then did I divine
That every heave and coil and move I made
Within my brain, and in my mood and speech,
Was in the glass portrayed
As long forestalled by their so making it;
The first of them, the primest fuglemen of my line,
Being fogged in far antiqueness past surmise and reason's reach.

V

Said I then, sunk in tone,
'I am merest mimicker and counterfeit! —
Though thinking, *I am I,*
And what I do I do myself alone.'
— The cynic twist of the page thereat unknit
Back to its normal figure, having wrought its purport wry,
The Mage's mirror left the window-square,
And the stained moon and drift retook their places there.

(1916)[7]

The first stanza sets the 'literal' scene of the poem. The poet studies his pedigree by moonlight. Already a figure enters the poem, however, as well as an echo before and after of other texts. The image is an ugly one, but powerful. The moon is an old woman with a watery eye, like Yeats's moon, in its old age, variant of Shelley's: 'Crazed through much child-bearing/The moon is staggering in the sky.'[8] Or rather the moon, for Hardy, *is* the old eye, grotesquely detached from its body, open and yet alien, green-rheumed, mute and cold, a dead eye, closed mysteriously in on itself, keeping its secrets, 'like a drifting dolphin's eye seen through a lapping wave'. A detached eye is, Freud argues in his reading of Hoffmann's *The Sandman*, the symbol of something else missing, of castration in short, or of the female pudendum.[9] Is this equation at work here? The poet's confrontation of a female moon which turns into his own image in the mirror matches, in any case, the meeting of male Narcissist and sisterly counter-image in Shelley's 'To the Moon'. It matches also that strange passage in *The Well-Beloved* I have quoted. In the latter, the reader will remember, Jocelyn bows the knee three times to his 'sisterly divinity' the moon, seeing in her 'his wraith', his double 'in a changed sex'.

In the second and third stanzas of Hardy's poem, the major figurative transformation takes place. The window turns into a mirror and the pedigree into the face of an enchanter who produces magic visions in that mirror. A scene of necromancy superimposes itself in palimpsest on the 'realistic' scene of the first stanza. That realism has already been perturbed by the turning of the moon into an uncannily detached eye, with its disturbing sexual implications.

The change into a scene of magic potentiality goes by way of another figure, the figure of figuration itself. The word 'pedigree' comes from the Old French *pie de grue*, crane's foot, called that from the lines in a genealogical tree. The spectacle of a man poring over his lineage, trying to confirm who he is by identifying who he has come from, studying that crane's foot like a soothsayer reading tea-leaves, palms or bird entrails, must have struck those Old French as more than faintly ludicrous. The lines of genealogical 'descent' mapped out on the page are of course a schematic graphing of that descent. They make a spatial figure for a temporal process which does not involve 'lines' as such at all. This figure is as arbitrary and artificial, and yet as socially binding, as the tangled network of kinship names itself. In response to an irresistible instinct of sign-making and sign-reading, men have seen those graphed lines in turn as an emblem: as a tree, as a map, or as writing in hieroglyphs, or as a crane's foot, or as a seared and cynic face. What was already a conventional sign is further metamorphosed into another sign, according to that irrepressible tendency in signs, since they are metaphorical in the first place, to proliferate laterally into further metaphors and metaphors of metaphors. The end point of this series of transformations of figure into figure is a prosopopoeia, a face, or rather, it is appropriately an endless series of faces, one behind the other, as though there were no end to the power of personification, no getting behind or beneath this figure to some literal ground.

Hardy's poem depends throughout on the figure of lines. It depends on the inherent tendency in man the sign-making and sign-using animal to take any configuration of lines, natural or artificial, as a hieroglyph, as some kind of signifying token. The poem depends also on the inherent tendency of such hieroglyphs to be multiple, to multiply metaphors. In Hardy's poem the pedigree becomes a tree, becomes a text in 'hieroglyphs', becomes a map, becomes a face. The lines 'charactered' on a man's face are, of course, an index to his 'character', as 'cynic', for example, or naive, according to a play on the word and the concept of 'character' which is implicit in Hardy's poem, though the word itself does not appear. A 'character' is an incised sign, made of crisscrossing lines. It is a hieroglyph, but the ultimate hieroglyph may be a character, a face.

What each man reads in the signs confronting him, characters, hieroglyphs, tree, crane's foot, is his own face in the mirror. This is so because there are no meanings in any configuration of intersecting lines but those man has put into it or has had put into it by his 'begetters'. Those begetters are sower sires who have begotten him by begetting the languages within which he is inscribed. In the third stanza of 'The Pedigree', the window turns into a mirror, and the sisterly image of the moon, the speaker's double in a changed sex, turns into his own face or rather into the faces of all those forebears, 'with the kindred look', one behind the other, 'dwindling backward each past each'. The face in the mirror is *mise en abime*, as if there were a double mirror, not a single one. The multiple image in the mirror is like that in Charles Addams's cartoon of the man in the barber chair confronting in reflection a receding series of men in barber chairs.

The result of the poet's encounter with all his doubling ancestors, 'generation and generation of my mien, and build, and brow', is not, as might perhaps have been expected, the making solid of his selfhood by grounding it in his heritage, as a tree is rooted in the earth, but, characteristically for Hardy, just the opposite. It is the reduction of his every thought and gesture to a hollow repetition. He becomes a mere copy and fake. For Hardy, in this poem at least, authentic selfhood lies only in originality and autonomy. The speaker discovers that when he most seems to have these he least has them. He is the copy of his image in the mirror rather than the source of an image that copies him. It is as though the infinitesimal time lag between original and copy went the other way. It is as though my mirror image were to make a movement or gesture an instant before I do, coercing my every move, even anticipating my thoughts, feelings and speech, things that would seem hidden from mirroring:

> Said I then, sunk in tone,
> 'I am merest mimicker and counterfeit! —
> Though thinking, *I am I,*
> *And what I do I do myself alone.*'

For 'archaic' or traditional man, scholars such as Mircea Eliade say, an action has validity only if it is a copy of some ancestral archetypal pattern. For Hardy it is the opposite. All his work, including *The Well-Beloved*, finds one of the most disastrous ways in which it is impossible to 'undo the done' to be the way I am forced, in spite of myself, to repeat what has already been done before. I am forced to make myself one of a long row. I am nothing if I am a mere copy, and yet as soon as I think or do, whatever I think or do. I am nothing but a mere copy. The image in 'The Pedigree' of the 'heave and coil and move' within the speaker's brain not only picks up from elsewhere in the poem the figure of tangled lines. It also parallels a grotesque image in the 'Forescene' of *The Dynasts*. There the whole universe is a gigantic pulsating brain made of 'innumerous coils, / Twining and serpentining round and through. / Also retracting threads like gossamers — / Except in being irresistible.'[10]

In 'The Pedigree', the 'I am I' of God, generating himself in self-reflexive relation to himself, is the model for Hardy's impossible ideal of independent human selfhood. This would be another 'I am I', a self-enclosed circuit of reflection, I looking at the other I in the mirror, as Narcissus beheld his image and loved it, making and sustaining himself in self-admiration. In 'The Pedigree' this becomes a mocking parody in which the I is a false mimicking copy of that previous I in the mirror. That specular I does not copy me but has 'forestalled' me, has paralysed my every move even before I make it. Rather 'they have' forestalled me, since the image in the mirror is doubled and redoubled to infinity, image behind image. They force me to copy them. Moreover, the original image behind the row of images is not single but multiple. It is a multiplicity lost in the fogs of past time, unreachable by guesswork or by logical deduction, 'past surmise and reason's reach'. The initiating 'origin' cannot be grounded in the principle of reason, the *logos*. The row is, rather, groundless. It is abyssed.

Even those grand multiple ever-repeating originals, moreover, were not fathers, potent generators, initiators laying down a line. They were sign-makers, signal-swingers, tokeners. They offered a copied model for others to imitate, according to Hardy's striking use here of one of his odd words: 'The first of them, the primest *fuglemen* of my line, / Being fogged in far antiqueness . . .' (my italics). A fugleman, according to the *NED*, is a 'soldier especially expert and well drilled, formerly placed in front of a regiment or company as an example or model to others in their exercises'. The word comes from the German *Flugelmann*, 'leader of the file', from *Flugel*, 'wing', plus *Mann*, 'man'. To fugle is 'to do the duty of a fugleman; to act as guide or director; to make signals', or, figuratively, 'to give an example of (something) to someone'. To fugle is also slang for 'to cheat, trick'. The example given by the *NED* has a sexual implication. To fugle is to mislead, to seduce: 'Who fugell'd the Parson's fine Maid?' (1729). A fugleman is not an originator. He is himself a well-drilled copy who stands at the wing and who passes on to others a pattern, perhaps a deceitful pattern, by the wing-like beating of his arms and legs, making signals. Hardy uses this strange word at least one other time in his work. This is in the extraordinary episode in *The Woodlanders* that describes John South's belief that his life is tied to the great elm tree which stands outside his window: 'As the tree waved South waved his head, making it his fugleman with abject obedience.'[11]

For Hardy in 'The Pedigree', as I have noted, 'the first of them' are already multiple, not single. He says 'primest fugle*men* of my

line' where one might expect fugle*man*. The later always mimics
the earlier in a perpetual reversal of time, or in a treading water of
time, forbidding any novelty, any autonomy, any new beginning,
any '*I am I, / And what I do I do myself alone.*' Whatever I do my
fuglemen have already been there first. I can never be more than
a follower, the momentary last of the line, never be an initiator, a
first. The concept of 'archetype', as 'The Pedigree' shows Hardy
knew, is inherently contradictory. Any type (from the Greek word
tupos, 'informing matrix'), is already divided within itself. It is
multiple, and it is an iteration. It is already secondary to any *arche*
or origin.

At the end of 'The Pedigree' the mirror becomes a window again.
Through that window the poet sees the moon again in its drift of
clouds. The poet returns to the situation of Jocelyn when he bows
the knee three times to his sisterly divinity the moon. The sorry
wisdom the poet learns from his magic mirror is the knowledge
Jocelyn tries, unsuccessfully, to avoid acquiring. Jocelyn's half-
knowledge, his attempt to avoid being a merest mimicker and
counterfeit, inhibits him from joining himself to any of the Avices,
so repeating his ancestors. By an inescapable law in Hardy's
universe, Jocelyn becomes as much a repetition by doing nothing,
by refraining from action or marriage, as he would have if he had
plunged into them. For Hardy, either way you have had it. The
tangle of hieroglyphic lines marking out an heredity is a double
bind.

If 'The Pedigree' is a kind of commentary or footnote on *The
Well-Beloved*, the novel, on the other hand, may be said to be in
the poem, folded into it, waiting to have its implications unfolded
along the narrative line of the novel proper. Just as Jocelyn's
attempt to ground himself in a relation to an ideal beloved leads
ultimately to a form of depersonalisation, so the sequence of
figures, figure behind figure, in 'The Pedigree' leads to the figure
of prosopopoeia as apparently the ultimate or grounding figure in
the line. Nevertheless, the figure of prosopopoeia, for Hardy, far
from being a solid ground for the self, dissolves into a receding
series of faces that is ultimately devastatingly destructive for the
poet's sense of himself.

I turn now to Wallace Stevens's 'Not Ideas about the Thing but
the Thing Itself'. Here is the poem:

Not Ideas about the Thing
but the Thing Itself

At the earliest ending of winter,
In March, a scrawny cry from outside
Seemed like a sound in his mind.

He knew that he heard it,
A bird's cry, at daylight or before,
In the early March wind.

The sun was rising at six,
No longer a battered panache above snow . . .
It would have been outside.

It was not from the vast ventriloquism
Of sleep's faded papier-mâché . . .
The sun was coming from outside.

That scrawny cry — It was
A chorister whose c preceded the choir,
It was part of the colossal sun,

Surrounded by its choral rings,
Still far away. It was like
A new knowledge of reality.[12]

  The title of this poem, one of Stevens's last, is a little strange. It
is not a complete sentence, but hangs in the air: 'Not Ideas about
the Thing but the Thing Itself'. The title is a label for the poem, as
a painting may be labelled by its title, a title that may be written
on the painting itself. In this case, does Stevens's title name the
poem? Is the poem itself not ideas about the thing, but the thing
itself? And what would that mean? Or does the title name the
experience that the poem records? That would give the title a
rather different meaning. Or does the title simply mean: 'I wish I
could have access to, or write a poem that was, not ideas about
the thing but the thing itself'? Is the title optative, a kind of wish,
or is the title some form of hypothesis? There is no way to know
for sure. The poem does not confirm certainly any reading of the
title.
  The word 'thing' is, moreover, a pregnant word here. It is not

easy to be sure what Stevens means by 'the thing'. Does he mean, by 'thing', the sun? Is the thing rather the scrawny cry? In what sense is a scrawny cry a thing? Either to call the sun a thing, or to call a scrawny cry a thing, does not seem quite right. The sun is not something that one normally thinks of as a thing. In attempting to pin down the meaning of 'thing', the reader might move in the direction of emphasising the word 'it' that occurs over and over in the poem. 'It' has a clear referent: the scrawny cry. 'He knew that he heard *it* / A bird's cry . . .' (my italics). But the word recurs: '*It* was not from the vast ventriloquism / Of sleep's faded papier-mâché . . . *it* was a chorister . . . *it* was like . . .' (my italics). By the time the reader reaches the end of those 'its', the 'it' has detached itself from the cry. *It* has become a name for 'the thing itself'. Stevens is using the word 'thing' in its full etymological and historical complexity, as a name for that which is manifested by the rising of the sun, or by the bird's cry or by the coming of spring, but still remains always hidden, an 'it' or 'unnamable X'.

'Not Ideas about the Thing but the Thing Itself' is, then, a poem about the appearance of something out of hiddenness, out of occultation: the sun; the cry; spring; the earliest ending of winter; the poet waking up out of sleep, coming into consciousness. These are all said to be like one another, metaphors for one another. They were all forms of appearance that are related to the thing itself, whatever *that* is: some kind of 'it'. A 'thing', in the sense of a gathering together, as in a medieval assemblage of people; a 'thing' in the sense of some substratum which is hidden and never appears, something that remains outside — these are versions of the thing.

The poem depends, in its lateral dislocations, circling around the thing itself, on synaesthesia: a visual thing is expressed in terms of an audible thing. The bird's cry announces the rising of the sun. There is a lateral metaphor in the poem that says 'a chorus', a great crowd of people singing something like a Bach mass, 'is like' the appearance of the sun. This displacement of sight to sound in the description of the sunrise reminds me not of Walt Whitman, as it does Harold Bloom, but of Goethe in the great opening of the second part of *Faust* where the sun rises as a loud noise, as a tremendous racket. In the passage in *Faust*, as in the poem by Stevens, there is the same displacement from sight to sound. In both cases this displacement has something to do with the impossibility of naming, in literal language, what is behind the

appearance of the sun. You cannot look the sun in the eye, and
you cannot name it as such, so it seems, so instead of naming it
you name the great chorus. The 'chorister whose c preceded the
choir' is that little pitch-pipe noise that you hear in an *a cappella*
choir, the muted, soft, scrawny 'c' you hear before the whole noise
begins. That sound is a figure here for the literal bird's cry that
announces the appearance of the sun, blinding and deafening,
and the earliest approach of spring too. The mixture or displacement
of senses is fundamental to this poem because it is a lateral
dislocation expressing another dislocation, the displacement from
the hidden 'thing' or 'it' to any manifestation or metaphors of it.

Like so many of Stevens's poems, this one too is fragile,
evanescent. It is a poem about thresholds. The poem says in effect
that 'it' — the cry that has become all these other things — is a
new knowledge of reality just at that borderline moment before
the sun rises. At that moment alone one learns something about
reality. Once the sun has risen above the horizon, and the chorus
is singing full-blast, one is in the ordinary world, where one has
only ideas about the thing. The thing itself takes place and instantly
vanishes only at that point: at the earliest ending of winter.

I come finally to the word 'panache' and to prosopopoeia in this
poem. A 'panache' is a tuft of feathers, as on a helmet. A 'panache'
is also a rare astronomer's word for a solar protuberance. The word
comes from the Italian *panachio*, which is from the Latin *penna*, 'a
feather'. Only secondarily does the word mean flamboyant or
flagrant behaviour. When Stevens says that 'The sun was rising at
six, / No longer a battered panache above snow', he must have
been reading the dictionary. Stevens must mean to describe the
sun rising as if it were that tuft of feathers on a helmet. This is a
latent personification of the sun. The sun is a person, like that
giant on the horizon he projects in 'A Primitive Like an Orb'. The
seeing of the sun as a person is another version of that displacement
from sight to sound, in the sense that it is both a revelation —
something that carries meaning — and at the same time another
covering-over. The prosopopoeia is another inadequate figure. It
is appropriate here to remember another poem by Stevens, 'The
Snow Man'. If the 'battered panache above snow' is a helmet with
a tuft of feathers on it, that seems a distant displacement of the
famous snow man.

Stevens's 'thing itself', so powerfully anthropomorphised in this
poem, is something like the Kantian *Ding an sich*. For Stevens as

for Kant the thing itself is always absent, imperceptible, always outside any perception, any idea, any image, though it is what motivates all perceiving, thinking and naming. It is what most demands to be perceived, thought, and named, though this is a demand that can never properly be fulfilled. Since the thing itself is always outside any perceiving, thinking or naming it can only be perceived, thought or named in figures or in negations, as not this or not that, or as no more than like this or like that, in a resemblance that is not an assimilation, nor a use of negatives as part of a dialectical sublation. The scrawny cry 'seemed *like* a sound in his mind'. 'It was *like*/A new knowledge of reality.' The sun was '*no longer* a battered panache above snow'. 'It was *not* from the vast ventriloquism/Of sleep's faded papier-mâché.'

Though one cannot say what the 'it' or the 'thing itself' is, one can know that it is always outside whatever can be said of it. Though the scrawny cry, for example, 'seemed like a sound in his mind', it was in fact 'from outside'. Or, 'it would have been outside' (an extremely odd locution: it would have been *if* what? What is the conditional here?). In another line, the poet affirms that 'the sun was coming from outside'. Outside of what? Presumably outside of everything. Outside the mind. Outside the house. Outside the world, where the sun is when it is invisible, after it has set and before it has risen again. Outside, most of all, language.

The thing itself is outside of everything, outside every perception, thought or name, whether proper, common or figurative. It is impossible to call it by name because it is neither sensible (not a thing like other things inside the world) nor intelligible (not inside the mind, not even in the depths of the mind below sleep). It is not a perception, nor a thought, nor a word, but is outside those oppositions or hierarchies between inside and outside (inside the mind as against outside it, and so on). The threshold between all those namable elements and the 'it' is before all those oppositions. The 'it', therefore, cannot be glimpsed or heard as such. It can only be apprehended in its vanishing in the 'sharp flash' at the border that is a kind of abyss between winter and spring ('at the earliest ending of winter'), night and day ('at daylight or before'), between sleep and waking, between mind and things, between the absolute outside and all those insides that divide again into insides and outsides.

The 'it', on the outside of these thresholds, is the thing itself, though, as I have said, it is not a thing in the sense that the sun is a thing when we can see it, nor an object of thought, nor able to be named except as what it is *like* or as what it is *not*, including especially and primarily *not like* the human form or face that always intervenes between inside and that absolute outside, between us and it.

Both poems, then, Hardy's and Stevens's, are about the necessity of prosopopoeia and at the same time they are, if I dare to use the word, deconstructions of prosopopoeia. Even the most powerful and purest of poets cannot not have prosopopoeia, and yet it is a fictive covering of a non-anthropomorphic 'X', what Stevens, in 'The Motive for Metaphor', calls 'The weight of primary noon, / The ABC of being, / . . . — the sharp flash, / The vital, arrogant, fatal, dominant X'.[13] However far back or far out or far in, far far back, out, or in, we go, the human form, face, figure, or rather the words or other signs that ascribe to 'the thing itself' a human visage, form, figure and language are there. Is not prosopopoeia still there, for example, when Stevens calls that X which metaphor allows us to 'shrink from' 'vital, arrogant, fatal, dominant', as though it were some virile hidalgo or that 'giant, on the horizon, glistening' of 'A Primitive Like an Orb'?[14]

In 'The Pedigree' prosopopoeia is present in the *mise en abime* of the multiple and multiplying ancestors arising from the dry bones and mathematic design of the poet's pedigree. Those ancestors, the poet says, have programmed me to think and feel according to their paradigms, though my recognising of this is a depersonalising of myself. My pedigree and its transmutations into a vision of my begetters, 'dwindling backward each past each', show me that 'I' am a fictive schemata of signs like the rest.

In 'Not Ideas about the Thing but the Thing Itself' one of the 'ideas' that irresistibly appears as a way of talking about the 'thing' that is always 'outside', outside of everything, is the image of the human form, present in 'panache' and in that chorister whose c precedes the choir. We cannot not see or hear the it as a person or persons, as a 'giant on the horizon' or as a great choir singing, but that seeing or hearing is disqualified by 'like' or 'not', that is, it is seen or heard as an idea about the thing, not the thing itself. The thing itself cannot be seen, heard or anthropomorphised. Therefore the poet's wish to have not ideas about the thing but the thing itself can never be fulfilled. It is for this reason, among others, that, as Stevens more than once says, the mind cannot be satisfied, ever.

Notes

1. Paul de Man, 'Hypogram and Inscription', *The Resistance to Theory* (Minneapolis: University of Minnesota Press, 1986), pp. 27–53.
2. Wallace Stevens, 'Credences of Summer', *Collected Poems* (New York: Knopf, 1954), p. 373.
3. Cited by Jacques Derrida in 'Of an Apocalyptic Tone Recently Adopted in Philosophy', *The Oxford Literary Review*, vol. VI (1984) no. 2, pp. 19–20. Translated from Immanuel Kant, 'Von einem neuerdings erhobenen vornehmen Ton in der Philosophie' (1796), *Werke*, vol. VI, edited by E. Cassirer (Berlin: 1923), pp. 494–5.
4. Thomas Hardy, *A Group of Noble Dames, Writings*, Anniversary Edition, vol. XIII (New York and London: Harper, no date), p. 48. Further references to this work will be by page number to this edition.
5. Sigmund Freud, 'Constructions in Analysis', *The Complete Psychological Works*, Standard Edition, vol. XXIII (London: The Hogarth Press and the Institute of Psycho-analysis, 1953), pp. 255–69. For the German original see 'Konstruktionen in der Analyse', *Gesammelte Werke*, vol. XVI (London: Imago, 1942), pp. 43–56.
6. Thomas Hardy, *The Well-Beloved*, New Wessex Edition (London: Macmillan, 1975), p. 148.
7. Thomas Hardy, *The Complete Poems* (London: Macmillan, 1976), pp. 460–1.
8. W. B. Yeats, 'The Crazed Moon', *Collected Poems* (New York: Macmillan, 1958), p. 237.
9. See Sigmund Freud, 'The "Uncanny"', Standard Edition, vol. XVII, pp. 218–56. For the German original see 'Das "Unheimliche"', *Gesammelte Werke*, vol. XII, pp. 229–68.
10. Thomas Hardy, *The Dynasts* (London: Macmillan; New York: St. Martin's Press, 1965), pp. 6–7.
11. Thomas Hardy, *The Woodlanders* (London: Macmillan, 1958), p. 97.
12. Wallace Stevens, *Collected Poems*, p. 534.
13. Ibid., p. 288.
14. Ibid., p. 442.

7
Buddhist Tendencies in Hardy's Poetry

Jagdish Chandra Dave

No reader of Hardy's work would deny that as a thinker, provocative and profound, Hardy compels serious attention. Yet if baffled critics, unable to grasp the coherence of tone and content and true character of his thought, complain that he is desultory and confused, the fault lies not with the thought, which easily could be put into the shape of its own, but with their approach, predisposed to find in it a faith of Christian or heretic assumptions, or a system of speculative philosophy which he consciously shuns. It is seldom realised that Hardy, curiously, strayed from the western tradition and tended positively towards the early Buddhist view of life both in his clear perception of the human situation and, to ease its rigours, a pursuit of spirituality which he unmistakably evinces but cannot consciously define. This is not to say, of course, that resemblance between the two is complete. The Buddha finds the darkness that Hardy sees to be far darker, and the liberating light, too, he finds far more effulgent than the faint rays familiar to the latter. The tendencies systematically developed to the point of consummation in one are but carelessly though consistently exhibited in the other. One is a fully-matured shapely thing towards which the other, still an unfinished embryo, seems to be growing. There are, then, welcome features of Hardy's thought foreign to Buddhism, and it is not assumed here that he was at all influenced by the Oriental tradition which, probably, was little known to him. Nevertheless, the resemblance is striking enough to call for a comparative study of Hardy's thought, as manifested in his poetry, and early Buddhism.

THE QUEST FOR PERFECT HAPPINESS IN THE LIGHT OF TRUTH

King Śuddhodan, so the legend goes, afraid that Prince Siddhartha, his sensitive son, later known as Gautama the Buddha, might become a monk, carefully concealed from his view life's disgusting evils, and, anxious to see his son become an emperor, kept him perpetually surrounded by plentiful luxuries and beauties which might increase his attachment to the earth. The Prince, consequently, was deluded into believing that the world was paradise. But then to startle him out of his intellectual slumber came a sudden perception of disease, old age and death which set him off in search of a higher happiness that no such evil could impair or undermine. His constant preoccupation had been absolute happiness, as his extremist nature could be content with no partial pleasure evanescent as dew-pearls. Since the world does not yield it ready-made to our longing, to realise it by an effort of will was the end and purpose of his quest. Truth is valuable only because illusions, however comfortable, do not last, and disillusionment proves to be painful. By truth is meant, not the ultimate stuff of reality said to exist behind the supposed veil of appearance, but a clear vision of the phenomenal world in relation to the desiring self which, far from being a paradise, is discovered to be a hell of misery. Ideal happiness is that which grows steadily to perfection in the lucid light of truth. The Buddhist quest is thus different from the western philosophical inquiry aiming dispassionately at rational knowledge of reality in abstract, or the popular Christian faith in the beatific heaven presumed to await us after death.

Hardy was never deluded into believing that the world was paradise, but longed always to see it as such. T. R. M. Creighton is quite right when he observes of Hardy:

He had the temperament of a pre-lapsarian visionary and intuitively expected a harmonious universe animated by divine purpose and meaning, an immortal condition of peace and well-being for all creatures, and for man in particular the life of Eden, willed and sanctified by the paternal love of an immanent God — 'as an external personality, the only true meaning of the word' — with whom he would be on terms of absolute devotion and reverent personal intimacy, and consummated by a perfect and innocent sexual union in an existence free of death, sin or evil.[1]

That exactly is the reason why Hardy had to recognise in despair
the world as an unfortunate product of the defective law which
permits no happiness to its creatures, and as such a bad contrast
to the mythical paradise. He ardently wished that 'this muddy
earth' be moulded into 'A spot for the splendid birth / Of everlasting
lives, / Whereto, no night arrives',[2] or that life could at least 'feign
like truth, for one mad day, / That Earth is paradise'.[3] But he knew
as well that it was an impossible hope, for dreams do not become
reality and delusions do not last. In all this the nature of Hardy's
quest should become clear to us. His is the quest for unalloyed
happiness in the lucid light of truth; something distinct from
speculations regarding the nature of ultimate reality on the one
hand and belief in the tales and pictures of the religious imagination
on the other.

THE ABSENCE OF GOD AND THE EXISTENCE OF ORDER

The Buddha had not inherited from Eastern tradition the idea of a
benevolent Creator. He was, moreover, temperamentally rational
and analytical, not emotional and imaginative. Hence, he had
never learnt to bank on God for help and support. The questions
relevant to his quest are: How could one who appears nowhere
and is indicated nowhere be the object of our inquiry? Does the
speculation either to affirm or to deny His existence serve any
practical purpose? Could it mitigate or undo *real* sorrow? Surely it
cannot, and there is no evidence to suggest that He is, or would
or could improve the scheme of existence so painful to us, for our
sake. God is, therefore, superfluous to the Buddhist way of
salvation from suffering. The Buddha studiously avoids futile
discussions of God, and lays it down that metaphysical speculations
(Ditthi) are wasteful of time and energy and are sinful. He was an
agnostic centuries before agnosticism was systematically formula-
ted. But in the *Buddhacarita*, a Sanskrit epic by Asvaghoṣa, a great
Buddhist monk of the first century AD, the Buddha is made to
argue with Anāthpiṇḍika, even for atheism, thus:

> If the world had been made by Īśvara (God), there should be no
> change nor destruction, there should be no such thing as sorrow
> or calamity, as right or wrong, seeing that all things, pure and
> impure, must come from him. If sorrow and joy, love and hate,

which spring up in all conscious beings, be the work of Īśvara, he himself must be capable of sorrow and joy, love and hatred, and if he has these, how can he be said to be perfect? If Īśvara be the maker, and if all beings have to submit silently to their maker's power, what would be the use of practising virtue? The doing of right or wrong would be the same, as all deeds are his making and must be the same with their maker. But if sorrow and suffering are attributed to another cause, then there would be something of which Īśvara is not the cause. Why, then, should not all that exists be uncaused too? Again, if Īśvara be the maker, he acts either with or without a purpose. If he acts with a purpose, he cannot be said to be all perfect, for a purpose necessarily implies satisfication of a want. If he acts without a purpose, he must be like the lunatic or suckling babe. Besides, if Īśvara be the maker, why should not people reverently submit to him, why should they offer supplications to him when sorely pressed by necessity? . . . Thus the idea of Īśvara is proved false by rational argument, and all such contradictory assertions should be exposed.[4]

But the absence of God does not indicate the sway of Chance in Buddhism. To quote Dr S. Radhakrishnan, 'Even in the mere mechanism of a soulless universe Buddhism sees an eternal cosmic law or ordered procedure . . . The wheel of the cosmic order goes on "without maker, without known beginning, continuously to exist by nature of concatenation of cause and effect."'[5]

However, it is not fair to equate the Buddha with a European materialist of the nineteenth century just because he abandons God 'as an external personality, the only true meaning of the word', for he sought single-mindedly and realised in full measure an impersonal spirituality not much different from Meister Eckhart's 'Godhead' of the Upaniṣadic 'Brahma' or the Sufi 'sea of love'. Only he thought that silence, not words, and behavioural repose, best bespeak the ineffable.

Hardy refuses to admit that he is a 'clamourous atheist', and calls himself quite justifiably a 'harmless agnostic',[6] for the temerity to pronounce emphatic judgments on the ultimate ontological issues is unknown to his nature. He just notes faithfully his impartial observation of the world, and recognises as truth what strikes him as obvious there. He thus recognises even as the Buddha does, the absence of God 'as an external personality', and his atheism, patent in all his poetry, even like the latter's, has the character of practical truth as distinct from a fanatical creed, to base his melioristic action upon. In 'God's Funeral' he clearly states that God is an anthropomorphic concept which has evolved from a 'jealous' primitive Deity to a merciful Providence in a long process of wishful thinking, not a reality corresponding to this concept:

> And, tricked by our own early dream
> And need of solace, we grew self-deceived,
> Our making soon our maker did we deem,
> And what we had imagined we believed.[7]

But 'Uncompromising rude reality' discovered to our view by the scientific enlightenment, at last

> Mangled the Monarch of our fashioning
> Who quavered, sank; and now has ceased to be.[8]

The death of God was a misfortune to Hardy, not a happy riddance as it was to Russell who wrote that after the process of the loss of belief was completed, 'I found to my surprise that I was quite glad to be done with the whole subject',[9] for Hardy was temperamentally emotional in spite of his readiness to see truth boldly and clearly and had loved God with the passion of a devout Christian. He was compelled against his will to admit that He does not exist. That is why he resented in 'The Impercipient' 'the charge that blessed things/I'd liefer not have be/O, doth a bird deprived of wings/go earth-bound wilfully!'[10]

There is nothing in Hardy's poetry to suggest the view that he held a heretic belief. There is no reference here to 'some indistinct, colossal Prince of the World' who had framed Eustacia's situation and ruled her lot, or to 'the President of Immortals' who had mercilessly dogged the footsteps of hapless Tess. There are no Henchards and Sues here to conjure up God in order to lay on Him the blame for their misfortunes. Here he has no reason to paint God as a Fiend to prove His absence, none to strike an aggressive posture against a possible critical uproar, for he knows that poetry, even if it runs 'counter to the inert crystallised opinion' will be let alone with 'merely a shake of head'.[11] That is why he avers in 'Hap' that the being of even a 'vengeful god' would be welcome to him, as it makes at least the attitude of revolt meaningful, but total spiritual absence in the universe is a fact which cannot be evaded just for such comfort.

Hardy's 'Immanent Will' which he often calls also God, is just physical Nature figuratively conceived, not an abstract idea of the ultimate real. The First Cause or, to be precise, the phenomenon of cause producing effect in a causal chain which has no terminal point on either side, is, to him, nothing beyond perceptible Nature evidently blind, creative and 'logicless'. His poems on the subject are self-admittedly 'weak phantasies', a mere fancy-play which moodily suggest now that the Will might wake up someday from Its sleep-working to frame consciously a better world, now that It may not wake at all, now that It may wake up after sentience upon this planet is extinct to rue Its cruelties to Life. They are not meant to embody any serious metaphysical proposition. Hardy's admirers, anxious to read a ray of hope in him, in order to defend him against the charge of pessimism, make unreasonably much of a few lines in *The Dynasts* on the Will's wished-for waking up to pity. But they would do well to consider side by side with them poems such as 'By the Earth's Corpse', 'I Have Lived With Shades', 'The Blow', 'The Aërolite' and 'V. R. 1819–1901', to realise that there are other directions, too, towards which the fancy-play drifts as freely, and that none of these is meant to be a prophecy.

Hardy's correct view of Nature, shorn of poetic phantasies and philosophical possibilies that may suggest themselves to a thoughtful mind in response to the question 'why we find us here!', are clearly expressed in 'Nature's Questioning':

1   Has some Vast Imbecility,
        Mighty to build and blend,
        But impotent to tend,
    Framed us in jest, and left us now in hazardry?

2   Or come we of an Automaton
        Unconscious of our pains?

3   Or are we live remains
    Of Godhead dying downwards, brain and eye now gone?

4   Or is it that some high Plan betides,
        As yet not understood,
        Of Evil stormed by Good,
    We the Forlorn Hope over which Achievement strides?[12]

These are just questions. None of them is meant to be an

affirmation. 'Thus things around. No answerer I . . .'[13] As for himself Hardy accepts as truth what plainly appears to our view, without seeking to go beyond the concrete into the realm of the transphenomenal, or to hazard a guess about the final shape of things in future:

> Meanwhile the winds, and rains,
> And Earth's old glooms and pains
> Are still the same, and Life and Death are neighbours nigh.[14]

This sad but certain reality need not be whitewashed with idealistic speculations, for 'if way to the Better there be, it exacts a full look at the Worst'.[15]

The disappearance of God unveils to our view the pervasive presence of *Chance*, a word which in Hardy's usage has a meaning of its own. He certainly does not mean to say that the universe is a chaos of 'Crass Casualty', for a lover of the scientific light which reveals the uniform operation of infallible laws of Nature would not perceive a causeless happening in the causal chain of events. 'Chancefulness' indicates, not that the movement of time is not well-ordered, but that the Prime Mover of the movement is absent; not that causation permits the occurrence of accident, but that the design of causation is not teleological. It means that events fall out according to the necessities of Nature, not the wishes of man, or the need to make a good man happy. But it also signifies Hardy's regret, lingering still in the subconscious, that the natural order is not (and the wish that it should be) the prelapsarian order. The absence of 'Chance' in the Buddhist phraseology indicates that the Buddha, disillusioned that the earth is not paradise, resolutely dismissed both the fruitless regret and unreasonable wishes of this sort, altogether. His 'Causal Order' has scientific precision devoid of equivocations and emotional overtones.

A METAPHYSICS DESCRIPTIVE OF THE HUMAN SITUATION

The Buddha accurately describes the human situation in the world in terms disturbing to those reluctant to face and inclined to flee its lucid perception. He finds man essentially alone, engaged in the futile strife of existence, as often shocked as sustained by the ever-changing pattern of social relationships. Man must boldly realise that he is alone by total renunciation of family, of the private sphere of relationships and the social world at large. The Buddha would not call him an alien here, for it would imply that he has a home or the possibility of a home elsewhere, or at least an unwillingness to realise clearly the fact of absolute loneliness. This life is the Buddha's immediate truth, the only truth that matters to him, and its pain is his all-absorbing concern:

> This, O monks, is the Ariyan Truth of suffering: Birth is suffering, old age is suffering, sickness is suffering, death is suffering, to be united with the unloved is suffering, to be separated from the loved is suffering, not to obtain what one desires is suffering; in short, the fivefold clinging to the earth is suffering.[16]

It requires only common sense to understand but courage to recognise the fact that the origin of suffering is 'the will to life . . . together with lust and desire, which finds gratification here and there; the thirst for pleasures, the thirst for being, the thirst for power'[17] in view of a natural world hopelessly indifferent to human desires. The Buddha altogether, and rightly, avoids as irrelevant the question that seems so natural even to the atheistic thinkers brought up in the western religio-philosophical tradition, as to why the world is made such a bad place of sorrow, or whether man's place in the universe is central or superfluous, for, according to him, there is no evidence that the wheels of time were ever set into motion by anybody and for man. Any change in the nature of the world being out of the question, his emphasis is on what *we* should do to suit it well. 'Annihilation of desire, letting it go, expelling it, separating oneself from it, giving it no room',[18] therefore, is his prescription for uprooting sorrow. There is no suggestion anywhere here of the unconscious wish that the world should be a place as we would have it.

Hardy knows, of course, that the prelapsarian order he is so nostalgic about never adorned this world. But he thinks exactly as the existentialists do that

> A TIME there was — as one may guess
> And as, indeed, earth's testimonies tell —
> Before the birth of consciousness,
>   When all went well.[19]

Beings of the earth, its true citizens, were happy with what they got, and did not crave for what Nature did not grant. This is the primal harmony of Nature, the only true paradise that existed.

> But the disease of feeling germed,
> And primal rightness took the tint of wrong.[20]

This brought about, as for Erich Fromm and Sartre, so for Hardy, man's expulsion from Nature's paradise, and instead of earlier consonance, conflict between the urges of consciousness, the new emergent in evolution, and Nature which has never promised to satisfy them. In fact, consciousness clearly is alien to this world, and must have come, Hardy thinks in 'The Aërolite', on a meteorite from another planet, its true home, where external conditions respond well to inner needs, where paradise is a reality, not a myth. But here it has spelt the absurd. Idealists, seeking to discern spiritual unity behind the supposed veil of phenomenal appearance, or naturalists, trying perversely to reduce mind to an 'aura' of matter, for a monistic explanation of existence, cannot with their vain speculations undo our direct experience of 'Our Old Friend Dualism', the irrefutable reality of consciousness at strife with Nature. The actual harmony, the primal one, will return only with the cessation of consciousness, someday. Hardy hopes: 'May be now / Normal unawareness waits rebirth.'[21] He even longs: 'Ere nescience shall be reaffirmed / How long, how long?'[22] But for the present the fact of discord has to be taken account of without evasions. Hence, the metaphysics that emerges from Hardy's work, even like the phenomenology of existentialists, is merely descriptive of the state of confrontation between man's quest for meaning and the universe that offers none, the will to life and necessity of death, human desires and the drift of time indifferent to them.

The power of thinking clearly has not made man happy. In 'Drinking Song' Hardy shows how scientific thought beginning with Thales, running counter to geocentric religious thought, through Copernicus, Hume, Darwin, Doctor Cheyne and Einstein particularly, has gone progressively on robbing us of sweet illusions and left us ultimately in the 'piteous case' of having none.[23] Hence, the crucial question in 'The Problem' is: should we court trouble by adopting the scientific view of life?

> Hearts that are happiest hold not by it;
>   Better we let, then, the old view reign:
> Since there is peace in that, why decry it?
>   Since there is comfort, why disdain?[24]

The questions here affirm that the old view is preferable to the
anguish of the new, for those still not awakened to the human
predicament in the world without God. But for himself, as ignorance once lost cannot be regained with its bliss, there is no option
to burning enlightenment.[25] In 'On a Fine Morning' Hardy clearly
implies that he did not believe in 'cleaving to the Dream / And in
gazing at the gleam / Whereby gray things golden seem'[26] either,
though spiritual solace comes 'Not from noting Life's conditions'.[27]
He, therefore, sees the human situation lucidly and writes of it
disturbingly. 'The Caged Goldfinch' is obviously a symbol of man
in the midst of Nature, and in *Jude* and *The Return*, too, the world
is likened to a prisonhouse. The bird does not know who put him
into the cage, and why, to long for liberty and to die without it.
But Hardy's recognition of the human situation, like that of the
existentialists, though bold and clear, is not free from an irrational
wish that the world should be the place that we would have it be.

AWARENESS AND THE TRANSCENDENCE OF IMPERMANENCE

The Buddha's doctrine of *anicca* (impermanence) is the strongest
part of his philosophy. Existence is a river that ever flows. Human
desires are out of place here because they have no objects that
could stay unchanged, sweet as ever, no eternally youthful body
to be harboured in, and they themselves do not keep unalterably
the same. Ceaseless succession makes for the illusion of stability
in time. But a beautiful baby is not the same as the withered old
man he eventually grows into. The seed is the tree only in so far
as the process of change between the two is unbroken. The changes
are causally related as antecedents determine succeeding events
and appearances. The stream of becoming, never stilled into a pool
of being, thus flows eternally and permits no lasting happiness to
man.

Corollary to *anicca* is *anattā* (no soul). The Buddha is at one with
Sartre in calling the self 'nothing' which means that it has no
permanent 'thinghood' or 'being-in-itself'. It is also in a state of

flux more dynamic than that discerned in material objects, and the illusion of its identity, too, is the result of a constant succession of changes in its continuity. A calm analysis of subjectivity discovers nothing pure, incorruptible and ever the same in its stream that could be named as self:

Body, monks, is not the Self.

Feeling is not the Self . . . perception is not the Self . . . the constructions are not the Self . . . Consciousness is not the Self.[28]

What is impermanent, that is ill; what is ill is not the Self. What is not Self, that is not mine, that am I not, that is not my Self.[29]

There is no question of the soul's survival after death because during life, too, it has never existed as a fixed entity. Hence, the Buddha does and does not believe in rebirth. If by reincarnation is meant the soul's casting off the old garment and putting on the new, he does not believe in its possibility, for he sees only the garments and no identical wearer. But if it means the continuity of the stream of consciousness growing into bodies one after the other, governed by the causal law of karma which, in the words of E. A. Burtt, *'is the principle that good choices, earnest efforts, good deeds, build good character, while bad choices, inertia, and evil deeds build bad character'*,[30] then he did observe it as a fact. From the ashes of the dead Phoenix rises a new one which is never quite the same. Coomaraswamy and Horner observe:

Just as for Plato, St. Augustine, and Meister Eckhart, so here, all change is a sequence of death and rebirth in continuity without identity, and there is no constant entity (*Satto*) that can be thought of as passing over from one embodiment to another as a man might leave one house or village and enter another.[31]

The universe, all history, things animate and inanimate, mental (*nāma*) and material (*rūpa*), are in a process of endless change. Sorrow comes from our futile quest of permanence in the self and the world. This quest is called *tanhā* or thirst. We must always remember that

There are five things which no samanā and no Brāhman and no
god, neither Māra, nor Brahmā, nor any being in the universe,
can bring about. What five things are those? That what is subject
to old age should not grow old, that what is subject to sickness
should not be sick, that what is subject to death should not die,
that what is subject to decay should not decay, that what is liable
to pass away should not pass away.[32]

Seeing in what's impermanent the permanent, in what is ill what
   is well,
In what's not-Self the Self, in what is ugly beauty,
These are the erroneous views of the scatter-brained and
   unintelligent . . .
They tread the round of becoming, theirs is the road of birth
   and death.[33]

Constant meditation on all this gradually turns desires into
dispassion and taste for the world into distaste. Constant awareness
of self as a flux of consciousness, as *anatta* or not-self, ultimately
makes for the dissolution of the illusory 'I' sense, the individuality,
the will to life and realisation of oneness with all existence. 'When
the thought "I am" has been eradicated, the monk is no more on
fire.'[34] This is Nirvāṇa which literally means 'dying out', the true
death wherein the cycle of lives terminates, the final deliverance
from suffering. It is the experience of the Infinite, covering all time,
ineffably tranquil, positive and profound, though never positively
named by the Buddha, who transcended all change mystically but
disdained any metaphysical notion of being that all along the
stream of becoming had surely been implicit, for there can be no
movement without reference to a still point. This is true spirituality
without personal God. The discord of existence is transformed
here into absolute harmony. Explusion of the craving consciousness
from the primal paradise of Nature is over, and man's return to
her realm, final, royal, triumphant, is staged. There is, however, a
difference between the citizens of Nature who obey, and the
Buddhist sage who has no wish to command, though both alike
make strife impossible. The former are in a state of stupor below
normal human consciousness, having no power to yearn and
aspire; the latter is above normal human consciousness in a state
of quiet awareness of all things, free from the turmoil of desires
that had existed long and are undone now. 'Having already died

to whatever can die, he awaits the dissolution of the temporal
vehicle with perfect composure and can say: "I hanker not for life,
and am not impatient for death. I await the hour, like a servant
expecting his wages; I shall lay down this body of mine at last,
foreknowing, recollected."'[35] The death of Nirvāṇa, realised while
the body is still alive, is stillness that lives even after the body
disintegrates. It is called *Parinirvāṇa*.

Hardy, too, tends positively towards the Buddhist way back to
the primal paradise, though his views are rather raw than refined,
and the poet understandably is less systematic than the prophet.
His perception of existence as 'this never truly being, / This ever-
more becoming'[36] is clear and constant. He, too, sees that nothing
stays identically the same, and that the stream of change flows
through causal channels. Thus two Rosalinds, the youthful one of
'eighteen sixty-three', and 'the hag' whose 'voice — though raucous
now — was yet the old one', at 40 years' remove from each other,
are totally different persons in an identical flux.[37] Agnette of 'The
Revisitation' shocks her lover who meets her after a lapse of 20
years because she looks old, so opposed to the earlier damsel,
though she has been the same unbroken process of change that
has had in it no still points either before or after they first met.[38]
Hardy asks in 'Former Beauties':

> These market-dames, mid-aged, with lips thin-drawn,
> > And tissues sere,
> Are they the ones we loved in years agone,
> > And courted here?[39]

But it is only to affirm that they are as a continuity of change and
not of permanence. In 'The Second Visit' he writes of a place which
looks the same as before when he revisits it many years later:

> But it's not the same miller who long ago I knew,
> Nor are they the same apples, nor the same drops that dash
> Over the wet wheel, nor the ducks below that splash,
> Nor the woman who to fond plaints replied 'You know I
> do.'[40]

The only permanent phenomenon in this world is the ceaseless
succession of changes which give the illusory impression of
stability.

Constant, clear understanding of the self as nothing does not emerge from Hardy's work. But, surely, he was not unaware of the fact that in the stream of consciousness there is no entity that remains ever identically the same. He writes: 'December 4 (1890). I am more than ever convinced that persons are successively various persons, according as each special strand in their characters is brought uppermost by circumstances.'[41] But he was principally a poet drawn by the charms and transience of the external world, not a psychologist like the Buddha interested in analysing mind.

Trouble arises because we expect to see happy times and things still in the stream of change. That is why Time appears to Hardy in his darker moods as a 'tyrant fell' that 'tools away' beauties of the earth, as a Sportsman that 'rears his brood to kill'. Death, then, seems to hold absolute sway over the world. The dead man is often said to survive in others' fond memory of him. But this Comtian concept of immortality does not satisfy Hardy, and cannot hearten anyone anxious to preserve individuality intact, particularly as memory, too, gradually wears away,[42] and man dies a second death when all those who knew him pass away.[43]

But in his positive moods (more frequent than the darker ones) Hardy, too, like the Buddha, does not want Time to change its character. Constant brooding over the perishability of all things makes in Hardy, too, for want of zest in life's dance.[44] His desires weaken and wane, and he learns to accept with open arms all that Fate brings unasked. This is the attitude of affirmative resignation to life's 'neutral-tinted haps and such', that makes for Hardy's establishment of harmony with the world. 'I NEVER cared for Life; Life cared for me', he writes in 'Epitaph', because he does not seek in it much more than he finds and is finally prepared to die reposefully.[45] In 'He Fears His Good Fortune' the poet, in a mood not different from that of Elizabeth-Jane at the end of *The Mayor of Casterbridge*, reflects that no 'glorious time' of life has come to stay for good. 'Its spell must close with a crash/Some day!' Well-established in the vision of impermanence, he is prepared for such a crash which does come:

> Well . . . let the end foreseen
> Come duly! — I am serene.[46]

Here lies the difference between the denizens of Nature's paradise and the poet resigned to natural happenings. They are asleep, he is self-aware and serene. Craving, the trouble-maker, is not awakened in them, and is overcome by him.

As the spirit of resignation resolves itself into a higher unity the existential discord between the self and the universe that the will to life had conjured, a kind of monism not speculatively arrived at, but actually observed in phenomena and inwardly felt, emerges from Hardy's poetry. Reality is one, and life and matter are its two modes, one ceaselessly turning into the other and returning to itself. The dead body mouldering beneath the earth shoots alive as grass and plants, as their sap, colour and fragrance, to feed the cattle who die in man's food and relive as the human vitality. The identical Life-force runs on thus everlastingly through changing forms of inertia and sentience. This is the cycle of reincarnation to Hardy. The difference between things and beings, between one thing or one being and another, is just formal, not substantial. Shelley's skylark appears to Hardy to be just an ordinary bird who

> Lived its meek life; then one day, fell —
> A little ball of feather and bone,

not the 'blithe spirit', the Platonic idea abstracted from the stream of impermanence. But it is immortal, nevertheless, in the sense that perishability is the characteristic of the form, not of its substance:

> Maybe it rests in the loam I view,
> Maybe it throbs in a myrtle's green,
> Maybe it sleeps in the coming hue
> Of a grape on the slopes of yon inland scene.[47]

The same idea continues to recur in Hardy's poetry, and is particularly expressed in 'Life Laughs Onward', 'Transformations', and 'Voices from Things Growing in a Churchyard'. If living means this ceaseless flow of Life-force through changing forms, death is inconceivable. But if life means staying still in the same form immune against the universal sweep of change, nothing has ever lived for a moment. Life is eternal being from one point of view, and eternal non-being from another. So is death. Hardy in his most philosophical moods serenely observes the permanence of Life even as in his darker moods he sees distressfully the pervasive presence of death. However, the immortality of Hardy's view, the perception of daisies thriving gaily upon the grave, could gladden only those who no longer hanker after the stillness in the stream of becoming, whose will to life as identical shape of body and mind, has markedly thinned if not quite dissolved. That is why this kind of materialistic monism probably did not yield to Buchner and Haeckel, its chief exponents, any spiritual satisfaction in the way it does to Hardy. In fact, the monist who feels with self-effacement, instead of just conceiving objectively, the oneness of reality, is a mystic whether he knows it or not, and he unconsciously contradicts himself as Hardy seems to do, if he calls this reality material, for awareness of identity with the totality of existence, is essentially subjective, and hence idealistic. The Buddha, too, appears to be a materialist to Rhys Davids whose approach to the Buddhist philosophy is Comtian. But refuting Davids, Arthur Lillie rightly states: 'In point of fact, Buddhism, like the philosophy of Vedas and Vedantic school, has always been a pure idealism.'[48]

Hardy's egoity is attenuated even more at times, and his monistic feeling, consequently, deepens further into a mystical state transcending time. Thus in 'The Absolute Explains' Time, together with the other dimensions of space, exists, not as a stream, but as infinite stillness simultaneously present from end to end. All becoming is now transformed into all being. Then 'in a sane purview / All things are shaped to be / Eternally':

> As one upon a dark highway,
>   Plodding by lantern-light,
> Finds but the reach of its frail ray
>   Uncovered to his sight,
>   Though mid the night
>
> 'The road lies all its length the same,
>   Forwardly as at rear,
> So, outside what you "Present" name,
>   Future and Past stand sheer,
>   Cognate and clear.'[49]

Similarly Time in 'So, Time', 'Heretofore held to be / Master and enemy' is discovered to be

> . . . placid permanence
> That knows no transience:

Firm in the Vast,
First, last;
After, yet close to us.[50]

The opposition between the self that seeks fixity and the flux that frustrates the quest, has disappeared. This is the result of what the Buddhists call *prajña* or true insight which integrates dualism, 'our old friend', stubborn and unyielding, into the wholeness of being, even as *avidya* (ignorance) divides existence into the ego-consciousness and the external world. That Hardy, content with the positive feeling of the Absolute, does not care to explain the psychological process that makes for it, does not matter. The feeling is powerful and joyful enough, and mystical in the Indian sense unknown to him.

METAPHYSICAL ETHICS AND THE MORALITY OF UNIVERSAL COMPASSION

Buddhist ethics are basically metaphysical, for they aim at a harmonious relationship of consciousness and the phenomenal world, to be realised by conquest of passions and dissolution of individuality. But full awareness of the painful situation of sentience in the world generates in one sympathy for one's co-sufferers. Moreover, kind concern for others accelerates the process of dissolving personal egoity which leads ultimately to the goal of Nirvāṇa. Hence, the Buddha's compassion embraces all creatures from the smallest fly to man, and even gods who are said to be mortal, who have to be born upon the earth again after the effects of their meritorious actions are exhausted according to the law of karma. Vicarious suffering is the highest ideal of the Buddha's compassionate ethics. Writes E. A. Burtt:

As long as one is completely absorbed in his own grief, arising from the death of a dear one, there is no way of gaining victory over pain or release from the numbing bitterness of loss . . . If, instead, one can identify in feeling with the experience of others who similarly suffer, he will be freed from his own grief by and in a compassionate oneness with all living beings. This oneness intrinsically brings an enduring peace and joy that are superior to grief — superior because they spring not from hopelessly trying to evade its causes or stoically steeling the mind to its impact, but through overcoming the evil to oneself by the good of a deep and fully satisfying love for others.[51]

The Buddha lays down the noble eightfold path of ethical behaviour 'to wit: Right Belief, Right Aspiration, Right Speech, Right Living, Right Effort, Right Recollectedness, Right Rapture'[52] which liberates the self from the cycle of reincarnations, and achieves others' good as well.

Hardy's concern, too, is man's actual being in conflict with the world, and the realisation of harmony with it by the ethical effort of resignation. Its natural offshoot, too, is the ethics of compassion embracing all beings. As his own personal grief did not disturb him much, Shelleyan self-pity is nearly absent in his poetry. 'What does often depress me', he writes, 'is the sight of so much pain in the world, constant pain; & it did just as much when I was an orthodox Churchman as now; for no future happiness can remove from the past sufferings that have been endured.'[53] He felt, not as an individual apart from other beings, but as organically identified with them, their pains as his. That is why the wind-blown words along the skies and 'through the wide dusk', command him:

. . . 'Lift up your eyes,
   Behold this troubled tree,
Complaining as it sways and plies;
   It is a limb of thee.

'Yea, too, the creatures sheltering round —
   Dumb figures, wild and tame,
Yea, too, thy fellows who abound —
   Either of speech the same
Or far and strange — black, dwarfed, and browned,
   They are stuff of thy own frame.'

I moved on in a surging awe
   Of inarticulateness
At the pathetic Me I saw
   In all his huge distress,
Making self-slaughter of the law
   To kill, break, or suppress.[54]

This monistic feeling of oneness with all life, and its pain that is not personal, should be, according to Hardy, the basis of morality in a world deserted by God. He writes:

> Altruism, or The Golden Rule, or whatever 'Love your neighbour as Yourself' may be called, will ultimately be brought about I think by the pain we see in others reacting on ourselves, as if we and they were a part of one body.[55]

Hardy's compassion embraces even God, the imaginary being, when he plays poetically with the idea, just as it does the smallest crawling thing. That is why he fondly describes Nature or the Immanent Will (synonymous with God) as mother, omnipotent but blind. Often he pities God that he pities man but is powerless to mend the matters for him. In no poem do we discern even the slightest suggestion of His malice or wilful cruelty. It is because Hardy's imagination of God in poetry is his, while in fiction Henchard's or Eustacia's heretical belief in Him is theirs. The two must never be confused.

THE CHARGE OF PESSIMISM

The charge of pessimism is levelled against both the Buddha and Hardy again and again but with little justification. The Buddha had, of course, waded through despair, but just to reach the 'other shore' of plenary peace. Consider the following dialogue between him and Tissa:

> Suppose now, Tissa, there be two men, one unskilled and the other skilled in wayfaring. And the one who is unskilled asks the way of the other who is skilled in that way. And that other replies: 'Yes. This is the way, good man. Go on for awhile and you will see the road divide into two. Leave the path to the left and take the right-hand path. Go on for a little and you will see a thick forest. Go on for a little and you will see a great marshy swamp. Go on for a little and you will see a steep precipice. Go on for a little and you will see a delightful stretch of level ground.'
>   Such is my parable, Tissa, to show my meaning and this is the meaning thereof. By 'the man, who is unskilled in the way'

is meant the manyfolk. By 'the man who is skilled in the way' is meant a Tathagata, an Arahant, a Fully Enlightened One. By 'the divided way', Tissa, is meant 'the state of wavering'. The 'left-hand path' is a name for this false eightfold path, to wit: the path of wrong views, wrong intention, and so forth. The 'right-hand path', Tissa, is a name for this Ariyan Eightfold Path, to wit: Right Views, and so forth. The 'thick forest', Tissa, is a name of ignorance. The 'great marshy swamp', Tissa, is a name for the feeling-desires. The 'steep precipice', Tissa, is the name for vexation and despair. 'The delightful stretch of level ground', Tissa, is a name of Nibbana.[56]

It is obvious here that despair follows desires and disappears with them. It is the last of the hurdles to be crossed on the way. On the far side of it lies the goal of Nirvāṇa, actually reached by the Tathagata, and attainable for those who walk the path guided by him. The state of Nirvāṇa-consciousness, totally empty of both the mind-stuff and the world, serene and immovable in the face of the worst calamities, spontaneously compassionate and craving nothing is, in fact, the state of inward fullness which the Buddha had left to Śaṁkarācārya, the great Hindu philosopher of the eighth century AD, to describe positively as *Sat-Cit-Ānanda* or Existence–Consciousness–Bliss absolute. The mind of a pessimist, never happy with being alive because the conditions of life do not satisfy his obstinate loves and longings, is the opposite pole, while optimists known to us, always struggling to be cheerful, often touching despair though steering soon away, rejoicing in life's transitory pleasures but unable to endure its pains stoically, are infinitely removed from the Buddha's radiant tranquillity on the one hand, and not very far away from pessimism on the other. Yet the Buddha is charged with pessimism just because his clear-sighted view of the world and valiant struggle to win authentic spirituality through insuperable obstacles as stated in the just-quoted dialogue, profoundly disturb the desire-ridden minds of his critics who prefer sweet delusions to bitter truth.

That Hardy, too, in his spirit of affirmative resignation, his visitations of the monistic feeling, and his constant compassion for all living beings, has tended positively towards a Buddhist spirituality, should be obvious now. His critics, too, assume that because his constant awareness of the chance-governed transience of all existence disturbs them, it must have kept him disturbed as well. But this is far from the truth. Hardy writes in a letter to A. G. Gardiner, dated 19 March 1908:

> By speaking of it [Hardy's philosophy] as 'downward, ever downward', 'a journey towards despair' & c., you & all optimists, seem to imply that everybody who does not hold your own views of life must be very miserable, which strikes people who think as I do as having something comic about it. 'Pessimism' — as the optimists nickname what is really only a reasoned view of effects & probable causes, deduced from facts unflinchingly observed — *leads to a mental quietude that tends rather upwards than downwards, I consider.* As for professional optimists, one is always sceptical about them: they wear too much the strained look of the smile on a skull.[57]

POINTS OF DIFFERENCE

Attitude to Love

The Buddha in his single-minded pursuit of eternity altogether ignored the evanascent beauties and blessings of life, and even called them snares. Early Buddhism is essentially a religion of ascetics, which regards love as the strongest of passions and, hence, the greatest source of misery. Ananda Coomaraswamy observes:

> 'To fall in love is a form of *Moha*, infatuation: and just as the monastic view of art takes note only of its sensuous elements, so the monastic view of woman and the love of woman takes into account none but the physical factors. To compare Nibbana — as the *Brihadāranyaka Upanishad* compares the bliss of Atman intuition — to the self-forgetting happiness of earthly lovers, locked in each other's arms, would be for Buddhist thought a bitter mockery. No less remote from Buddhist sentiment is the view of Western chivalry which sees in woman a guiding star, or that of Vaishnava or Platonic idealism which finds in the adoration of the individual an education to the love of all.[58]

Hardy never runs to this Buddhist extreme of total turning away from the world. His dispassion does not mean unwillingness to enjoy its pleasures when he stumbles upon them.

> Let me enjoy the earth no less
> Because the all-enacting Might
> That fashioned forth its loveliness
> Had other aims than my delight.[59]

Cyder, dance and love had always been 'great things' to him, particularly love. Hardy's poetry, to quote Lance St. John Butler, 'is as often about love as about all other topics put together'.[60] Though Hardy's view of love as raw passion, as the most compulsive form of desire, as the force of Nature that frequently spells ruin and death of lovers, symbolised by the hungry night-hawk in 'A Hurried Meeting', is not much different from that of Schopenhauer who added greater gloom to the Buddhist view, Hardy knows how to transform its force into 'The hand of friendship down Life's sunless hill'[61] in wise marriage with 'one of kindred pursuits', or into the mystic devotion for the spiritual image of the beloved not dissimilar to Platonic idealism. Self-sacrifice, not self-indulgence, is the characteristic of ideal love of Hardy's notion.

Hardy's rationalism, unlike the Buddha's, was limited to viewing the world lucidly. Hence, while the ascetic saviour disdained all emotions as unsteady waves with varying intensity of force and magnitude that keep the consciousness in constant turmoil, the sensitive poet confined himself to cleansing love, and the other noble emotions that he loved, of earthly selfish ingredients in order to turn them into a still and steady spiritual shape. The emotions thus purified stay self-fulfilled instead of conflicting with the world. Hardy was misunderstood as a champion of permissiveness because he reacted strongly to the puritanic aversion of his Victorian contemporaries to normal human passions and emotions. He should not similarly be treated as an exponent of abstinence simply because like the Buddha he regarded raw desires as the root-cause of sorrow. He simply aimed at transmutation of the physical into the spiritual. Hence, while the Buddha looks distant and divine, Hardy is more human and nearer to us. This is an additional reason why the charge of pessimism against Hardy carries no sense at all.

The Social Absurd and Its Amelioration

There is little substance in the oft-repeated statement of the
Buddha's western admirers that he was Auguste Comte born two
thousand years too soon. The Buddha, of course, shunned as evil
all metaphysical speculations like any positivist. It is also true that
a tremendous wave of compassion roused by him achieved some
social good as well, and did make an indelible impression upon
the Indian ethos. But this does not make him essentially a seeker
after social harmony even as Comte's founding a religion of
Humanity does not make him a pilgrim or prophet of eternity.
One was never a sociologist, and the other never a mystic. Social
concern does not figure in the Buddha's message which is, strictly
speaking, relevant only to a few men agonisingly aware of their
entanglement in the meshes of Time and seized with a fiery quest
for the imperishable. He only taught how an individual should
learn to live alone, away from society in self-communion for the
realisation of Nirvāṇa, and had no wish to reorganise society on
any new lines.

Social concern is never absent in Hardy's work. He is not an
extremist like the Buddha preoccupied entirely with the human
situation in the temporal universe. He is much influenced by
Auguste Comte and western enough to know that social amelior-
ation cannot be left alone to take care of itself. It is necessary in
his view to dissociate meliorism from God, who is a myth, and
from temptations of reward and fears of punishment that are false.
It should be made entirely secular and based on the altruistic
sentiment born of monistic intuition. Not the 'pleasure' of his
contemporary utilitarians, but gratuitous self-sacrifice for others'
well-being, as set forth in 'The Old Workman', is his ultimate
value. Formal virtue, devoid of compassion, is just a dead habit, a
mere custom, and compassion, to alleviate human misery, often
assumes unconventional forms. Thus a virtuous lie is illustrated
in 'Her Dilemma', 'Her Death and After' and 'Mock Wife'. The
husband in 'The Burghers' come to kill his wife and her paramour,
lets them depart with valuables, because he is convinced that the
lovers truly love and deserve each other more than he, 'the licenced
tyrant', deserves her or she loves him. Always Hardy's emphasis
is upon the spirit rather than the form of action.

Hardy's compassion, unlike the Buddha's, is enraged at times,
as evident particularly in *Tess* and *Jude*, when he sees the spectacle

of social exploitation of an individual or human apathy to his suffering. But as such spectacles are nearly absent in Hardy's poetry, his indignation, too, does not appear there.

Does anything of Hardy's social ethics, as manifested in his poetry, indicate pessimism?

It is not claimed here that Hardy was a perfect saint competent to found a new faith for modern humanity. Yet, it is certainly true that he was more religious, not only in his essential quest, but also in substantial realisation of harmony with the world and visitations of monistic feeling, than his Christian critics outraged by his non-conformity to received dogma. Facile belief that all is well with the world in contravention of open-eyed observation of phenomena might satisfy naive optimists engrossed in the mundane round of evanescent blisses, seeking nothing higher, who would rather evade than face the facts which might painfully disillusion them. But clear recognition of the fact that all is ill with the world has been the indispensable first step towards Eternity of great mystics.

Hardy wished very much to interfuse essential 'religion, which must be retained unless the world is to perish, and complete rationality, which must come, unless also the world is to perish'.[61] to evolve an acceptable new faith. He had turned for the purpose to the study of other religions, too. 'He read widely in "other moral religions within whose sphere the name of Christ has never been heard", and which taught the same doctrine "of nobler feelings" towards humanity and emotional goodness and greatness.'[63] It is not known how far his reading included Indian thought. But he notes with amazement the atheistic Sāṃkhya view that *prakṛti* (Nature), blind and soulless, is responsible for creation, and Richard Taylor comments that 'The Hindu notion appeals to Hardy's ideas of an insentient Will.'[64] Hardy, however, if he had studied the system in detail, would not have found the Sāṃkhya-view of the soul's immortality acceptable, even as the Buddha did not. The Buddha drove the tradition of the Sāṃkhya system, which he had probably learnt from Ālāra Kālāma, his first Guru, to the bitter end, eliminating soul from man after seeing the departure of God from the universe. Hardy's dream of realising a viable faith, thoroughly rational and yet spiritual, would have come true if he had known intimately the radiant personality of the Enlightened

One, and studied in depth his path of crossing over to the 'other shore', if he had known 'the only one of the great religions of the world that is consciously and frankly based on a systematic rational analysis of the problem of life, and of the way to its solution'.[65]

Notes

1. T. R. M. Creighton, 'Some Thoughts on Hardy and Religion', in Lance St John Butler (ed.), *Thomas Hardy After Fifty Years* (London: Macmillan, 1978), p. 73.
2. 'In a Whispering Gallery', in James Gibson (ed.), *The Complete Poems of Thomas Hardy* (London: Macmillan, 1981), p. 522.
3. 'To Life', *Complete Poems*, p. 118.
4. Quoted from S. Radhakrishnan, *Indian Philosophy*, vol. I (Bombay: Blackie & Son, 1983), p. 456.
5. Ibid., p. 374.
6. F. E. Hardy, *The Life of Thomas Hardy 1840–1928* (London: Macmillan, 1962), p. 127.
7. 'God's Funeral', *Complete Poems*, p. 327.
8. Ibid.
9. Bertrand Russell, *The Autobiography of Bertrand Russell 1872–1914*, vol. I (London: George Allen and Unwin, 1967), p. 41.
10. 'The Impercipient', *Complete Poems*, p. 68.
11. F. E. Hardy, *The Life*, p. 127.
12. 'Nature's Questioning', *Complete Poems*, pp. 66–7.
13. Ibid., p. 67.
14. Ibid.
15. 'In Tenebris II', *Complete Poems*, p. 168.
16. Quoted from Ananda K. Coomaraswamy, *Buddha and the Gospel of Buddhism* (New Delhi: Munshiram Manoharlal, 1974), pp. 81–2.
17. Ibid., p. 82.
18. Ibid.
19. 'Before Life and After', *Complete Poems*, p. 277.
20. Ibid.
21. 'The Aërolite', *Complete Poems*, p. 770.
22. 'Before Life and After', *Complete Poems*, p. 277.
23. 'Drinking Song', *Complete Poems*, pp. 905–8.
24. 'The Problem', *Complete Poems*, p. 120.
25. 'To Outer Nature', *Complete Poems*, p. 61.
26. 'On a Fine Morning', *Complete Poems*, p. 129.
27. Ibid.
28. A. K. Coomaraswamy and I. B. Horner (eds), *The Living Thoughts of Gotama the Buddha* (London: Cassell, 1948), p. 155.
29. Ibid., p. 161.
30. E. A. Burtt (ed.), *The Teachings of the Compassionate Buddha* (New York: The New American Library, no date), p. 18.

31. Coomaraswamy and Horner, *Living Thoughts*, pp. 14–15.
32. Quoted from A. K. Coomaraswamy, *Buddha and the Gospel of Buddhism* (New Delhi: Munshiram Manoharlal, 1974), p. 84.
33. Coomaraswamy and Horner, *Living Thoughts*, p. 161.
34. Ibid.
35. Ibid., p. 38.
36. 'According to the Mighty Working', *Complete Poems* p. 571.
37. 'The Two Rosalinds', *Complete Poems*, pp. 199–201.
38. 'The Revisitation', *Complete Poems*, pp. 191–5.
39. 'Former Beauties', *Complete Poems*, p. 239.
40. 'The Second Visit', *Complete Poems*, p. 892.
41. F. E. Hardy, *The Life*, p. 230.
42. 'His Immortality', *Complete Poems*, p. 143.
43. 'To-Be-Forgotten', *Complete Poems*, pp. 144–5.
44. 'For Life I Had Never Cared Greatly', *Complete Poems*, p. 537.
45. 'Epitaph', *Complete Poems*, p. 695.
46. 'He Fears His Good Fortune', *Complete Poems*, pp. 509–10.
47. 'Shelley's Skylark', *Complete Poems*, p. 101.
48. Arthur Lillie, *The Life of Buddha* (Delhi: Seema Publications, 1974), pp. x–xi.
49. 'The Absolute Explains', Stanzas IV and V, *Complete Poems*, p. 755.
50. 'So, Time', *Complete Poems*, pp. 757–8.
51. Burtt, *The Teachings*, pp. 43–4.
52. Coomaraswamy, *Buddha and the Gospel of Buddhism*, p. 82.
53. Hardy's letter dated 19 March 1908, to A. G. Gardiner in Richard Little Purdy and Michael Millgate (eds), *The Collected Letters of Thomas Hardy*, vol. III (Oxford: Clarendon Press, 1982), p. 308.
54. 'The Wind Blew Words', *Complete Poems*, pp. 446–7.
55. F. E. Hardy, *The Life*, p. 224.
56. *Some Sayings of the Buddha*, translated by F. L. Woodward (Oxford University Press, 1951), pp. 325–6.
57. Hardy's Letter to A. G. Gardiner dated 19 March 1908. (Italics are mine.)
58. Coomaraswamy, *Buddha and the Gospel of Buddhism*, p. 155.
59. 'Let Me Enjoy', *Complete Poems*, p. 238.
60. Lance St John Butler, *Thomas Hardy* (Cambridge University Press, 1978), p. 162.
61. 'She, to Him' I, *Complete Poems*, p. 15.
62. 'Apology' to *Late Lyrics and Earlier* in *Complete Poems*, p. 562.
63. Harold Orel, *The Final Years of Thomas Hardy 1912–1928* (London: Macmillan, 1976), p. 118.
64. *The Personal Notebooks of Thomas Hardy*, edited by Richard H. Taylor (London: Macmillan, 1979), p. 61.
65. Burtt, *The Teachings*, pp. 22–3.

8

A Flame Unseen: The Mystery at the Heart of Hardy's Vision

Lance St. John Butler

She Who Saw Not

'Did you see something within the house
That made me call you before the red sunsetting?
Something that all this common scene endows
With a richened impress there can be no forgetting?'

' — I have found nothing to see therein,
O Sage, that should have made you urge me to enter,
Nothing to fire the soul, or the sense to win:
I rate you as a rare misrepresenter!'

' — Go anew, Lady, — in by the right . . .
Well: why does your face not shine like the face of Moses?'
' — I found no moving thing there save the light
And shadow flung on the wall by the outside roses.'

' — Go yet once more, pray. Look on a seat.'
' — I go . . . O Sage, it's only a man that sits there
With eyes on the sun. Mute, — average head to feet.'
' — No more?' — 'No more.' Just one the place befits there,

'As the rays reach in through the open door,
And he looks at his hand, and the sun glows through the fingers.
While he's thinking thoughts whose tenour is no more
To me than the swaying rose-tree shade that lingers.'

No more. And years drew on and on
Till no sun came, dank fogs the house enfolding;

And she saw inside, when the form in the flesh had gone,
As a vision what she had missed when the real beholding.

What does this poem mean? What can it teach us about Hardy?
What can have impelled him to write it?

For Michael Riffaterre the first of these questions would be quite
simply answered, for in his terms 'meaning' is restricted to the
surface mimesis by performed by a poem, what he calls the result
of the *first* reading of it.[1] The mimesis in 'She Who Saw Not' is clear
enough: we have little difficulty in understanding the references to
the sunset, the house, the Sage, the Lady, the sunlight, the roses
and so on. Here Hardy's deceptive simplicity is at work.

But if we employ Riffaterre's other term, the 'significance' of the
poem, we come up against a number of opacities that challenge
the critic. The 'significance' is what emerges on a second reading
and relates to the non-mimetic unity of the art work. Hardy throws
down the challenge in the last line where the word 'vision' floats,
apparently an undetermined signifier, hinting at the most extensive
significance but offering no immediate handle to be grasped. We
wonder for an instant whether there might not be, 'over the page'
as it were, another stanza in which the 'vision' will be explained.

Perhaps a way of approaching this enigma is to pick up what
we can at the mimetic level and see if there are any patterns that
can point us towards significance. If we do this, starting with the
word 'vision', we at once discover that it connects up with
'beholding' (the last word of the poem) and therefore with the 'Did
you see?' that opens the poem. This leads us in to the whole range
of details about sight, light, sunset, shadow, glow, eyes, shining
and light-excluding fog that make up the main motifs of these six
stanzas.

To see what all these details can mean we are driven to a range
of other, more famous lyrics by Hardy. It may be some time before
we are able to return to 'She Who Saw Not'. In the meantime we
can look at 'When I Set Out for Lyonnesse' and 'The Second
Night'.

'When I Set Out for Lyonnesse' strikes its readers with the
beauty, delicacy and mystery of its references to starlight and to
the 'magic' left in the poet's eyes in the last stanza.

> . . . starlight lit my lonesomeness
> when I set out for Lyonnesse
> A hundred miles away.

And:

> When I came back from Lyonnesse
> With magic in my eyes,
> All marked with mute surmise
> My radiance rare and fathomless,
> When I came back from Lyonnesse
> With magic in my eyes!

The exclamation mark that concludes the poem underlines the bright-eyed air of visionary mystery that love has wrapped the poet in.

In the ballad 'The Second Night' (printed immediately before 'She Who Saw Not' in *Late Lyrics and Earlier*) the lover fails to meet the girl he wants to jilt one night at the appointed place on a cliff. The second night he goes and tells her that he is due at a 'differing scene' and she vanishes, turning out to be a ghost who has committed suicide the previous evening when he did not appear. In this situation Hardy turns once more to the stars for help; this time to a shooting star:

> A mad star crossed the sky to the sea
> Wasting in sparks as it streamed,
> And when I looked back at her wistfully
> She had changed, much changed, it seemed:
>
> The sparks of the star in her pupils gleamed,
> She was vague as a vapour now,
> And ere of its meaning I had dreamed
> She'd vanished — I knew not how.

In the first of these two stanzas we are being asked to take the shooting star as a symbol of the dying love the poem's narrator feels for the girl: it was fiery and splendid, but now it is 'wasting in sparks' and will go out or disappear. Later, when we realise that the girl is a ghost, we might take the shooting-star to represent the girl's life burning itself out, and perhaps there is a literal association between the falling trajectory of the star and her having thrown herself from the cliff on the previous night.

But when we read the second stanza quoted we find that this will not quite do: the 'sparks of the star' are reflected in the girl-ghost's 'pupils': her vision is at once illuminated and obscured by the sudden flare of light in the sky. Somehow the girl has become a ghost and the ghost is nothing more than the reflected light of a heavenly accident: she is only seen, at last, because of her eyes, her ability to see.

In 'The Second Night' we have another theme that is pregnant with interest for our unravelling of 'She Who Saw Not': the theme of repetition. On the first night a real woman stood on the cliff, on the second night her ghost. On the first night she expected the exclusive love of her man, on the second night the ghost hears only a ghostly echo of his love, a grimacing simulacrum of passion. The man has moved from one love to another, he is now enacting the same events (the eternally repeated events of courtship) on a 'differing scene'.

In 'When I Set Out for Lyonnesse' Hardy celebrates his meeting with Emma Gifford but we know, from 'The Wind's Prophecy' and elsewhere, that he was moving from a first love, Tryphena Sparks (or Eliza Nicholls) to a second, from the black hair or the girl he left behind to the 'tresses flashing fair' of the blonde Emma. We notice the vocabulary: only Hardy would think of blonde hair as 'flashing' — the mere sparks have become brilliant, though intermittent, light.

Hillis Miller has, of course, pointed out[2] how repetitions of this sort work so powerfully in *The Well-Beloved* where for Jocelyn Pierston a magical quality that inspires passion passes mysteriously from one woman to another so that he is doomed to fall in love with three generations of women from the same family. As the third of these incarnations of the Well-Beloved hints, it is only the brevity of natural human existence that has prevented Jocelyn from having been in love with her *great*-grandmother, too. In our own poem, 'She Who Saw Not', the repetition is of visits, obviously symbolic, to an establishment that must be considered as un-changing. To understand what can be seen in the house seems to require a certain *in-sight* on the part of the lady. The *second* time she looks into the house she sees the light and the *third* time she sees the man. And then there is the implication at the end of the poem that it is some sort of seeing, or seeing-plus-remembering, that finally and fully brings home to the lady the meaning of what she is beholding. This sort of repetition-when-it-is-too-late or repetition-in-the-absence-of-the-protagonist is famously enacted in Hardy's own life in 1912 when he recreates his love for Emma, 40 years on, in a brilliant series of poems. Many of these operate specifically through the mechanism of repetition. 'The Walk' is a good example: it rehearses a walk *with* Emma, the same walk without Emma *because she was infirm* and the same walk without Emma *because she was dead*; the poem ends with the fundamental question of the *difference* between these repetitions:

> What difference, then?
> Only that underlying sense
> Of the look of a room on returning thence.

To recapitulate: we have seen:

(a) that Hardy makes special use of light, starlight, shine, and that this is associated with *vision*;
(b) that Hardy is inclined to connect this vision, this *en-lightenment*, with repetition, re-enactment, with the second occasion of things.

The next clue also concerns the *Poems 1912–1913* and Emma's death and it is to be found in the epigraph. From Virgil Hardy, famously, take the three words '*Veteris Vestigia Flammae*'. Here is the episode, in Book IV of the *Aeneid*, in which these words occur; I give it, appropriately enough, in Dryden's translation, as presented to Hardy by his mother when he was a child.

> But anxious Cares already seiz'd the Queen:
> She fed within her Veins a Flame unseen:
> The Heroe's Valour, Acts, and Birth inspire
> Her Soul with Love, and fann the secret Fire.
> His Words, his Looks imprinted in her Heart,
> Improve the Passion, and increase the Smart.
> Now, when the Purple Morn had chas'd away
> The dewy Shadows, and restor'd the Day;
> Her Sister first, with early Care she sought,
> And thus in mournful Accents eas'd her Thought.

My dearest Anna, what new Dreams affright
My lab'ring Soul; what Visions of the Night
Disturb my Quiet, and distract my Breast,
With strange Ideas of our Trojan Guest?
His Worth, his Actions and Majestick Air,
A Man descended from the Gods declare:
Fear ever argues a degenerate kind,
His Birth is well asserted by his Mind.
Then, what he suffer'd, when by Fate betray'd,
What brave Attempts for falling Troy he made!
Such were his Looks, so gracefully he spoke,
That were I not resolv'd against the Yoke
Of hapless Marriage; never to be curs'd
With second Love, so fatal was my first;
To this one Error I might yield again:
For since Sichaeus was untimely slain,
This onely Man, is able to subvert
The fix'd Foundations of my stubborn Heart.
And to confess my Fraility, to my shame,
Somewhat I find within, if not the same,
Too like the Sparkles of my former Flame.[3]

This passage contains the seed of a remarkable element in Hardy's make-up. He, who in his 20s would write the 'She to Him' sonnet sequence had perhaps already, as a child, empathised with the passions of an older woman.

In it, of course, we see Queen Dido suffering from what might be called Repetition-phobia. She is profoundly distressed by feelings which arise within her for a *second* time, she is horrified by the thought that she could love *again* and this sense of guilt will be one of the things that will drive her to suicide. But what is so interesting from our point of view is that she automatically chooses to express herself through a series of light-related metaphors:

Within her veins burns 'A flame unseen' which, like Milton's 'darkness visible' has an oxymoronic ring about it; flames cannot burn unseen. Only if 'flame' is used in the entirely metaphorical sense in which it usually *is* used when connected with affairs of the heart can it be understood in this context.

This oxymoronic flame is echoed or repeated two lines later when it is transformed into a 'secret fire'. This expression is less exclusively metaphorical, a fire could be secret, at least for a while, but it contains the same elements of self-contradiction as 'a flame unseen', the elements of public effect and private emotion.

Dido spends a bad night and in the morning, when '*shadows*' have given place to '*day*', she tells her sister about the 'dreams' and '*Visions*' that have disturbed her.

Then, after a brief mention of 'hapless' marriage and her resolve not to be 'cursed with second love', we approach Dido's clearest expression of her plight and the words that Hardy chose as a prefix to his great series of poems *in memoriam*:

> Somewhat I find within, if not the same
> Too like the Sparkles of my former Flame.

Leaving aside the near-coincidence of 'Sparkles' and 'Sparks', which makes this peculiarly appropriate as an epigraph for poems about the woman who supplanted Tryphena Sparks in the poet's affections, here we have again Hardy's combination of light and repetition.

Veteris Vestigia Flammae, 'The sparkles of my former flame' or 'The remains or traces of an old flame'. Flames, seen or unseen, *burn* and this constrains us to add heat to light, to remember not only the cool silver light of the stars but also the warm golden light of the sun, and that takes us a step nearer to 'She Who Saw Not', a poem about sunlight.

The sun can be a strong presence in Hardy. We remember the 'golden-haired divinity' that rises over the misty meadows at Talbothays to beam genially at Tess and Angel one summer morning and we remember Hardy's comment that worship of this divinity at such a time must seem entirely rational.

We may remember, too, the effect of sunlight on the red painted wall in the hall of the old house at Bockhampton, or rather the effect of this effect on the young Hardy.

> In those days the staircase at Bockhampton (later removed) had its walls coloured Venetian red by his father, and was so situated that the evening sun shone into it, adding to its colour a great intensity for a quarter of an hour or more. Tommy used to wait for this chromatic effect, and, sitting alone there, would recite to himself 'And now another day is gone' from Dr. Watts's

Hymns, with great fervency, though perhaps not for any religious reason, but from a sense that the scene suited the lines.[4]

And perhaps we remember the repetition (once in the autobiographical but fictional *Life* and once in the fictional but autobiographical *Jude the Obscure*) of the moment when, lying with a straw hat over his face, the young Hardy/Jude, enjoying the sunlight shining through the interstices of the straw, decides it might be better never to grow up.

One event of this date or a little later stood out, he used to say, more distinctly than any. He was lying on his back in the sun, thinking how useless he was, and covered his face with his straw hat. The sun's rays streamed through the interstices of the straw, the lining having disappeared. Reflecting on his experiences of the world so far as he had got, he came to the conclusion that he did not wish to grow up.[5]

Connecting the ideas of light and heat might be that word 'radiance' (from 'When I Set Out for Lyonnesse') which combines *shine* with *glow* and both of these with something of a metaphorical suggestion of the emanation of a mystic aura.

Now some of all this seems to imply that the light, the heat and the repetition are all phenomena associated with passion, with erotic love. The 'radiance' is that of a man just newly fallen in love, Queen Dido burns with love, the *Poems 1912–1913* are love poems, and so on. But this is clearly not the whole story: the 'golden divinity' may beam down on Tess and Angel but his warmth and geniality seem to be of broader implication: the sun is a god for all the world. The 'radiance' of 'When I Set Out For Lyonnesse', which is clearly erotic, is matched by the 'radiance' which Clym Yeobright feels to emanate from his mother in *The Return of the Native*: Clym refers to her as 'the sublime saint whose radiance even his tenderness for Eustacia could not obscure'. Clym, incidentally, is the bright yeoman who swaps the bright lights of Paris and jewellery for the humbler task of bringing the light of knowledge to Egdon Heath. Nearly blinded, he comes to learn 'earth secrets' during his spell as a furze-cutter.

So there is a *motif* in Hardy of light and heat — let us call it 'Flame' — which has a secret or private aspect — let us call it 'Unseen' — which seems to involve, by a mysterious and more than merely symbolic process, a vision of love, beneficence, wisdom and cosmic harmony that may be quite at variance with our common assumptions about Hardy's view of the universe. Hence I have called this essay 'A Flame Unseen: The Mystery at the Heart of Hardy's Vision'. The implication which I am testing is that there *might* be an interpretation of Hardy that saw him as a mystic, at least in a limited sense, who believed that a certain *perception*, a certain *vision* would give insight into the deep love and even harmony that at some level form a profound strand of reality. 'She Who Saw Not' certainly *appears* to demand some such interpretation.

Before returning to the poem itself let us continue our brief survey of some more familiar Hardy poems. In 'The Fallow Deer at the Lonely House' the deer looks in through the 'curtain-chink' as the poet (and others) sit by the fire. Of the two stanzas the second reads:

> We do not discern those eyes
>   Watching in the snow;
> Lit by lamps of rosy dyes
> We do not discern those eyes
> Wondering, aglow,
>   Fourfooted, tiptoe.

Here is the tension that we found in 'The Second Night' between the perceiver and the perceived: the deer looks in but the humans, in the cosy lamplight, do not see its eyes which themselves glow as much as the fire or the lamps. Ironically it is the light *within* the house that prevents its occupants from seeing what is outside it. The deer is 'wondering' — it cannot possibly understand what is within the house. In 'She Who Saw Not' it is a human who looks in, and who is also in a kind of ignorance about what she is seeing, but, unlike the deer, she can return and return until she understands, and she can remember, that is return in her mind, until she sees all. The deer is a passer-by arrested an instant by the unfathomable light. Both he and the static occupants of the house are missing out on wisdom, he because as an animal it is beyond him and the humans because they cannot see the beauty and wonder that is just outside their circle of cosy firelight.

In 'An August Midnight' the insects, attracted by the 'shaded lamp' humble the poet by reminding him that 'they know Earth-secrets' that he does not know. In company with a human they get stuck (in the ink) or hurt themselves (they 'bang at the lamp') and we feel that it might have been better for them to dodge the light of wisdom and remain, with their opaque 'Earth-secrets' outside in the primaeval darkness.

'The Self-Unseeing' ends:

> Everything glowed with a gleam:
> Yet we were looking away.

The poet here realises that he has not seen himself or the world properly: a certain magical aura hung around the room where he danced as a little boy but he was not observant enough to catch it nor, according to the title of the poem, was he able to see himself. By leaving the connection between the blindnesses merely tacit, Hardy implies that sight of the self and sight of things (true insight into the one and into the other) are perhaps mutually dependent.

In 'His Immortality' the poet sees 'a dead man's finer part/Shining within each faithful heart' of those who remember him. Memory, too, glows.

In 'The Last Signal' it is a flash of light from William Barnes's coffin that startles Hardy into a realisation that his friend is finally dead.

This catalogue could be continued at considerable length but it might be best to bring it to an end with a reference to a novel. In *Far From the Madding Crowd*, a novel for which it has been suggested that 'Lead Kindly Light' might act as a backdrop, the moment at which Bathsheba is finally aware of the full value of Oak comes when, towards the end of the novel, she sees him saying his prayers. To this typically Hardyan situation of one character looking in through a window to see another must be added what is equally Hardyan: Bathsheba sees Oak by *candlelight*; it is evening and he is romantically illuminated behind the glass.

When we remember the usual assessment that is made of Hardy's view of the universe we might feel that we are coming close to establishing a subversive vein of sentimental nonsense in his work. Can he *really* believe, given all the other things that he so clearly feels about the world, that insects know 'earth-secrets'? Is there truly a *meaning* in Gabriel Oak saying his prayers by candlelight? Does the darkling thrush with his 'happy good-night air' and his putative knowledge of 'some blessed hope' really represent a serious possibility of optimism? Is the vision of the fallow deer (albeit an unseen vision, except in Hardy's imagination) truly a *vision* or is it only one more insight into the blind weaving of the Immanent Will? *Is* there light at the end of the famous tunnel of Hardy's gloom?

As a test case we can now look at 'She Who Saw Not'. The title, immediately, must remind us of Psalm 115: 'They have mouths and they speak not; they have eyes and they see not.' The implication is that 'she' is a heathen as the psalmist is referring to blind and dumb heathen idols. 'She' does not see, in the same way that a wooden idol, for all its eyes, does not see, and the contrast is with a true God, not made of wood, who *can* see. 'She' is thus the object of false worship or, at least, is excluded from some religious truth.

In the opening question the Sage asks the Lady if she saw the thing that made him call her, 'Did you see something within the house . . .?' It must be an unusual 'something' if it provokes him to this summons. The *red* sunset implies a mild optimism (unless the colour of blood outweighs the delight of shepherds), but sunset *per se* implies the end of something: she had better take a look before it is too late. The 'common scene', that is, man's everyday earthly lot, is made richer, unforgettably richer, by this 'something' that is in the house. The repetition of the something, as it were, means something.

In the second stanza she finds ('I have found'), but she finds *nothing*. She is respectful to the Sage but firm in her opinion that there is nothing uncommon within the house: nothing to '*fire*' the soul, no flame to be seen (or felt burning unseen); we notice the connection of *fire* and *soul*. She adds that there is nothing of special aesthetic interest in the house either, nothing 'the *sense* to win'.

Then she shows a moment of petulance: she calls the Sage a liar: 'I rate you as a rare misrepresenter.' Why the strength of feeling here? Obviously it comes from disappointment, but the exclamation is ambiguous: 'I rate you' could mean 'I estimate you' or 'I criticise you', while 'a rare misrepresenter' could be a specially good and fine rearranger of the truth or an exceptionally wicked liar.

'Go anew Lady.' Why the Sage and the Lady? Has Hardy now grown up from the days when Ladies went together in his imagination with Poor Men? Is the Sage, as F. B. Pinion suggests in his commentary on the poems,[6] Hardy himself and the Lady Emma, who never fully understood his writing? Perhaps, but they seem to have a profounder significance, too.

'In by the right.' We remember that in the chivalric romances and medieval literature generally the *right* means the proper way to go. When knights take turnings in forests they show their true knightliness by turning right. So perhaps the right, here too, implies a truth in the vision to be seen in that part of the house. 'Well', says the Sage, who is now watching the lady enter the house for a second time, 'Why haven't you seen God?' That at least is the first thing that springs to mind. The collocation of Moses and Sinai is in itself enough to suggest man meeting God but the *shining* face (we notice the light imagery that Hardy reaches for instinctively in these matters) takes us even more definitely to *Exodus* 34, verses 29–35:

> And it came to pass, when Moses came down from Mt. Sinai, with the two tables of testimony in Moses' hand, when he came down from the mount, that Moses wist not that the skin of his face shone while he talked with him. And when Aaron and all the children of Israel saw Moses, behold, the skin of his face shone; and they were afraid to come nigh him. And Moses called unto them; and Aaron and all the rulers of the congregation returned unto him: and Moses talked with them. And afterward all the children of Israel came nigh: and he gave them in commandment all that the Lord had spoken with him in Mount Sinai. And till Moses had done speaking with them, he put a vail on his face. But when Moses went in before the Lord to speak with him, he took the vail off, until he came out . . .

Hardy was interested in this phenomenon of the shining face. He uses it elsewhere, notably in the poem of 1916 'I Met a Man', in which he imagines meeting a man who has spoken with God (God, not surprisingly in Hardy, is a little ashamed at having allowed the First World War to get out of hand). 'I Met a Man' begins (and roughly ends) with the lines:

> I met a man when night was nigh,
> Who said, with shining face and eye
> Like Moses' after Sinai . . .

The man then quotes what he has heard God saying to himself. Interestingly for us God, 'The Moulder of Monarchies', is pictured

'Sitting upon the sunlit seas' and 'Sitting against the western web of red/Wrapt in His crimson robe'. The God in whom Hardy did not believe seems to be associated with light, with evening sunlight (with the 'luminous numinous' as one might say) and if that is so then there is more to be said: it might oblige us to account for our earlier assertions about erotic love, magic and repetition; we might also have to account for Hardy's famous, even notorious, use of the colour red, of firelight, of flame and of sunlight (and even of sunset) to connote the devilish and the malign. There are ambiguities here, to say the least, but for our purposes the critical point is that God (in Hardy) is not immune from the rule that the mystery (for we seem to be approaching the heart of a mystery) is to be contemplated at sunset.

The Lady returns to the Sage a second time and says that she has seen 'no moving thing' except the light. The light *moves* because the roses outside are being blown about and their shadow moves on the wall (in the penultimate — fifth — stanza this will be confirmed by the reference to the 'swaying rose-tree shade'). On her first visit the Lady saw 'nothing to fire the soul', that is, nothing to move her emotionally; now she sees something, the light, and the light is *moving*. Perhaps there is the ghost of a pun here.

F. B. Pinion suggests that we should look at another poem, 'The Spell of the Rose', to understand about these swaying roses in 'She Who Saw Not'.[7] If we consult 'The Spell of the Rose', one of the *Poems 1912–1913*, we discover echoes of Hardy and Emma: 'She' plants a rose, secretly, at the Manor Hall that 'He' has built (Max Gate?). 'She' dies and the poem is spoken by her ghost wondering what he now feels about her; whether, *post mortem*, 'he, *as of old*/Gave me his heart anew' (italics mine.) 'As of old' here hints at the epigraph *'Veteris Vestigia Flammae'*. If this cross-reference to 'The Spell of the Rose' is an accurate one it only serves to emphasise the difference (and therefore the similarity) between the two poems. The *difference* arises from the stark fact that for the 'She' who is the voice of 'The Spell of the Rose' the rose symbolises all that there may or may not have been in her love for 'him', while in 'She Who Saw Not' the rose is an irrelevance, a distraction from the main vision. The *similarity* arises from the title 'The Spell of the Rose' — magic is involved, the magic that we are trying in a roundabout way to associate with 'She Who Saw Not' — and from the fact that without the rose she would not have noticed the light. Only the movement of the rose's shadow draws her (and our) attention to the light. Perhaps the shadow of love alerts us to a deeper mystery in the universe, a mystery that is akin to love but that is not love. Something signalled by the rose but greater than it.

In these third and fourth lines of the third stanza we encounter the first hint of Plato's allegory of the cave, to which we shall return.

In the fourth stanza the Sage tells the Lady to go in once more. Vague Biblical echoes sound from this thrice-repeated action.

She goes in and returns to say, a little sharply perhaps, 'It's only a man that sits there.' But in Hardy 'only a man' is oxymoronic, an offensive way of speaking because no man can be *only* a man. We all remember the disdainful reference to divine morality at the end of Hardy's description of Alec d'Urberville's violation of Tess: 'Though to visit the sins of the father upon their children may be a morality good enough for divinities, it is scorned by average human nature . . .'[8] With this in mind, we must be alerted to something *fine* by the words 'only a man' ('average human nature', that is, somebody who is 'only a man', for Hardy, is somebody better than God) and this impression is increased in the next line when we read that the man is 'average head to feet'. In the holograph manuscript of 'She Who Saw Not' it is apparent that Hardy considered two possible adjectives, not counting 'Mute', to describe the man. The first seems to have been 'common' and the second the 'average' that we see printed. I would suggest that it is probable that Hardy first thought of 'common' in the sense of 'general' or 'universal', together with its overtones of human solidarity, as in a word such as 'commonwealth' (which is the way it is used in the third line of the first stanza), and that he then balked at the implication of inferior social class that is also present in 'common' and of which he, of all people, was bound to be conscious. He therefore selected a less attractive and in some ways less effective word, but one which conveyed the special quasi-mystical point that he had in mind — 'average'. It is the very averageness of the previously unseen man sitting in the house that guarantees for Hardy that he can be part of the secret vision. This Beckettian figure, motionless in the evening light, is somehow attuned to the mystery of the universe, he is in a manner God, and yet he is so insignificant as to be unnoticed twice. It is as if the Lady, or her subconscious, has denied her master twice, and though she does not entirely miss him a third time she is not aware of his significance until much later.

There is a stubbornness in the Lady's refusal of meaning to the 'average' man: 'It's only a man', she says; 'No more?' asks the Sage; 'No more', she says and follows it with a full stop. And yet she starts at once to give herself away: so powerful is the insignificant sunset mystery that it has started to work on her subconscious mind. She sees, at least, that the man is *suited* to the place where he is sitting. This is extremely odd if we stop to think about it; what on earth can the Lady mean? What exactly would it be about any man that would make you say that he was 'befitted' by that seat in that house that evening? Here, surely, we are again in the world of the medieval romance, where what is stated as a physical fact ('he turned *to the right*') is to be taken as a moral fact ('he did *what was right*'). The fittingness of the man to the scene is at a deep level of spiritual suitability, as the lady inarticulately realises.

The sunlight 'reaches in through the open door'. There is no effort needed on the part of the 'average' man to feel the sunlight. All he need do is to sit still. But we notice another extraordinary fact: the man has at least one hand in front of his face. He is 'looking at his hand' and the sun is glowing through the fingers. If you hold your hand up in front of a bright light you can see the light coming through *between* the fingers but you can also see a pinkish translucency through the fingers themselves, and I think it is this latter idea that Hardy has in mind: the word 'glows', a typical Hardy usage in a context like this, implying a warmth, a steady and life-giving light, makes us think of the sunlight actually co⌐ ⌐g through the flesh. But, either way, the man looks at his ⌐ ⌐d ⌐ ⌐d observes the masked flame of the sun glowing through ⌐ ⌐wing through *him*.

⌐he Lady doesn't just leave her subconsciously generated interest ⌐ the man at the level of surface description, she speculates on his thought processes. She makes it appear, of course, as though she is protesting to exactly the opposite effect; we at first think that she has said that the man's thoughts are nothing to her, but what she in fact says is that the '*tenour*' of his thoughts is 'no more' to her than the shadow that also occupies the room. This is a subtle distinction which implies that she has considered what his thoughts might be, and there is a faint implication not so much that she dismisses these as beneath her as that she is excluded from them. Perhaps this is too faint an implication to bear analysis,

but even if the more obvious meaning is considered we can
certainly notice that she declares her separateness simultaneously
from the man's thoughts and the shadow cast by the rose. In other
words, just as she did not understand the light in the third stanza
or the significance of the man in the fourth, she now associates the
further elements (the shadow cast by the light, the thoughts
entertained by the man) and protests that she does not understand
them either, while the very act of protesting and the very association
of these two elements themselves reveal her nascent capacity for
understanding.

Then a new voice enters the poem, a voice that is neither that of
the Sage nor that of the Lady. This voice is responsible for the
sixth Stanza which thus becomes something like a moral appended
to the earlier five and which starts by picking up the words that
we have heard three times in the previous two stanzas: 'No more.'
What do these words refer to? They seem to echo the 'no more/To
me' of two lines earlier, in which case the new voice is simply
telling us that the Lady has not understood her experience. Or
they might be purely the poet's own, in which case they indicate
that the Sage did not try to push his point and that no more was
said between him and the Lady on this occasion. But either way it
comes to the same thing: the Lady remains unenlightened by the
glow of this sunset. The years go by and the light is taken away,
'dank fogs' enfold the house. In the interpretation, no doubt right
as far as it goes, that has this poem as a meditation on Hardy's
first marriage, we must think of the fogs as the gloom that
descended on a relationship that had started so brightly, but how
are we to interpret this final stanza if we pick up the hints we have
found elsewhere in Hardy and try to push home an interpretation
of broader significance?

The key must lie in the last two lines. Here we find that it is *she*
who survives *him*, which puts a question-mark over the Hardy-
and-Emma interpretation, especially in view of the fact that this
poem was first published as late as 1922, ten years after Emma's
death. At all events, once he has 'gone' she, the Lady who has so
far 'seen not', starts to see: without the sunlight, without the Sage
and without the man to look at she sees 'as a vision' what it was
she missed when looking at the 'real' man years before.

The question remains, what does she now see? She has seen,
successively, Nothing, the Light, a Man and a Vision; by repetition
alone she moves towards meaning, but what is it that forms her

vision? What is the meaning? What, in Riffaterre's terms, is the significance?

Let us add up the evidence. Light, from Hardy's earliest boyhood, had a special, intimate and ambiguous significance for him. He finds it to be a stimulus to what in other writers would be called religious experience. As a boy it excites in him a mystical melancholy or a quasi-Buddhist self-abnegation and as a man he associates it with love. It comes in the guise of starlight (though I think not often moonlight, *pace* the Shelleyan Dr Fitzpiers) and firelight and lamplight, but first and foremost it is sunlight that works its magic on him, and the light of sunset above all. Although he did not believe in God he used sunlight as a symbol for a quasi-divine mystery at the heart of existence. When personifying the deity in poems he will have God, as we have seen, 'sitting upon the sunlit seas' but when he wishes to talk about the mystery itself he abandons his rather lightweight simulacra of the divine and resorts to light itself, not forgetting however to steal from theistic religion the convenient symbol of Moses's shining face.

Of course, because it is light that stimulates the mystery, it is *vision* that humans need to penetrate it. And here I think we come to the core of Hardy's meaning: the light is not *merely* symbolic, the 'vision' is not just a metaphor for understanding. For Hardy, as for young Jude under his straw hat, the sunlight is real enough and the 'red sunsetting' of 'She Who Saw Not' is intended to be real.

But this is what we should expect. Although Hardy knows, nobody better, the value of a symbol, and although the flame is *unseen* and therefore metaphorical, the mystery behind these metaphors is a trick: it is not *beyond* them, it is *back on this side of them*. Symbol, allegory and metaphor are usually used in religious writing to refer beyond themselves in a tripartite pattern: there are real vines, there are the metaphorical vines about which Christ says 'By their fruits ye shall know them' and then there is the spiritual meaning that emanates from this and refers to *another world*, a *beyond* in which grace is accrued and good works *count*. But for Hardy the situation has only two parts: there is the real sunlight, the metaphor of the sunlight and then . . . just the real sunlight again. The mystery is that there is no mystery. The faculty of sight leads men to imagine the metaphor of vision, but the vision that is the ultimate wisdom is just the vision of . . . the faculty of sight.

This is why at the end of the poem the woman *sees without* the aid of light.

In all this Plato's allegory of the cave is at work. In Plato the average man cannot look at the real nature of the universe, cannot face the sunlight, because he is in the darkness of ignorance or, rather, takes shadows to be reality. In 'She Who Saw Not' the Lady first takes the room to be empty, then sees only the shadows of the roses on the wall; the man within the room, however, is able to look at the sunlight directly or, rather, looks at it through his fingers. Plato is thus subtly developed by Hardy: the mystery of the universe does not lie in an ineffable beyond, it lies in man himself; the light is essential to the vision but the vision is not through the light to a beyond of a more real reality, the light is itself given meaning only by the presence of the man, of Man. The Lady does not have to be taken *out* of a room and shown the light — she has to go *into* a room, *see* a man, see not the light but his ability to see the light and, indeed, his ability to see light through himself (his fingers).

And it is the simple *physical* ability to see a man sitting in a house in the sunlight, just to see him, that is the first step to wisdom. And wisdom itself is the vision of him *as what he is* which is not another, further thing *beyond* what he seems, but is just him, as he is. This is the huge strength of Hardy's descriptions of nature; he can allegorise with the best, but at the end of the day (an appropriate cliché in this context) his landscapes are real landscapes and their significance is no more than that they are what they are. The deer in the snow, looking in through the curtains, stimulates all Hardy's religious instincts in its magical glowing: here he antici- pates the moment of vision, the mystery revealed. But when the poem ends nothing new has happened, no third party has joined the scene, no metaphysical regions have appeared. There is just the greater mystery, the older mystery, the mystery that was there all along for our vision to see: just the deer in the snow. There 'should' be a third stanza, a stanza implying significance, but Hardy has no extra stanzas, no significance to add.

What Hardy does add, in the last two lines of 'She Who Saw Not', is his typical note that we usually get this vision rather too late, but the nature of the vision is clear enough: the mystery is not the secret of *what* things truly are, it is the non-miraculous Zen miracle *that* things are.

I call it a Zen miracle to distinguish it from the Heideggerian plenitude of Being. We are not faced here with an ultimate presence — far from it — the vision comes too late not because of Hardy's predilection for missed opportunities but because it is in absence that presence is signified. It is only when the man is *not* there that the Lady can see him; only disappearance can achieve the miraculous vision of appearance. If this is anybody's world we are in it is Derrida's.

Derridean self-contradiction thus underpins Hardy's view of the world. Presence is nothing, presence is absence. The Will is, of all impossible things, an Immanent Will. The Will weaves a garment that is nothing but a series of repetitions, as all weaving is. The Lady's visits to the house in 'She Who Saw Not' are repetitious: every time she goes in she sees something but she sees no relationship between the somethings: Nothing, a Man, Light; what have they in common? The vision is at once a principle of identity (they have presence) and of baseless difference (they can remain unseen or be seen when not there).

In Riffaterre's terms Hardy attempts to square a hermeneutic circle: for him the mimetic surface *meaning* is identical with the constructed *significance*, and a poem such as this appears utterly inconclusive because of that attempt. Conclusions being only a special mythology of their own, this may be a space which Hardy has liberated from the tyranny of metaphysics.

Notes

1. Michael Riffaterre, *The Semiotics of Poetry* (London: Methuen, 1980; 1st edn: Indiana University Press, 1978), ch. 1.
2. In *Fiction and Repetition* (Oxford: Oxford University Press, 1982).
3. 'The Fourth Book of the Aeneis', lines 1–31, in James Kinsley (ed.), *The Poems of John Dryden*, 4 vols., vol. III (Oxford: Clarendon Press, 1958), p. 1145.
4. F. E. Hardy, *The Life of Thomas Hardy 1840–1928* (London: Macmillan, 1965), p. 15.
5. *Life*, pp. 15–16.
6. F. B. Pinion, *A Commentary on the Poems of Thomas Hardy* (London: Macmillan, 1976), p. 190.
7. Ibid., p. 190.
8. *Tess of the d'Urbervilles* (London: Macmillan, 1949), p. 91.

9

Hardy's Alternatives in *The Woodlanders*, Chapter 39

Henri Quéré and Janie Sénéchal

---

1 INTRODUCTION

1.1 A Semiotic Description

The point of view deliberately adopted in this paper is that of 'narrative and discursive semiotics', best illustrated by the work of A. J. Greimas and then developed in the context of the GRSL (Groupe de recherches sémio-linguistiques) and of what is now known as the 'Paris School'.[1]

Such a choice implies a certain commitment as regards the concepts and descriptive language which belong to the theory. This immediately raises the problem of the metalanguage. Although ideally motivated, the metalanguage remains fundamentally arbitrary and its adequacy entirely depends on the aptness of the definitions attached to each term. That is why we shall keep it as it is, at least as far as this translation will allow.[2]

The aim of semiotic description is the construction of meaning, a meaning which is apprehended at the various levels of the 'generative path'.[3] The selection of a short passage — in this case the beginning of Chapter 39 of *The Woodlanders*[4] — enables us to combine micro- and macro-analysis by replacing the excerpt concerned in the larger context which gives it its full significance. Within those limits, what is attempted here is a reconstruction of Thomas Hardy's 'semantic micro-universe' which will at the same time account for at least some of the specific features of fiction and discourse.

CHAPTER THIRTY-NINE

ALL night did Winterborne think over that unsatisfactory ending of a pleasant time, forgetting the pleasant time itself. He feared anew that they could never be happy together, even should she be free to choose him. She was accomplished: he was unrefined. It was the original difficulty, which he was too thoughtful to recklessly ignore as some men would have done in his place.

He was one of those silent, unobtrusive beings who want little from others in the way of favour or condescension, and perhaps on that very account scrutinize those others' behaviour too closely. He was not versatile, but one in whom a hope or belief which had once had its rise, meridian, and decline, seldom again exactly recurred, as in the breasts of more sanguine mortals. He had once worshipped her, laid out his life to suit her, wooed her, and lost her. Though it was with almost the same zest it was with not quite the same hope that he had begun to tread the old tracks again, and had allowed himself to be so charmed with her that day.

Move another step towards her he would not. He would even repulse her — as a tribute to conscience. It would be sheer sin to let her prepare a pitfall for her happiness not much smaller than the first by inveigling her into a union with such as he. Her poor father was now blind to these subtleties, which he had formerly beheld as in noontide light. It was his own duty to declare them — for her dear sake.

Grace, too, had a very uncomfortable night, and her solicitous embarrassment was not lessened the next morning when another letter from her father was put into her hands. Its tenor was an intenser strain of the one that had preceded it.

After stating how extremely glad he was to hear that she was better, and able to get out of doors, he went on:

'This is a wearisome business, the solicitor we have come to see being out of town. I do not know when I shall get home. My great anxiety in this delay is still lest you should lose Giles Winterborne. I cannot rest at night for thinking that while our business is hanging fire he may become estranged, or in his shyness go away from the neighbourhood. I have set my heart upon seeing him your husband, if you ever have another. Do then, Grace, give him some temporary encouragement, even though it is over-early. For when I consider the past I do think God will forgive me and you for being a little forward. I have another reason for this, my dear. I feel myself going rapidly down hill, and late affairs have still further helped me that way. And until this thing is done I cannot rest in peace.'

He added a postscript:

'I have just heard that the solicitor is to be seen tomorrow. Possibly, therefore, I shall return in the evening after you get this.'

The paternal longing ran on all-fours with her own desire; and yet in forwarding it yesterday she had been on the brink of giving offence. While craving to be a country girl again, just as her father requested; to put off the old Eve, the fastidious miss — or rather madam — completely, her first attempt had been beaten by the unexpected vitality of that fastidiousness. Her father on returning and seeing the trifling coolness of Giles would be sure to say that the same perversity which had led her to make difficulties about marrying Fitzpiers was now prompting her to blow hot and cold with poor Winterborne.

If the latter had been the most subtle hand at touching the stops of her delicate soul instead of one who had just bound himself to let her be mute on all that appertained to his personality, he could not have acted more seductively than he did that day. He chanced to be superintending some temporary work in a field opposite her windows. She could not discover what he was doing, but she read his mood keenly and truly: she could see in his coming and going an air of determined abandonment of the whole prospect that lay in her direction.

O, how she longed to make it up with him! Her father coming in the evening — which meant, she supposed, that all formalities would be in train, her marriage virtually annulled, and she be free to be won again — how could she look him in the face if he should see them estranged thus?

1.2 The Title: 'Hardy's Alternatives'

Chosen for its variety of potential uses the term 'alternative' can be applied here in several different ways:

– from the point of view of the underlying axiology, it refers to the opposition between the values of /Nature/ and /Culture/, and

to the way in which these values are dramatised in the novel;
- from the point of view of the development of the story, it refers to *'la logique des possibles narratifs'*[5] and to the syntactic 'pivot' (closure/new start) around which the redirection of the story is organised;
- from the point of view of the 'actants' and their respective 'moves', it refers to the principle of alternation which regulates the transfer of Objects (acquisition/deprivation) within the general framework of the circulation of values;
- from the point of view of the 'thematic-narrative'[6] content, it refers to the veridictory and fiduciary configuration of 'misunderstanding' with the various 'plot effects'[7] which it entails;
- finally, from the point of view of discourse, it refers to the different modes of enunciation and to the choices dictated by Hardy's discursive strategies (direct vs indirect speech, 'shifting out' vs 'shifting in').

2. BEING OR NOT BEING, DOING OR NOT DOING: POSITIONS AND MOVES

2.1 The Canonical Narrative Pattern

2.1.1 *An Assessment of the Situation*

In its canonical form, the full syntactic course (or narrative algorithm) can be divided into the following logically ordered phases: Manipulation – Action – Sanction.

Within this framework, the action undertaken so far by the two protagonists has failed.

As regards Grace, she has put into operation a narrative programme of /union/. This narrative programme, it must be remembered, resulted from the Contract that she had drawn respectively with her father (in the form of submission to authority: modality of /HAVING TO DO/) and with herself (at least in the form of 'passive acceptance'[8]: modality of /NOT WANTING NOT TO DO/). It has been fully carried out, but without bringing the expected results. In syntactic terms, Grace's marriage with Fitzpiers — i.e. the statement of BEING: S1 (= Grace) ∩ O (= Fitzpiers)[9] — has led to a transformation such that she, as a Subject of DOING, has not obtained (disjunction) or has rapidly lost (non-conjunction) her value-Object: /happiness/. Ironically, the success of the 'auxiliary narrative programme' — marriage being supposedly conducive to happiness — is the very reason for the failure of the 'basic narrative programme', and Fitzpiers, in that respect, appears as an anti-Subject who deprives the heroine of her value-Object. It can be noticed that here, at the beginning of Chapter 39, the same distinction can be found between 'union' (i.e. marriage) and 'happiness': to Giles, the narrative programmes corresponding to each of these value-Objects appear as antagonistic (marriage becomes an instrument of unhappiness) and thus he is led to choose between them and to discard the one (renunciation: reflexive disjunction) in favour of the other (attribution: transitive conjunction).[10]

As for Giles's own narrative programme, it is the result of a self-destined Contract: S2 (= Giles) → /S2 ∩ 01(02(03))/ with 01 = the Object of knowledge with which Giles reflexively conjoins himself, 02 = the modal state of /WANTING/ in which he, as a Subject, finds himself, 03 = the virtualised narrative programme which corresponds to the statement of DOING: S2 → S2 ∩ O (= Grace). At first, his narrative programme meets with comparative success, but then it is thwarted until eventually it comes to be completely abandoned. The reason is that Winterborne has neither the material possessions nor, as in the case of his rival Fitzpiers, the education and social standing which could make of him an acceptable suitor. Because of these deficiencies, as a Subject he is made incompetent (he lacks the modal value of /BEING ABLE TO DO/) and as an Object he is considered ineligible (a case of modalisation of BEING: /NOT BEING CAPABLE OF BEING chosen/). Furthermore, he himself exercises a cognitive /DOING/ of a reflexive kind through which he acknowledges his own unworthiness (i.e. /S2 ∩ 01(02))/, with 01 = the Object of knowledge and 02 = the statement of BEING that expresses his own shortcomings, his own faulty 'modal existence'). According to the prevailing system of values, what would appear to be a mismatch turns Giles, at least in a first stage, into a Subject that is placed in a state of 'modal confrontation', torn as he is between opposed modal values: /WANTING TO DO/ vs /NOT BEING ABLE TO DO/ and /HAVING NOT TO DO/. The latter modality corresponds to an obligation imposed upon him by Grace's father, who assumes the actantial role of anti-Destinator while being himself manipulated by the social Destinator, namely the dominant axiology which regulates matrimonial transactions and inspires the desire for social promotion. A 'consenting Subject'

Giles eventually comes to accept a kind of 'anti-Contract' which itself is inspired by the 'injunctive Contract' binding Grace and Melbury together and determining that the girl's desire be in accordance with her father's will. In the context of this anti-Contract, Giles is induced (by Grace) or forced (by Melbury) to give up his own narrative programme (i.e. $S2 \rightarrow /S2 \cup O(= NP)/$). Consequently, he ceases to be an 'actualised Subject', disjoined as such from his value-Object, and resumes the state of 'virtualised Subject'.[11]

In the frame of reference concerned — i.e., mimetically, the rural Victorian society within which the events of the novel take place — marriage, both as a figure or discursive configuration and as a type of process or possibility of action offered to the female actors, is liable to be invested with contrasting values. The following terms can sum up these values in a 'semiotic square' bringing together the various axiologised contents:

/promotion/   /decline/

/suitability/   /mismatch/

Furthermore, these contents themselves take on a modal value (a case of modalisation of the deontic type) which places them respectively in the negative and positive deixis, according to a term-to-term correspondence:

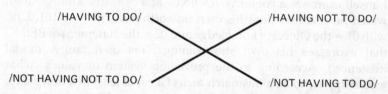

/HAVING TO DO/   /HAVING NOT TO DO/

/NOT HAVING NOT TO DO/   /NOT HAVING TO DO/

The 'square' made up in such a way has double scope, both taxonomic and syntactic. On the one hand, it determines positions corresponding to various possibilities which the story may or may not actualise through the actors' moves and relationships. On the other hand, it defines trajectories and makes it possible to follow the transformations which come about as a result of the putting into action of the narrative programmes and which alter the actantial and modal status of those concerned. From this point of view, the array of characters makes up a sort of network in which the ever-changing relationships which constitute the plot of the novel are woven together, along with their successive implications as regards the system of contents and values.

The effectuation of the /programme of union/ is therefore largely instrumental, even though, in the context in question, it may itself constitute a sort of obligation: it is as if society imposed its law upon the heroine and her kind and 'manipulated' them (modality of /NOT BEING ABLE TO DO/). Thus there is an opposition between the 'state of marriage', both desirable and euphoric, and the unacceptable and dysphoric 'state of spinsterhood' to which corresponds the stereotype of the 'old maid' greatly used in fiction[12] and particularly exposed to satire. Yet, here, the foreseen /union/ *does* aim at bringing about the conjunction of the Subject of DOING with the basic values of /happiness/ and /social standing/. As can be seen, the system of personal values blends with the system of collective values — which is itself a kind of moralisation of the various actions, a moralisation depending on a general social ethics. This system of personal values, linked to the subjects' modal state of /WANTING/, is based on the opposition: /desired/ vs /feared/. Besides, it is overdetermined by the thymic category (euphoria vs dysphoria) and produces accordingly the effects of meaning /happiness/ or /unhappiness/. In actual fact, considering both the 'discretion' of the novel as regards the intimate relationships of the characters and the tragic turn of events, the two types of Objects ('individual happiness' and 'social promotion') more or less coalesce, and it is above all failure and unhappiness which are manifested.

2.1.2 *'Terminus ad quem': the Sanction*
The typical phase of the Sanction marks the end of the canonical narrative development corresponding to the first part of the story. In Grace's case, it is translated by a 'persuasive doing' which, supported by her spectacular demeanour (languor and voluntary seclusion) aims at having her father — the Subject of the correlated 'interpretative DOING' — acknowledge the state of unhappiness in which she finds herself. As for her father, identified with the final Destinator, the Sanction is translated both by the recognition of this final state and the admission of his own unjust behaviour as initial Destinator and manipulating Subject whose manipulation is now

seen as having been wrong. Accordingly, the cognitive /DOING/
exercised at this point by Grace's father has two dimensions:
transitive as regards his daughter and reflexive as regards himself.
This explains why his ensuing action takes on a twofold orientation
when the story is given a new start.

2.2 The Narrative 'Pivot'

2.2.1 *'Terminus ab quo': the Manipulatory Sanction*
Ending on a double failure, this first part of the novel makes up a
sort of circle, or indeed constitutes a whole sequence totally
completed and characterised by its *'finition structurale'*.[13] All in all,
things could have been left there, were it not, of course, for the
fact that the story continues and that this entails the obligation to
motivate the new phase in the narrative development. The cohesion
of discourse, already noticeable through its strictly linguistic marks,
finds its semiotic expression in the articulations of the narrative
syntax. What we get here is a striking phenomenon of syncretism
which endows the connecting procedures with even greater
strength and provides a good example of efficiency and economy
of means. It is as if the same unit, facing in two different directions,
meant at the same time the end of one episode and the beginning
of the next one. From a functional point of view, this means that
the Sanction, which is terminative, becomes the equivalent of a
Manipulation, itself inchoative.

   In the case of Grace's father, the recognition of his error — in
other words the negative Sanction which, as final Destinator, he
applies to himself — is what leads him to manipulate 'himself' into
doing something else. His previous manipulative /DOING/ now
seems to him to be adverse to the goal sought after so that he sees
himself in retrospect as an axiological anti-Destinator whose action
was conducive to the heroine's unhappiness (i.e. S3(= father)
→ /S1(= Grace) ∩ O(= unhappiness)/). From then on, no longer
manipulated by an /ambition/ which would have allowed him to
gain fulfilment through his daughter's 'success', but by /remorse/,
the father suggests a new programme of action which is designed
to strike in two directions. For Grace, it is a /programme of
replacement/ and for him a /programme of reparation/ which is
both transitive, since its purpose is to make amends for the wrong
done, and reflexive, since it is the way for Melbury to ease his
conscience (S1 → /S1 ∩ O(= 'peace')/). The narrative 'pivot' which,

like a 'risky moment' in the story (or, as Barthes also said, a 'cardinal function'[14]) links together the successive episodes and establishes their interdependence, therefore corresponds here to this new structure of manipulation or rather, one should say, to this 'manipulatory Sanction' which, combining past and future, is the formal translation, as regards the underlying syntax, of the 'alternative' opened up at this point in the story.

Organised around this narrative pivot, the new start in the story is translated syntactically by the setting up (virtual, at first) of a new contractual relationship between the father and the daughter, the proposed Contract reading: $S1 \rightarrow /S2 \cap 01(02(03))/$, with 01 = the Object of knowledge transmitted, 02 = the /WANTING/ of $S1$ and 03 = the virtualised NP of $S2$, namely, this time, to 'marry Winterborne'.

It should be noted that this new Contract, similar to the preceding one, according to which Grace was to marry Fitzpiers, represents in fact a substitution of Objects which, taking place in an unchanged syntactic framework, manifests itself figuratively by a rotation of characters (Fitzpiers $\rightarrow$ Winterborne) and axiologically by the transformation of the values brought into play. It must then be considered that this transformation and the definition of this new Contract are matched by a modalisation of the veridictory type which aims at redistributing contents and values. Thus, the expected 'promotion' which was held to be 'true' (/APPEARING TO BE/ + /BEING/: Grace's marriage with Fitzpiers standing both as a guarantee and a visible sign of individual and social 'success') turns out to be illusory or even deceptive (/APPEARING TO BE/ + /NOT BEING/) so that the value /social promotion/ proves to be a delusion which hides the anti-values of, at best, /mismatch/ and, at worst, /social decline/. At first kept secret (/BEING/ + /NOT APPEARING TO BE/), Grace's misfortune suddenly comes out in the open (/BEING/ + /APPEARING TO BE/) with the spectacular revelation (/CAUSING TO APPEAR/[15]) which the separation of the couple amounts to.

2.2.2 *The 'Matrimonial Transaction'*

The putting into practice or even, one might say, this negotiation of values is carried out in the context of a 'fiduciary Contract' in which the Objects are assessed both intrinsically and comparatively. It was already so in the case of Grace's marriage with Fitzpiers: the material goods, present or to come (in the form of a dowry or an inheritance) were, so to speak, exchanged or bartered for the standing and social prestige which Fitzpiers could contribute on his side. It is, then, worth noticing the way in which the 'thematic roles' — here, for instance, those of 'marriageable daughter', 'heiress', 'accomplished young lady', or those of 'eligible young man', 'cultivated gentleman', 'member of the professions' — are not only pregnant with specific narrative virtualities as can be seen through the various figurative or thematic developments of the 'functions' corresponding to these different roles, but are also connected with the values brought into play and with the axiology that underlies the whole story.

The fiduciary Contract has for its basic aim the establishment of 'the value of values' and it brings into action different systems which, should the case arise, compete with each other until a sort of balance is reached. From this point of view, it can be said that the story, like so many of the same type,[16] revolves around the 'eligibility' of the characters wanting to get married;[17] this 'eligibility' is nothing but the translation in fictional terms of the contents and values of the deep level, themselves 'converted'[18] syntactically into 'modal structures' in the heart of which the modalities prove to be either compatible or incompatible.

In this case, it is at least a triple model[19] — individual (/desired/ vs /feared/), social (/prescribed/ vs /prohibited/) and also economic (/profitable/ vs /unprofitable/) — which regulates the relations of exchange within the framework of the fiduciary Contract. Thus, the father's 'ambition', both for himself and his daughter as Destinatees, is directed not only towards the 'realisation' of personal objectives and social imperatives, but also towards the 'profitability' of the operation. To the values of /happiness/ and /social promotion/ which marriage is supposed to bring there is added the /profit/ or, at the very least, the /non-loss/ which this type of /DOING/ is also meant to represent. In the case of Fitzpiers, what is exchanged and what is accordingly seen fiduciarily (taking into account 'the value of values') as exchangeable is, on the one hand, Grace and her material possessions and, on the other hand, the prestige of the profession and social environment. However, in actual fact, the failure of the marriage turns this relationship which was based on equal exchange and which was considered mutually /profitable/ into a state of affairs which is /non-profitable/ and even /prejudicial/, Fitzpiers appearing as a 'money-grabbing' or 'squandering' anti-Subject who obtains his value-Object without giving in return the expected 'counter-gift'. From this point of view, there is a breach of Contract and consequently both father and daughter become the 'wronged' or 'duped' party. The meeting between the father and the solicitor can accordingly be seen as a step — an 'auxiliary narrative programme' — towards rectifying the situation, and the potential annulment of the marriage seen in that light amounts to getting back the material goods that have been lost (i.e. the following transformation: $/S4(= \text{Fitzpiers}) \cap O \cup S3/ \rightarrow /S4 \cup O \cap S3/$).

As for Giles's eligibility as an 'alternative' solution, it certainly raises a problem, precisely because of the systems of prescriptions and prohibitions which are at work in the novel. Within the framework of the fiduciary Contract which contributes to the elaboration of values, Giles is at first set aside as being /ineligible/ because of his rural origins, his inferior social status, his lack of education and patrimony,[20] in short his lack of everything that could serve as a medium of exchange in the 'matrimonial transaction'. Marrying him would mean the actualisation of the (anti-) values of /mismatch/ and even of /social decline/, since the amount of possessions available would have to be divided into two, without anything to make up for it. Because of this, whatever his intentions may be, Giles appears as a 'money-grabbing' and 'exploiting' anti-Subject. How then can the same Giles and what he represents be proposed as a value-Object by the new Contract and the narrative programme resulting from it? One may say that for 'want of anything better' and on account of Grace's feelings, precarious status and 'obligation' to marry,[21] poor Winterborne turns out to be /non-ineligible/ and therefore capable of representing the virtual value of /suitability/. Furthermore, this assessment which makes of him an acceptable Object (his 'modal existence' being /NOT HAVING NOT TO BE chosen/) means the re-establishment for Grace's father of the initial Contract which he had drawn with himself[22] and which promised the two young people to each other. Let us remember that it had been broken precisely in favour of the other Contract which had selected Fitzpiers as the value-Object.

These substitutions of Objects, first studied from the point of view of the heroine and her father are paralleled, as regards the two 'heroes', by configurations and moves which are the typical manifestation of a topological syntax of 'transfers of Objects' and which, placed under the sign of a rivalry, are the realisation of a series of polemical transfers.[23] These polemical transfers can themselves be represented in terms of 'syntagmatic' (i.e. S1∪O → S1∩O) and/or 'paradigmatic' (i.e. S1∩O = S2∪O) 'junctions'. In that light, the Object 'Grace' circulates as it were between the two antagonistic Subjects, and this circulation is regulated axiologically, as has already been seen, by the interplay of Contracts and programmes and syntactically by the interplay of competences and performances. This brings about sequences of the following type: /conjunction/ → /non-conjunction/ → /disjunction/, or: /disjunction/ → /non-disjunction/ → /conjunction/. These sequences, resulting from the 'square of junctions' and referred to the isotopy of marriage, yield states or phases such as 'union' → 'disunion' → 'parting' or, conversely, 'rejection' → 'drawing together' → 'union'. It can therefore be said that Fitzpiers's and Giles's respective trajectories illustrate in parallel and/or successively these different configurations: thus, Fitzpiers's 'good fortune' alternates paradigmatically with Giles's correlated 'misfortune', while the latter alternates syntagmatically, at least potentially, with the 'good fortune' promised to him who, from then on, represents the 'accepted suitor'. This is whether we now stand, at this point in the story when the protagonists are struggling with their own future which is also the future of the story.

2.3 Contracts, Programmes and Competences

2.3.1 From /KNOWING/ to /WANTING/

Chapter XXXIX opens on a dysphorical note with Giles's admission of failure ('that unsatisfactory ending of a pleasant time'). In this way, Giles sanctions negatively the /programme of union/ that had just started with the encounter or rather, one should say, the organised meeting[24] between him and Grace. At the same time, as a subject of BEING, he is conjoined with /'fear'/, an emotional state or 'patheme' that is brought to bear on his future relationships with Grace, that is, on the narrative programme which they have in common. From a cognitive point of view, his present state of mind can be equated with a modalisation of the 'epistemic' kind (= 01) applied to the value-Object 'happiness' taken here as an Object of knowledge: $S2 \cap 01(02)$, which reads: S2 BELIEVING 02 NOT CAPABLE OF BEING. The reason for this is that Grace's own /DOING/, that is, her 'dissuasive' behaviour of the day before, has been construed by Giles as a 'true' manifestation (/BEING/ + /APPEARING TO BE/) of all that stands between them and, in particular, of their belonging to two separate worlds or 'deixis'. Syntactically, that corresponds to a double 'junction' of the $S2 \cup O \cap S1$ type, in which O represents the value 'refinement'. It is in fact the same kind of 'estrangement' that was expressed figuratively in the previous chapter by means of the opposition between the 'inn' and the 'hotel', the Abbey itself appearing as an intermediate or unmarked space, a sort of neutral ground. Thus, as a cognitive Subject, Giles is seen to exercise a two-tier 'interpretative DOING' which he applies first to the meeting itself, and then to the lesson that can be drawn from it. The result of all this is that his relationship with Grace is viewed in terms of /incompatibility/ and of /impossibility/. He thus finds himself in a state of /BELIEF/[25] which is going to determine his future modal and actantial development.

Giles's unsuccessful meeting with Grace may be said to echo Grace's own unsuccessful story with Fitzpiers. These structural identities, whether local or global, are one of the mainsprings of irony in the book: the parallel situations (that is, in both cases, the non-conjunction of the Subjects with their intended Objects) belie the changes recorded on the surface, what with the replacement of Fitzpiers by Winterborne and the latter's newly defined role, from 'jilted lover' to 'accepted suitor'. Thus, despite the change of programme, the story tends to repeat itself.

As an 'operating Subject' bent on carrying out her own narrative programme of /union/, Grace also sanctions herself negatively by anticipating the Sanction that her father virtually inflicts upon her. She sees him potentially acting both as the Subject of an 'interpretative DOING' ('seeing the trifling coolness of Giles') and as the final Destinator whose negative judgment is expressed in terms of /BEING/ ('the same perversity') as well as of /DOING/ ('to blow hot and cold with poor Winterborne'). One should note here that this Sanction is aspectualised both prospectively (in the present circumstances) and retrospectively (in the case of Fitzpiers) and that, for Grace who sees herself conjoined with such an Object of knowledge, it amounts to a form of Manipulation. In fact, that is yet another instance of the syncretic configuration previously described as the 'manipulatory Sanction'. Melbury's disapproval is a negative value-Object with which, as a 'Subject of representation',[26] Grace is virtually threatened. Consequently, in order to disjoin herself from such a negative possibility, i.e. in fact yielding to the 'intimidation' that it represents for her, Grace takes up the actantial role of 'self-destined Subject' and sets herself a new task which is 'to make it up with [Giles]'. In addition to its being in line with the basic narrative programme of /union/, this /programme of reconciliation/ has an immediate function which is to enable her to manifest (i.e. to /CAUSE TO APPEAR/) such dispositions as are in keeping with her father's own wishes, in his double capacity of initial ('I have set my heart on seeing him your husband') and of final Destinator ('how could she look him in the face if he should see them estranged thus?').

It should be observed, at this point, that there are striking similarities in the situations of the two actants. For one thing, there is the putting side by side of the segments of discourse devoted respectively to Giles and Grace, this being emphasised by the repetition of the same temporal indications which may be said to behave as demarcations ('All night did Winterborne . . .'/'Grace, too, had a very uncomfortable night . . .'). The juxtaposition of the two segments takes on symbolic significance and may be said ironically to emphasise or even literally to 'iconise' the characters' estrangement and misunderstanding. Besides, there is the 'dysphoria' that pervades the two 'utterances of BEING' in which we find Giles and Grace respectively conjoined, as 'thymic' Subjects, with the 'pathemes' of /'fear'/ in the one case and of /'solicitous embarrassment' / in the other. In fact, we are dealing here with two cognitive subjects who conjoin themselves with an Object of knowledge which is their own recent past ('that unsatisfactory ending' / 'she had been on the brink of giving offence') or even, for Giles, his whole past history ('He had once worshipped her, laid out his life to suit her, wooed her, and lost her'). This kind of recall, a case of 'semantic anaphora', contributes to reinforce the cohesion of discourse by anaphorising the events that preceded it in the syntagmatic development of the story. But, chiefly, it stresses the fact that what the characters remember is also at the same time what 'manipulates' them.

Thus, just as the 'thymic Subjects' are seen to be dysphorically conjoined with a past that is evaluated negatively ('unsatisfactory', 'uncomfortable') and so modalised (in terms of 'modal existence') as /HAVING NOT TO BE/, in the same way — and that is another example of structural equivalence — the two cognitive Subjects see themselves conjoined with negative value-Objects, namely /'perversity'/ in the case of Grace and now, with Giles, a /sense of guilt/ ('It would be sheer sin . . .'). Those two 'Objects of representation' play the part of an 'intimidation' and, as such, virtually set in motion narrative programmes that can be summed up as /CAUSING NOT TO BE/. By confronting themselves with such Objects, Giles (2S $\cap$ O = 'sin') and Grace (S1 $\cap$ O = 'perversity') exercise a reflexive 'persuasive DOING' in which they syncretically assume the actantial roles of 'manipulating' as well as of 'manipulated' Subject. One should note here that it is not only the syntactic framework that is the same, but also the semantic content of the Subject–Object relationship. In both cases, the values at stake are of a 'moral' nature and belong to the same isotopy. Grace and Giles stand as two 'ethical' Subjects at grips with their sense of moral values ('as a tribute to conscience'). This interiorised figure of the ethical Destinator is what partly accounts for the moral and psychological complexity which is imparted to the actors when they are treated as 'real' persons.[27] It is also what dictates to the characters their respective courses of action. Hence Grace's /programme of reconciliation/ — of 'reconjunction', and Giles's /programme of renunciation/, that is to say of 'non-conjunction' ('Move another step towards her he would not') or even, according to the distinction introduced here in discourse, of 'disjunction' ('He would even repulse her').

As we have already pointed out, the two protagonists have in common a /programme of union/ which, in both cases, is the result of a 'Self-' as well as of an 'Other-destined' Contract. Each may be said to be acting of his/her own free will, while at the same time both are equally 'commissioned'[28] by Melbury. Yet, whereas Grace's resolve is in keeping with her father's plans, Giles views his union with her as an 'anti-programme' that runs counter to his own self-assigned duty which is 'to make her happy' (S2 $\rightarrow$ S1 $\cap$ O = 'happiness') or, at any rate, 'not to make her unhappy' (S2 $\rightarrow$ S1 $\cup$ O = 'happiness'). In his own view, which is also that of the inbuilt moral Destinator, to get on with the /programme of union/ would be to act as an 'anti-Subject' invested with the 'thematic role' of deceiver or traitor ('by inveigling her into a union . . .'). Interestingly enough, what we have here is a transformation of the 'stationary' type[29] in which the operating Subject's performance consists precisely in *not* bringing about any change. Thus, in the present instance, Giles is set on acting in such a way that Grace should remain disjoined from what is once more threatening her ('to let her prepare a pitfall for her happiness not much smaller than the first').

2.3.2 *From /WANTING/ to /DOING/*

The 'cognitive DOING' exercised here by the two actants takes the form of a ratiocination which seems all the more likely and probable as it agrees with what 'natural logic' says about night being the right time to 'take counsel'. In terms of the mental processes involved, Giles and Grace may be said to draw on their experience of the past in order to calculate — that is, in fact, to envisage and evaluate — their future actions. Semiotically, this calculation is a kind of 'simulacrum' which consists in examining alternative narrative programmes (for instance, 'to blow hot and cold with poor Winterborne' vs 'to make it up with him') and/or in comparing and assessing different value-Objects (e.g. 'union' vs 'happiness'). As such, it throws light on the process of 'decision-making' which is to the cognitive dimension of discourse what 'execution' is to the pragmatic one.

To the temporal and aspectual distinction between past and future, or between /terminative/ and /inchoative/ ('he had begun to tread the old tracks again' vs 'they could never be happy together'), there corresponds the syntactic opposition between those two 'modes of semiotic existence', known respectively as the 'effected' and the 'virtual' or perhaps rather the 'virtualised'. Within the framework of the 'referentialisation process' which takes place in discourse itself, these two modes of existence along with the actual or potential narrative programmes which they encompass are taken as the 'internal referent' to which the actants' comparative and/or evaluative cognitive DOING is applied. What happens then is that these Objects of knowledge are systematically confronted and estimated in terms of their feasibility and/or of their intrinsic value.

We have seen already how the Subjects and Objects 'of representation' played a distinctive part in the operations of Manipulation and we now see how the cognitive DOING that is exercised by the two protagonists can be semiotically construed as an 'anticipated Sanction' which is there, so to speak, to decide about the decision that has to be made. Thus, it is with reference to the ethical Destinator in its double capacity of 'manipulating' and of 'judicating' Subject that Giles disjoins himself from the 'anti-Destinator' represented here by his own 'hope' or desire and decides to abandon his /programme of union/ in favour of another which he thinks is worth more. This renunciation can be technically interpreted as an 'actualising stationary transformation', that is one which is aimed at maintaining the Subject and Object in their present state of disjunction. At the same time, this choice is made to contrast with the alternative option — a dynamic transformation of the 'effecting' type — which would have been for Giles to go on acting with a view to marriage.

At this stage, one can homologate the various syntactic components that go into the making of Giles's 'deliberative DOING' and which 'programme' his subsequent course of action:

Destinator (D^1)	:	moral D1 ('conscience')	vs	personal (anti-)D1 ('hope')
modal Subject	:	/HAVING TO DO/ ('his own duty')	vs	/WANTING TO DO/ ('zest')
value-Object	:	Grace's 'happiness' (= O1)	vs	Giles's own satisfaction ('union' = O2)
virtualised NP	:	attribution–renunciation (S2 → /S1 ∩ O1/, and S2 → /S2 ∪ O2)	vs	appropriation (S2 → /S2 ∩ O(= S1)/)

From the point of view of Giles's competence, the resulting configuration is a modal structure in which the modality of /HAVING TO DO/ that is dictated by the hero's conscience is made to contrast with the /NOT WANTING NOT TO DO/ that summed up his previous attitude ('had allowed himself to be so charmed with her that day'), while it fully agrees with the /NOT WANTING TO DO/ or the /WANTING NOT TO DO/ that correspond to his present abstention or even deliberate refusal. Hence the /programme of dissuasion/ which he is now set on carrying out in order to 'manipulate' or rather, one should say, in order to 'counter-manipulate' Grace's father. That is what he intends to achieve through the communication of a knowledge ('It was his own duty to declare them', i.e.: S2 → /S3 ∩ Os (= 'subtleties')/) that will transform — that is, in fact, reinstate — Melbury's competence ('Her poor father was now blind to these subtleties which he had formally beheld as in noontide light'). By restoring the latter to his former clear-sightedness, i.e. to his /BEING ABLE TO see/, Giles avails himself of the capacity to 'dissuade' him, that is to /CAUSE him NOT TO (WANT TO) DO/. This, in fact, is the latest development to date in Melbury's modal and actantial history. In his dealings with Giles, he may be said to have acted first as 'Destinator' when he was still planning Giles's union with Grace.

He then took up the role of 'anti-Destinator' when he changed his plans in favour of Fitzpiers. His next move was the position of 'non-anti-Destinator' when he had to fall back on Giles as an alternative son-in-law, until eventually he was seen to resume his former identity of Destinator who urges the hero to win back his daughter's affections. Yet now, with Giles's proposed counter-action, he is offered yet another role which is that of 'non-Destinator' whose action consists precisely in /NOT CAUSING TO DO/. As for Giles, his next step is the /programme of 'estrangement'/ which enables him to manifest — i.e. to /CAUSE TO APPEAR/ — his own detachment ('an air of determined' = /WANTING/ 'abandonment' = /NOT TO DO/).

The irony here is that this programme which is aimed at persuading Grace of the truth of Giles's renunciation: S2 → /S1 ∩ 01(02)/ (with 01 = the epistemic attitude of /BELIEVING/ which modalises 02 = Giles's state of detachment) is seen to work at cross-purposes and, instead of dissuading her from taking any further steps, encourages her to act through an increase of her own /WANTING TO DO/ ('he could not have acted more seductively').[30] Thus, Grace appears as a competent cognitive Subject ('she read his mood keenly and truly') who can make out the true nature (/BEING/ + /APPEARING TO BE/) of Giles's feelings, but whose accurate 'interpretative DOING' paradoxically turns the latter into his own 'anti-Subject'! This distortion between what was intended and what actually happens is but one of the many ways in which irony makes itself felt throughout the book, the result being a series of misunderstandings which largely account for the story's tragic turn. In Giles's case, for instance, it is at the very moment when he ceases to be considered /ineligible/ and comes to be viewed as /non-ineligible/ that he sees himself as /non-eligible/ and decides to act accordingly. Similarly, after being submitted to a 'modal confrontation' of the /WANTING/ vs /NOT BEING ABLE TO/ type, it is precisely when Giles is finally recognised as being 'acceptable' that there occurs the sudden reversal which leads to a renewed conflict between the two modal states of /BEING ABLE TO DO/ vs /NOT — or rather no longer — WANTING TO DO/.

At this point in the story Grace appears as a complex entity whose modal and actantial status is in keeping with the structural instability and intermediate or 'interfacial' positioning of the 'narrative pivot'. On the one hand, there is the /WANTING TO DO/ that corresponds to her own /programme of union/, while on the other hand there is the /NOT BEING ABLE NOT TO DO/ which expresses the way in which she cannot help behaving in a distant supercilious manner ('She had been on the brink of giving offence). Thus, as an actor, she may be said syncretically to assume the antagonistic actantial roles of Destinator and anti-Destinator as well as those of Subject and anti-Subject. Her present task, as she sees it, is to divest herself of those pretensions that 'manipulate' her ('her first attempt had been beaten by the unexpected vitality of that fastidiousness') and to take up instead the role ('country girl') and the narrative programme ('to put off the old Eve, the fastidious miss — or rather madam — completely') that are dictated to her both by her father's wishes ('the paternal longing') and by her own yearnings ('her own desire'). The potential result of all this is an image of herself which would make her stand as a Subject in a state of 'modal quietude', that is, one in whom the two modalities of /WANTING/ and of /HAVING TO DO/ would prove to be fully consonant.

The irony in this case is that at the moment when Grace is about to show her good will there should arise a polemical relationship between herself and Giles who, through his refusal to cooperate, plays the part of 'anti-Subject'. Hence, later in the same chapter, the active role that Grace, as a Subject of Doing, will have to assume in order to overcome Giles's reluctance, that is, in other words, in order to 'counter-manipulate' him. The fact is that, through his renunciation,[31] Giles is forcing Grace to abandon her usual passive attitude, so that she is turned into a 'manipulated' Subject placed in the position of /NOT BEING ABLE NOT TO DO/. Were it not for Giles's acknowledged sincerity and truthfulness, one might be tempted to construe his present aloofness as a form of 'provocation' which itself would be made to serve a strategy of 'seduction'.[32] As for Grace's shift from a passive to an active role, it brings further confirmation of the focal or nodal character of the 'narrative pivot'.

As an actant in his own right, Melbury is the subject of various narrative programmes or sub-programmes which may be of a transitive or of a reflexive kind, but which all appear as a continuation of the newly drawn up Contract that has Grace's union for its object.

Thus, within the framework of the 'contractual relationship' set up between the father and daughter, there is first Melbury's /programme of Manipulation/ through which he urges Grace to take immediate action. Particularly revealing in this respect is his letter which amounts to a downright 'intimidation'. Indeed, by perusing it, Grace finds herself virtually conjoined with a succession of negative value-Objects which we can detail as follows: first, there is the 'wrong-doing' which would be Grace's if, by not complying with her father's wishes, she in fact prevented him from carrying out his own narrative programme and from finding the 'peace' he is looking for ('until this thing is done I cannot rest in peace'). Besides, when Melbury hints at his oncoming death ('I feel myself going rapidly down hill'), his pathetic appeal is but a way of putting even more pressure on his daughter.

Next, there is the 'responsibility' that is ascribed to Grace when her father suggests that she too had a share in those events which are endangering his life ('and late affairs have still further helped me that way'). In this way too, Grace is made to feel 'guilty'.

Thirdly, there is the 'risk' which Grace and her father are running of seeing Giles move away from them, both physically and mentally ('he may become estranged, or in his shyness go away from the neighbourhood'). If that were to happen, it would, of course, be impossible for Grace to carry out her own narrative programme: in terms of the operating Subject's 'modal competence', she would be cut off from her /BEING ABLE TO DO/. Thus, when Grace's father urges her to action ('Do then, Grace, give him some temporary encouragement'), his aim is in fact to 'counter-manipulate' Giles by means of a 'temptation'. By lending herself to him, Grace virtually deprives Giles of his power to leave and thus ultimately gets the better of him by placing him in the position of /NOT BEING ABLE NOT TO DO/.

To this rather subtle or even wily manoeuvre there is added yet another form of Manipulation which is in fact an operation of 'seduction'. By placing himself and his fate in his daughter's hands, Melbury virtually conjoins her to a flattering image of herself and of her own competence. Syntactically, the positive value-Object with which, as a 'Subject of representation', she finds herself conjoined is the recognition by her father of her own superior power, that is concretely of her /BEING ABLE TO DO/ what he himself couldn't do without her. Besides, that strategy which is aimed at furthering the programme of /union/ as well as Grace's quest of 'happiness' is also made to serve Melbury's own purposes, namely his desire to renew the Contract that he had previously broken and to put his conscience at rest by disjoining himself from what is troubling him (i.e. S3 → /S3 ∪ O(= un-'rest')/). In this way Melbury's reflexive /programme of reparation/ is seen to coincide with his 'transitive DOING' which was meant to 'manipulate' Grace in order that she herself should 'manipulate' Giles. This kind of syncretism — that is, in fact, the interpenetration of several narrative programmes — may then be viewed as the formal equivalent of what is traditionally described in terms of the characters' psychological wealth or depth or of the author's perceptiveness and insight.

What we have in the second place is Melbury's /programme of 'competentialisation'/, a programme which is both transitive and reflexive. Thus, Melbury's interview with the solicitor may be viewed as an 'auxiliary narrative programme' which is meant to 'free' Grace from what prevents her from marrying Giles ('her marriage virtually annulled and she be free to be won again'). Syntactically, what is at stake is Grace's competence. By taking up the actantial role of 'Helper', Melbury is in fact trying to provide her with the modal value of /BEING ABLE TO DO/. But there is also another difficulty, which is that the proposed course of action is socially as well as morally reprehensible ('though it is over-early'; 'for being a little forward'). By invoking what may be described as 'extenuating circumstances' ('when I consider the past') while at the same time appealing to God's forgiveness ('I do think God will forgive me and you'), Melbury is in fact disjoining himself from the inhibiting modal state of /HAVING NOT TO DO/ and turning it into something that is less forbidding, namely the modality of /NOT HAVING NOT TO DO/. In this way, God and the past are made to play the part of 'non-anti-Destinator'.

Chapter 39 thus appears as a kind of 'narrative cell' in which the characters' identities and positions are defined. This is achieved in terms of their respective courses of action, but also through the 'modalisation process' that affects them both individually and in their relations to each other. The actants' narrative programmes are made to rest on a definition of the various value-Objects that are at stake, this corresponding to the typical phase of the Contract in which values are estimated as such and/or exchanged on a 'fiduciary' basis. Besides, the carrying out of those narrative programmes obviously depends on the 'competentialisation process' which takes in the actants' previous modal history and prepares them for their future tasks.

3. FINAL REMARKS

3.1 The Narrative Pause

Without trying to be exhaustive or to give a formalised description of the phenomenon, we shall simply bring out a few characteristic features which may usefully contribute to a definition of the discursive type or subtype known as the 'narrative pause'.

The first thing to be said about the narrative pause is that it presents itself empirically as a kind of 'suspension' between two series of events. From a rhetorical point of view, its intermediate position makes it a place where prolepsis and analepsis are seen to interlock. Semiotically, it may be viewed as a 'tensive' unit stretching between the two poles respectively identified as the /end of continuation/ and, symmetrically, the /end of stoppage/.[33] We have confirmation of this with the demarcations built up on one side by the opening of a new chapter and the change in referential bearings and, on the other side, by the resumption of the narration of events, with the return of 'pragmatic DOING' and of 'somatic' activities ('He chanced to be superintending some temporary work in a field opposite her windows'), and by the temporal disjunction ('It being a fair green afternoon in June').

From a syntactic point of view, the narrative pause typically appears as a kind of 'interface' whose semiotic equivalent is the 'narrative pivot'. In functional terms, it combines 'Sanction' and 'Manipulation', whereas, from an aspectual point of view, it is /terminative/ as well as /inchoative/. It echoes what preceded it in the syntagmatic development of the story and paves the way for what is to follow. It is also a place where the actants' competences are defined or redefined and, as such, it is a kind of 'turning-point' in their modal history.

Another major aspect of the narrative pause is the importance of the 'cognitive dimension'. This is made obvious by the number of lexemes pertaining to that isotopy ('think', 'thoughtful', 'scrutinise', 'discover', 'read', 'see', etc.). That indeed is no surprise since it is precisely this aspect which formally characterises the two canonical phases of Manipulation and Sanction, as opposed to Action which constitutes their internal referent.

What is remarkable here is the 'projection' into discourse of various cognitive subjects that belong either to the narration itself (they are actors in the story) or to the communcation that takes place between, say, 'narrator' and 'narratee'. In the present instance, the actants belonging to that second level are in fact reduced to a single anonymous 'narrative voice'. This 'narrative voice' syncretically assumes the two actantial and thematic roles of 'Observer' (as regards the story-as-referent) and of 'Informant' (as far as the 'addressee' is concerned) within the framework of the 'epistemic relationship' that establishes itself both in and through discourse.[34]

What this 'projection' yields is a hierarchy of cognitive Subjects. Thus, on a first plane, we have Subjects like Giles or Grace whose cognitive DOING consists in identifying and/or evaluating Objects of knowledge which are in fact, 'utterances of BEING' or of 'DOING'. Then, at a higher level, we have a cognitive 'meta-Subject' whose 'observative' or 'informative' DOING is brought to bear on what makes up the first plane and views it as from a vantage-point.

In the present case, the 'narrative voice' can be semiotically interpreted as a cognitive role that is taken up by an actant whose competence, that is, in fact, whose knowledge (/BEING ABLE TO KNOW/) is practically unlimited. This actant whom we may call the implicit narrator or Observer indulges in a 'comparative DOING' which leads to Giles being placed on the side of /restraint/ ('he was too thoughtful') among a variety of alternative categories of a 'psychological' or rather 'metapsychological' nature. Hence the following 'semiotic square', which groups those various 'moods' or 'tempers' and relates them to their modal equivalents:

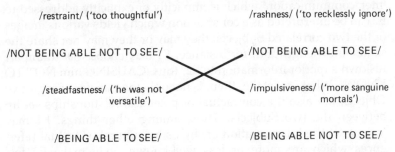

/restraint/ ('too thoughtful')   /rashness/ ('to recklessly ignore')

/NOT BEING ABLE NOT TO SEE/   /NOT BEING ABLE TO SEE/

/steadfastness/ ('he was not   /impulsiveness/ ('more sanguine
versatile')   mortals')

/BEING ABLE TO SEE/   /BEING ABLE NOT TO SEE/

What should be noted here is that these (meta) terms and the various positions which they represent are in fact descriptions of different types of competence in which /KNOWING/ (that is here concretely /(NOT) BEING ABLE (NOT) TO SEE/) is seen to modalise /WANTING/, so that eventually what we get is a classification of actors in terms of their actual or potential dispositions and roles.

As for the distinction that is established here in discourse between the cognitive Subjects and the structural planes to which they belong, it may be said to coincide with another distinction which has to do with the actants' semantic definitions. This enables one to homologate those various syntactic and thematic components:

cognitive Subjects	'moral' isotopy
cognitive meta-Subject	'(meta)psychological' isotopy

Owing both to this distribution of cognitive roles and to the relative restraint shown by the implicit narrator, it seems as if the reader were left to decide for himself, instead of being influenced or even thoroughly manipulated by the presence, within discourse itself, of value-judgments made by some authoritative axiological meta-Subject.

What this last remark suggests is that the narrative pause is a privileged 'locus' for the interaction that takes place between 'addresser' (or 'enunciator') = E1 and addressee (or 'enunciatee') = E2. The former's cognitive DOING consists in either /CAUSING TO KNOW/ or /CAUSING TO BELIEVE/. This we can see here when Grace's own 'interpretative DOING' is 'certified' through a direct 'veridictory' intervention of the cognitive meta-Subject ('she read his mood keenly and truly'). In fact, this 'metacommunication' which is implicitly or explicitly addressed to E2 can be interpreted as a construction which yields various images of the two correlated Subjects: they may or they may not share the same /knowledge/ and, for instance, E1 may choose *not* to impart his own superior information to E2, thus /CAUSING him NOT TO KNOW/. What is at stake, then, is not only the transfer of cognitive Objects, but also the contractual or polemical relationships set up between the two Subjects. Thus, among other things, E1 may 'orientate' the interpretation or, by using cultural or textual references which are more or less well-known, may make E2 feel inferior, or ignorant, or equally competent, etc.

Those are 'semio-pragmatic' considerations which perhaps should be extended to include E1's reflexive cognitive DOING. Viewed in this way, the narrative pause might well be an opportunity for the 'Subject of writing' to 'test' his own competence, to find his own way in the maze of the characters' actions and motivations. Thus, the transitive /CAUSING TO KNOW/ which is there to increase or simply to confirm the reader's competence would prove to be over-determined by the writer's self-applied controlling consciousness.

As a discursive unit, the narrative pause is clearly endowed with a double 'enuncive' and 'enunciative' functional value, and it is at those two levels that it can be formally described. Thomas Hardy's use of free indirect speech is of particular interest here, since, owing to its built-in structural 'ambivalence' or else, if one may say so, to its 'double bind', it enables one 'freely' to pass from one plane of discourse to the other. At the same time, it 'naturalises' the expression by reducing or even by completely obliterating the distance between the characters' own rumination and the narrator's metadiscourse.

3.2 From One Text to the Next

Thomas Hardy's novels are generally said to be based on the opposition between /Nature/ and /Culture/. The corresponding 'semiotic square':

$$s1 = /\text{Nature}/ \qquad s2 = /\text{Culture}/$$
$$\overline{s2} = /\text{Culture}/ \qquad \overline{s1} = /\text{Nature}/$$

is the 'deep axiological — but also topological — structure'[36] in which the actants' positions are defined. Thus, in the present case, Grace's successive 'moves' can be schematically represented as a sequence of the following type:

$$S1 \rightarrow \overline{S1} \rightarrow S2 \rightarrow \overline{S2} \rightarrow S1,$$

this 'final' state being, of course, only a stage in the character's overall development.[37] Semantically, these transformations correspond to a series of operations through which the values of /Nature/ and /Culture/ are successively asserted and negated. Broadly speaking, what we get is this:

– affirmation of /Nature/, on account of the girl's origins;
– negation of /Nature/, owing to her upbringing;
– affirmation of /Culture/, through her marriage;

- negation of /Culture/, with the separation and return;
- reaffirmation of /Nature/, when Grace is about to reintegrate her former familiar surroundings ('While craving to be a country girl again').

What should be noted here is that those basic logical operations, first syntactically 'converted' into narrative programmes, are figuratively translated into a series of movements which virtually take the heroine back to her starting-point.

It is, of course, important to see what particular meanings and values the two (meta) terms of /Nature/ and /Culture/ are made to cover. Judging from what we have been saying up till now, it seems here that it is mainly at the socio-cultural and socio-economic levels that the opposition between the two 'worlds' can be said to be relevant. Besides, one must guard against over-simplified views. Thus, as far as individual characters are concerned, Giles and Grace stand out as complex figures in which features pertaining to /Nature/ and /Culture/ are brought together. The former, for instance, has fully integrated the values of /Culture/ since he resorts to them in order to assess his own 'indignity' ('She was accomplished: he was unrefined.') or even to 'counter-manipulate' Grace's father ('these subtleties'). As for the latter, she, of course, bears the mark of those self-same values, but she is also closely associated with a /Nature/ to which she owes her identity — real or mythical — of 'perverse woman' ('the old Eve').

As matters stand, one might be tempted to think that those two basic categories are 'reductionist' in character and, indeed, that is what they are. The whole point, then, is to show how, starting from there — that is, starting from such 'primitive' data[38] — what one eventually gets is of a complex and irreducible nature. In other words, how, at what level and in what terms does the 'branching out' take place which leads to works that are 'unique', despite the similarities which one is bound to encounter as one passes from one text to the next? It is precisely to that kind of question that semiotic theory is set on providing tentative and perhaps also alternative answers, what with the model known as the 'generative path' and the distinctions it makes between various interrelated operational levels.

Here, we find ourselves in the domain of comparative studies. Thus, supposing that Hardy's novels should, in fact, be built on the same fundamental oppositions, what one has to find out is how those abstract meanings and values are thematically and figuratively translated into the 'language of fiction'. In particular, what are the actors and what are the actions that are selected in each case in order to concretise or, technically, to 'instanciate'[39] the underlying syntactic patterns? Are those patterns the same, in which case they would constitute a sort of common basis for the diversification that takes place at a later stage in the 'generative history' of the text? The present study could serve as a starting-point for such further developments by proposing a frame that can be applied elsewhere. One might then decide to use the term of 'co-texts' to designate such works as display the same 'deep' semantic and axiological structures. As for 'intertextual' relation-ships, they would rather belong to other — more superficial — structural levels in the 'generative path' and would thus lend themselves to a classification made precisely in those terms.

Notes

1. For a description of the theory, see A. J. Greimas and J. Courtés, *Sémiotique. Dictionnaire raisonné de la théorie du langage* (Paris: Hachette, 1979) (hereafter abbreviated to *Dictionary*), in which the main terms of the metalanguage, together with their English equivalents, can be found. See also, for a brief presentation, J. Courtés, *Introduction à la sémiotique narrative et discursive* (Paris: Hachette, 1976), and for a comprehensive view, J. C. Coquet (ed.), *Sémiotique: l'Ecole de Paris* (Paris: Hachette, 1982).
2. See, for instance, our brief French–English Glossary, below, and the English version of the *Dictionary: Semiotics and Language. An Analytical Dictionary* (Bloomington: Indiana University Press, 1982).
3. See the entry *'Parcours génératif'* in the *Dictionary*.
4. All the quotations are taken from Thomas Hardy, *The Woodlanders* (London: Pan Books, 1978).
5. See Claude Brémond, 'La logique des possibles narratifs', *Communi-cations*, vol. 8 (1966), and *Logique du récit* (Paris: Seuil, 1973). The 'logic of decision-making' propounded by Brémond (e.g. in *Logique du récit*, p. 99) is not without links with the 'deliberative' cognitive /DOING/ exercised here by the actants.
6. On that precise point, see J. Courtés, *Le conte populaire: poétique et mythologie* (Paris: PUF, 1986).
7. See P. Ricoeur, 'Figuration et configuration. A propos du *Maupassant* de A. J. Greimas', in Hermann Parrett and Hans Georg Ruprecht (eds), *Exigences et perspectives de la sémiotique/Aims and Prospects of Semiotics* (Amsterdam: John Benjamins, 1985), pp. 801–9.
8. As regards the various forms of 'acceptance' and 'refusal', and more

generally the system of 'modal confrontations', see A. J. Greimas, 'Pour une théorie des modalités, in *Du Sens II. Essais sémiotiques* (Paris: Seuil, 1983), pp. 82–90.

9. For a list of technical terms and a brief presentation of the metalanguage, see our French–English glossary at the end of this paper. The main diacritical signs and conventional symbols used hereafter are as follows: ∩ means 'conjunction', U means 'disjunction', while the arrow stands for the function 'Transformation'. Concerning these notions, see the entries '*Enoncé*' and '*Programme narratif*' in the *Dictionary*. See also the entry '*Carré sémiotique*' which provides a definition of the various terms and relations within the so-called 'semiotic square' (the bar '‾' placed above a given term means that this term is negated). As for the oblique strokes and inverted commas, they serve to designate descriptive meta-terms (e.g. /Nature/ vs /Culture/, etc.) and/or theoretical constructs (such as the modalities of /WANTING/, /KNOWING/, etc., or the actants' /narrative programmes/). Similarly, the initial capitals are used to single out actantial roles (viz. Subject, Object) and other syntactic units (Contract, for instance).

10. The various types of 'transfers of Objects' are described in the entry '*Epreuve*' of the *Dictionary*.

11. Thus, after the 'interdiction' signified by Melbury and recalled at the beginning of Chapter 15 ('the somewhat harsh suggestion to Giles to draw off from his daughter', p. 109), an 'interdiction' relayed by Grace ('For myself I would have married you — some day — I think. But I give way, for I am assured that it would be unwise', p. 100), Giles gives up his 'pretentions' and, as a consequence frees both father and daughter from their commitments ('he wished that it should be considered as cancelled, and they themselves quite released from any obligation on account of it', p. 113). Winterborne's 'renunciation' (first in Chapter 15 and then, again, in Chapter 39) is not unlike that of Gabriel Oak in *Far from the Madding Crowd*. Conversely, Tess appears as a 'refusing Subject', torn as she is between her love for Clare and the knowledge of her own 'sin'; this conflict can even lead at times to revolt (see, for instance, Chapter 38 in *Tess of the d'Urbervilles*).

12. See, for instance, *La vieille fille*, by H. de Balzac.

13. On this '*finition structurale*,' the counterpart of the '*programmation initiale*', see J. Kristeva, 'Problèmes de la structuration du texte', in *Linguistique et littérature, La nouvelle critique*, numéro spécial (1968), p. 58; and 'Le texte clos' in *Séméiotiké. Recherches pour une sémanalyse* (Paris: Seuil, 1969), pp. 113ff.

14. R. Barthes, 'Introduction à l'analyse structurale des récits', *Communications*, vol. 8, p. 10.

15. On these cognitive operations, see, for instance, Cl. Zilberberg, 'Notes relatives au faire persuasif', *Le Bulletin du GRSL*, vol. 15, (Sept. 1980), pp. 11–25.

16. For instance, D. H. Lawrence's short story 'Fanny and Annie' in *England, my England*, in which the issue is the same: will Fanny marry Harry, or not? See H. Quéré, *Problèmes et techniques de la narration* (Lille: Atelier National de Reproduction des Thèses, 1984 (microcards)).

17. The phrases 'free to choose him' or 'to be won' are a good illustration of the theme of eligibility, each of the actants offering itself as an Object to the other.
18. On these operations of 'conversion', see the corresponding entry of the *Dictionary*.
19. See A. J. Greimas and F. Rastier, 'Les jeux des contraintes sémiotiques', in *Du sens. Essais sémiotiques* (Paris: Seuil, 1970).
20. The loss of his house is the last element in Giles's disqualification, as is shown clearly in the well-known 'couplet': 'O Giles, you've lost your dwelling-place / And therefore, Giles, you'll lose your Grace' (p. 113). This settles the matter for Melbury: 'as a pretender to the position of my son-in-law, that can never be thought of more' (p. 109). Such a loss, in fact ascribable to an adverse fate, is at the same time a proof of Giles's carelessness and thus of his 'incompetence' (/NOT KNOWING HOW TO DO/).
21. Let us remember that Grace has been forsaken by her husband and that she is seeking a divorce. Thus, in the context of the novel, Giles's faithfulness is her only 'chance'. Marrying him would mean for her a sort of social rescue.
22. This Contract based on a desire to make up for the wrong caused to old Winterborne ('he determined to do all he could to right the wrong by letting his daughter marry the lad', p. 23) was not, it must be remembered, easily accepted by Melbury himself ('I feel I am sacrificing her for my own sin', p. 23, or else: 'I am ruining her for conscience's sake!', p. 87), so that he at once appeared as a 'split Subject' who was placed in a state of modal confrontation.
23. On all this, see J. Petitot-Cocorda, *Morphogenèse du sens I* (Paris: PUF, 1985), pp. 236–47.
24. Thus Grace asserts herself as a Subject of /DOING/ ('it crossed her mind that Winterborne would probably be there, and this made the thought of such a drive interesting', Ch. 38, p. 280) whose /WANTING/ for once corresponds to that of her father.
25. Giles, as the text makes clear, 'misjudges' Grace's real frame of mind: 'How could she explain in the street of a market-town that it was her superficial and transitory taste which had been offended, and not her nature or her affection?'. Culture, with the social conventions and good manners that it generates, has played a nasty 'veridictory' trick on Nature.
26. As regards this 'simulacrum', see A. J. Greimas, 'Le défi', in *Du sens II* (Paris: Seuil, 1983), p. 218.
27. On that, see, for instance, M. Zéraffa, *Personne et personnage* (Paris: Klincksieck, 1969).
28. Compare, in Chapter 37 (p. 277), the reference to the letters sent by Melbury respectively to Giles and Grace and in which he urges them to act.
29. On the typology of the various narrative programmes and a calculation of narrative possibilities, see the entry *'Programme narratif'* in the second volume of the *Dictionary*, (1986), pp. 177–9. See also the paper by E. Landowski and P. Stockinger, 'Problématique de la Manipulation:

de la schématisation narrative au calcul stratégique', in *Degrés*, vol. 44, (Winter 1985).

30. As far as love relationships are concerned, it is worth noticing the natural seductiveness (/KNOWING HOW TO DO/) with which Giles is here endowed and which at the same time differs from the 'culturalised' skill of the accomplished seducer and contrasts with his usual awkwardness and lack of insight ('You EVER will misunderstand me', Grace tells him in the previous chapter. See also the end of Chapter 15).

31. Contrary to 'dispossession' which implies a polemical relationship and, as it were, calls for further developments, namely a programme of 'reappropriation', 'renunciation' is a reflexive, self-imposed deprivation which rather marks a closure (see Greimas, *Du sens II*, p. 40). Hence, structurally speaking, the necessity for Grace to act, so as to counterbalance the 'apathy' of the renouncing Subject.

32. See the entry '*Manipulation*' in the *Dictionary*.

33. See Cl. Zilberberg, 'Conversion et réversion' in *Exigences et perspectives de la sémiotique*, p. 371. See also the (unpublished) essay: 'Pour introduire le faire missif' and, more generally, *Essai sur les modalités tensives* (Amsterdam: John Benjamins, 1981).

34. On the 'epistemic relation' and the roles of informing Subject/observing Subject, see J. Fontanille, 'Les points de vue dans le discours: de l'épistémologie à l'identification', Thèse de Doctorat d'Etat, Université de Paris III. This work provides a reformulation in semiotic terms of the narratological question of the 'point of view'.

35. We could speak here, with J. Fontanille, of a 'hyper-knowledge', or else a 'knowledge on knowledge'. In this precise case, the cognitive meta-Subject is supplied with the '*savoir référent*' (the greatest knowledge possible) and the other Subjects with the '*savoir référé*' (the particular and limited knowledge of the characters). On the distinction between the two types of knowledge, see the entry '*Véridiction*' in the *Dictionary*, vol. 2.

36. See A. J. Greimas, *Maupassant. La sémiotique du texte: exercices pratiques* (Paris: Seuil, 1976), pp. 139ff.

37. In fact, as is well known, 'the loop is not looped'. By accepting the resumption of married life with Fitzpiers, Grace goes back to /Culture/ and rejects /Nature/ once more. In a significant way, she ceases to visit Giles's grave in Little Hintock and finds herself again in the Wessex Hotel. Such is not the case with Bathsheba Everdene who, at the end of *Far from the Madding Crowd*, chooses /Nature/ for good. For a detailed comparative study of the syntactic courses in the two novels, see Janie Sénéchal, 'Stratégies énonciatives et pratiques narratives chez Thomas Hardy', 'Thèse de Doctorat d'Etat, Université de Lille III (to be published by the Atelier National de Reproduction des Thèses, Lille, microcards).

38. Data on which, needless to say, the analyses of Cl. Lévi-Strauss are founded.

39. On those operations of 'instanciation', see H. Quéré, 'De Sade à Yeats et retour: problèmes de la mise en discours', shortly to appear in *Cruzeiro Semiótico*, Lisbon (Portuguese Semiotic Association).

We wish to thank Ruth and Francis Kelly for their help with the translation.

A brief French–English Glossary of Semiotics

Actant = Actant
  (anti-)Sujet (S) = (anti-)Subject (S)
  Objet (O) = Object (O)
  (anti-)Destinateur (D1) (initial ou final) = (anti-)Destinator (D1) (neol.)
      (initial or final)
  Destinataire (D2) = Destinatee (neol.)
/être/ = /BEING/
/faire/ = /DOING/
  /faire/ pragmatique = pragmatic /DOING/
  /faire/ cognitif = cognitive /DOING/
  /faire/ persuasif = persuasive /DOING/
  /faire/ interprétatif = interpretative /DOING/
Enoncé d'état = statement, utterance of /BEING/
                junction either conjunction (S ∩ O) or disjunction (S ∪ O)
Enoncé de /faire/ = statement, utterance of /DOING/
                either reflexive (S1 → /S1 ∩ / ∪ O/)
                or transitive (S1 → /S2 ∩ / ∪ O/)
Programme narrative (PN) = narrative programme (NP)
  PN de base = basic NP
  PN d'usage = auxiliary NP
Sujet d'état = Subject of /BEING/
  Sujet de faire = Subject of DOING
  Sujet cognitif = cognitive Subject
  Sujet opérateur = operating Subject
Objet de valeur = value-Object
  Objet de savoir ou Objet cognitif = cognitive Object, Object of knowledge
      (Os)
Modes d'existence sémiotique = modes of semiotic existence
  virtuel = virtualised
  actuel = actualised
  réalisé = effected
Compétence = competence
Performance = performance
Modalisation = modalisation
Existence modale = modal existence
Etat modal = modal state
valeur modale = modal value

Alternative Hardy_

compétence modale = modal competence
Modalités = modalities
  /vouloir/ = /WANTING TO/
  /pouvoir/ = /BEING ABLE TO — CAPABLE OF/
  /devoir/ = /HAVING TO/
  /savoir/ = /KNOWING HOW TO/
  /croire/ = /BELIEVING/
/être/ vs /paraître/ /modalités véridictoires) = /BEING/ vs /APPEARING TO
  BE/ (veridictory modalities)
(ne pas) vouloir (ne pas) = (NOT) WANTING (NOT) TO
(ne pas) savoir (ne pas) = (NOT) KNOWING HOW (NOT) TO
(ne pas) pouvoir (ne pas) faire = (NOT) BEING ABLE (NOT) TO DO
  (ne pas) pouvoir (ne pas) être = (NOT) BEING CAPABLE OF (NOT)
    BEING
(ne pas) devoir (ne pas) = (NOT) HAVING (NOT) TO
(ne pas) faire (ne pas) être = (NOT) CAUSING (NOT) TO BE (action)
  (ne pas) faire (ne pas) faire = (NOT) CAUSING (NOT) TO DO (manipu-
    lation)
Contrat = Contract
  Contrat fiduciaire = fiduciary Contract
Catégorie thymique (euphorie vs dysphorie) = thymic category (euphoria
  vs dysphoria)
Deixis (positive ou négative) = (negative or positive) deixis
Parcours génératif = generative path, trajectory
Parcours narratif = narrative trajectory, development
embrayage/débrayage = shifting in/shifting out

10
Thomas Hardy and J. M. W. Turner

Annie Escuret

I have chosen Hardy and Turner as the subject of this article because their works constitute artistic events which reveal changes and breaches in Europe in the nineteenth century in so far as they both, one in the field of art and the other in that of literature, contributed to outdating the artistic experience of the generations which preceded them.

All eighteenth-century artistic culture was based on the premises of the Quattrocento. It must be remembered that at the beginning of the fifteenth century Florentine art had perfected a new organisation of space which was given the name of 'artificial perspective' or *trompe l'oeil*. Introduced by Filippo Brunelleschi (1377–1446) and systematised in about 1450 by Leo Battista Alberti (1404–72) in his *Treatise on Architecture*, the system made possible the illusion of an infinitely deep, fleeting space in which all objects were of a size on the scale of their distance with regard to the spectator's viewpoint. Gothic artists had introduced pictorial symbols which had no connection with reality as they saw it. In other words, their paintings were not supposed to be a reproduction of what they had around them. The desire to give an impression of depth was thus a revolution in pictorial art. The change which took place can easily be recognised in the works of Masaccio (1401–29), Fra Angelico (1387–1455), Paolo Ucello (1397–1475) and many others. All these artists tend to give up the use of bright colours, gold decorations, undulating lines and fussy details to concentrate rather on perspective, space, straight lines, balance between volumes and correct distribution of masses. After that Pollaiuolo, Verrochio and Leonardo da Vinci studied the anatomical workings of the body and the way in which its different parts are deformed by movements and tensions. The depiction of moving figures made possible a new assertion of depth and the continuity of pictorial space. It is to be remembered that Leonardo da Vinci's descriptions of the attitudes associated with basic emotions were fashionable in European academies right up to the eighteenth century. Some techniques helped improve this representation of space throughout the fifteenth century. It is thus that contours became less sharp and colours were softened by a slight mist. During the same period, in Flanders, Hubert (1370–1426) and Jan Van Eyck (1390?–1441) perfected a pictorial form which was characterised by great depth and extreme precision in realistic details. The past-masters of the illusion of depth and volume were undoubtedly Leonardo da Vinci, Michelangelo and Raphael, who managed to achieve harmony between movement, silhouettes and volume.

If we have considered it necessary to remind the reader of the important part played by the Italian tradition[1] of the *trompe l'oeil*, it is because it was a new technique in which everything was based on the (fictive) presence of a fixed viewer. The realistic novel reposes on the same principle, since it implies from the outset a particular 'angle' or a 'viewpoint' or a 'focalisation', that is to say, the eye of the imaginary viewer without whom nothing would be possible. The characters are dependent on the presence of this eye from which nothing can escape. The 'narrator', who is supposed to be all-knowing and ever-present, is above all the one who can see everything, who can explain everything, from the 'visible' to the 'invisible', from the most obvious attire to the most intimate secrets. He is this eye which looks on the painting from the outside or the authority supposed to relate the events in the past historic tense. But let us see what Roland Barthes has to say on this subject:

> By its past historic tense the verb is an implicit part of a causal chain, it takes part in a series of actions which are interdependent and guided, it works as the algebraic sign for an intention; upholding an ambiguity between temporality and causality, it calls for an unfolding, that is to say the unfolding of the narrative. It is for this reason that it is the perfect instrument for all creations of universes: it is the artificial tense of cosmogonies, of myths, of Histories and of Novels. It implies a well-built world which has been carefully planned, indifferent, reduced to basic lines, and not a world which has been thrown together, widespread, open to all. There is always a demiurge, god or narrator hidden behind the past historic; the world is not unexplained when one recites it, each one of its accidents is of no more than secondary importance and the past historic is the operational sign by which

the narrator reduces the bursting out of reality to a slight, pure verb, with no density, no volume, no expansion, whose sole function is to unite a cause and an end as quickly as possible.[2]

The past historic is thus the expression of an order since everything is such that it is as if reality gave no opaqueness to meaning. Nothing is absurd since all the elements are taken up in a series of coherent relationships. In choosing this kind of narrative, realistic authors have automatically accepted the criteria of the probable which designates the possible while, at the same time, showing it to be false. The probable is not Truth, which is the Idea or God Himself. To put it simply, the mission of realistic art is to express the essential in the artifice and the triumph of the third person — of the 'he' in preference to the existential 'I' — which marks the victory of essential man who competes with God in becoming an eye from which nothing can escape. The life of the character becomes a destiny and the length of a limited lapse of time heavy with meaning. This literature is that of a humanistic vision of the world, whose centre is man. If one is to understand fully all the epistemological implications of this kind of representation one must go back to one of the founders of this reduction of the visible to a physico-mathematical construction in which all that is sensitive is abolished, in favour of rational speech. We are of course referring to Newton[3] who, 30 years after Descartes, opposes his 'mathematical principles' to the metaphysical principles of Cartesian Physics. Newton's principles introduce a change of language but not of universe since mathematics succeeds figurative rhetoric in the mechanistic revolution in which Descartes, Galileo and Huygens were already present.

One of the first people to attack the Newtonian stronghold violently was Goethe, who saw in Newton's *Optics* a major epistemological obstacle. For the romantics Newton's theories are a dangerous, intellectualist alienation, for, in their conception, the eye is the perfect organ of presence in the world and the truth of what is sensitive is a human truth which cannot be reduced to mathematics. We all know today that the world is not ruled by numbers and that mathematics is a symbolic logic, or 'logistics', and not reality. By considering the ideal of an experiment without an experimenter to be the norm for knowledge, philosophy and mechanical science have denatured nature and have denatured man. All these mathematical and metaphysical principles form a 'master speech' in which man is supposed to *dominate*, from the outside, through his mind. Newtonian science is a practical science which claims to reveal the secret of the world or the truth of nature by giving access to the system which founds the harmony of moral, natural and political order. In other words, it states that the world is one, homogeneous and rational because there is a co-extensivity of mathematics as the language of both God and man. Thus there is no longer any room for the subject in this causal, harmonious world which is governed by legality, determinism, mechanism and rationality. Finally, time is reversible since, in this world which is subjected to causality, the cause is the effect and the effect is the cause; in other words, chance no longer exists, since one is supposed to be able to foresee everything.

What happens to creative liberty in such a scheme if God has decided everything and if, after Him, man can do no more than *imitate*?

Newton's premises are obviously totally opposed to those of the pre-Socratics, who had endeavoured to rid themselves of the superstition which, as is shown by its name, refers to 'that which is above', that is to say, God or the origin. We could, for example, mention the works of Democritus, which Plato wanted to burn in order to bring victory to Parmenides's theories (alias unity, permanence and immobility). The Heraclitean conception of evolution was indeed a threat to Platonism. After Democritus, Epicurus and, above all, Lucretius, new theories came into circulation. They no longer spoke of 'Nature' in the image of the One but of 'physics' and atomism. In a word, one no longer spoke of universal time but of evolution. One no longer spoke of the One, the Being, Harmony or the Whole but of the multiple, disparity, divergence, shock or deviation. Neither did one speak of predestination but of liberty and chance. This is how I. Prigogine sums up the confrontation between the theories of the atomistic philosophers and those of idealistic (or metaphysical) science:

> Philosophers in Antiquity had already stressed the fact that each natural process, interpreted in terms of the movement and the collisions of atoms in space, can be the object of a multitude of explanations, all plausible and all different. This is of little importance for the atomistic philosopher since his aim is, above all, to show that this type of explanation is sufficient and that it is useless to have recourse to the supernatural: it is to *describe a*

world with neither God nor norms, a world in which *man is free* and
is to expect no punishment and no reward of any kind, be it
divine or natural.[4] [The emphasis is mine.]

It was the progress of thermodynamics in the nineteenth century
which tore to shreds, atomised, broke into little pieces the rational
continuum which had been inherited from classical science or
Newtonian mechanistic dynamics. The subject was no longer
gravitation, plain rectilinear trajectories, but *fire* or *heat* which
transforms, dilates or evaporates. In a word, there was a movement
away from the straight line to the *cloud*. Industrial society is the
offspring of this new energy which made steam-engines work.
The subject was no longer clockwork propelled by the Divine
Clockmaker, but *motor*. Nature was no longer an automaton, but
a motor. It would nevertheless be simplistic to imagine that the
passing from automaton to the motor was brutal and took place
overnight. The great dream of the nineteenth century was to exploit
the new energy to its own advantage. In order to do this, a motor
which never stopped was necessary and that is why the nineteenth
century gave birth to a hybrid monster, the auto-motor, or the
everlasting motor. Society, man and nature are represented as
motors which produce energy. In keeping with Carnot's second
principle, these motors cool down and finally come to a stop.
However, as they are auto-motors, there immediately follows a
relaunching action, a move towards resumption, a new departure,
the eternal return which proclaims the triumph of the *same*. This
takeover of modern science by outdated science is like a conjuring
trick and yet it is what Zola does in all his works, as is shown by
Michel Serres in his book about the French novelist.[5] A novel
which does not build an auto-motor is one which admits that
chance is reality and that meaning is *local.*

The traditional novel differs from the works of modernity in that
it has a metaphysical content, which has no room for chance. Time
appears as a flawless, holeless continuum since the 'omniscient
narrator' allows himself the luxury of taking us back to the past
(by analepsis) or of foreseeing what is to come (by prolepsis). A
sequence from a classical narrative reveals only part of it to us but,
on the last page, the veil is invariably lifted. Nothing is left in the
dark or hanging over and the thread of the narrative speech or the
causal chain works its way through until it completes the circle.
The orphan hero who finds a family or the marriage which comes

off are the perfect symbols of the bonds which are tied anew. Failure or death do not question the value of the union but often intervene simply to add extra stress to it.

Thomas Hardy is not altogether an exception to this aesthetics of the *mimesis*, the cause, the whole, the One or the likely. Nevertheless, in several aspects, his works are forerunners of the modern acausal narration, or rather fiction, which speaks of, not mimetic duplication, but divergence or variation. To understand what makes a novel by Hardy different from a traditional novel one has only to compare *Jude* to *David Copperfield*. In the same way, if one of Jane Austen's heroines, like Emma Woodhouse, is able to understand her wrongdoings and 'make amends', the mistake made by Tess cannot be atoned for. In most of the Wessex novels there are still some shadowy areas left which cannot be accounted for by rational explanations. The past is continually denounced as a curse which it is preferable to avoid as it is always past events which make it impossible for the individual to express himself. But for the intrusion of the parson/genealogist, Tess would doubtless have been able to live. Without the return of Susan, Henchard would doubtless have been able to avoid being ruined. In the same way, without the fateful reminders of Aunt Drusilla, Jude would never have thought he was victim of a fatal inheritance. If Clym had not returned home Mrs. Yeobright, Eustacia and Wildeve would not have died. It can thus be noticed that, in Hardy's works, memory plays a negative part. Only the characters who are capable of forgetting manage to survive. We can mention Vilbert, who forgets Jude's books, or Arabella, who soils them with fat before throwing them out. This fatal memory is a fine condemnation of Platonic idealism in so far as a large number of novels can be read as a denunciation of the theory of reminiscence. Hardy obviously does not admit the Ideas or values independent of man or liable to impose themselves on all rational minds. In his works there is no philosopher capable of guiding the 'polis', nor is there any hero able to distinguish between truth and appearance. Even the narrator is constantly saying: 'It seemed that . . .' It is wrong of Jude to remember Phillotson, who forgets him immediately after his departure and, in the last novel (*The Well-Beloved*), the search of the idealistic artist (Jocelyn Pierston) is no more than buffoonery.

Hardy is not Joyce, but the modernity of the Wessex novels comes within the scope of classical narration which it gradually undermines. After *Jude the Obscure* Hardy gives up the traditional novel completely and devotes himself entirely to his poetical works. Turner acknowledges the same kind of failure, since he abandons clear lines and turns to painting what is called the 'hazy'. Hardy breaks a form to pieces, but this does not mean that he then offers modern works of fiction. Turner does the same thing since he is neither impressionist nor cubist. Thus they both represent a breaking-point, on the eve of the birth of new works.

There are several factors which make Hardy a forerunner of modernity. It can be noticed, for example, that he never gives up the habit of telling a story with a beginning, an unfolding and an end, but the end soon becomes the pre-text for a play on meaning. There is never a global meaning or a single system able to account for all the elements but a relationship of a negative critical dialogue with the principal myths of Western culture. The Bible, for example, is summoned only to be parodied and there are constant unresolved tensions between the mythical intertext and the realistic code. The overwhelming chronology of the earlier novels gives way to notations which indicate not an objective time-point but a subjective one which expresses the flowing of time, the 'decline' or the flux.

It is the 'end' of the day, the month or the year. Admittedly, it cannot be said that Hardy has done away with all reference to time but the last novels illustrate an increasing lack of interest in chronology, in favour of other elements. It is not until the novelists of the following generation that the repetitive chaos of time gets the better of 'clock time', but if we compare the *incipit* of the first novel (*Desperate Remedies*):

Chapter ONE
The Events of Thirty Years
December and January, 1835–6
In the long and intricately inwrought chain of circumstances . . .

to that of *Jude the Obscure*:

Chapter ONE
The schoolmaster was leaving the village and everybody seemed sorry.

we observe, in the first case, a desire to make the 'already lived' accessible to our wish for normative categories, whereas in the second the departure of the schoolmaster has a generic value. It is only a departure, one rupture among many others, and that is what the child is going to learn. The world of the linear chain is replaced by the time of evolution and rupture in which the individual feels disorientated.

By softening down the 'good will be rewarded' and the 'bad will be punished' categories Hardy engages in another kind of subversion of the traditional novel. The marriage or death which sometimes takes place at the end are not intended to give a final touch to a structural, coherent form but to question certain categories. Fancy Day triumphs without being really 'good', while Geraldine dies without being really 'bad'. The structure of the story becomes less and less coherent as the split, intermittent desire expresses itself. In the same way, it cannot be said that Tess or Jude personifies an enslaving passion, in opposition to other characters who would represent a well-organised subject or a centre of reference. All the actors are taken up in the dance but still remain members of common humanity. Finally, the splitting-up of the desire of the individual is always coupled with the splitting-up of the social. The 'values' which guarantee 'Harmony' no longer exist and the floundering of Tess, Jude or Sue was announced by that of Egbert in the very first novel. Hardy makes no effort to hide from his readers the disintegration of the individual and the social, the death of the name (which guarantees recognition), the end of the tree or the lineage. All sinks into the chaos of anonymity, and the loss of 'roots' tells of the loss of 'foundations/certitudes/concepts', which goes together with the urbanisation which draws people away from the country. The impossible return also tells of the collapse of the island submerged by the chaotic flow. The deaths of Tess and Jude are followed by the pure and simple abdication of the artist Jocelyn Pierston, who gives up his effort to bring order to chaos. *The Well-Beloved* was modified after the publication of *Jude the Obscure* and stress was deliberately put on the fact that any attempt at structuring would be vain. Faithful to his principles, Hardy gives up 'realistic' writing and devotes himself entirely to poetic writing.

Among the bastions which have collapsed is the family cell, which is ostentatiously absent or harmful:

'No, you are not Mrs. Phillotson,' murmured Jude. 'You are dear, free Sue Bridehead, only you don't know it.' Wifedom has not yet squashed up and digested you in its vast maw as an atom which has no further individuality.' (III, p. 9)

Sue's anguish at the thought of marrying Jude, the separation of Angel and Tess the day after the wedding, the parodical marriage between two old people which brings *The Well-Beloved* to an end, the deaths of Sorrow and Little Father Time, the trials of Tess in her parents' home, are all illustrations of the disintegration of the closed cell without which bourgeois power would not be able to last for ever. 'Nature', the Family, the University, Art are no longer in a position to offer a firm refuge against the flow of dissolution. *Jude the Obscure* is Hardy's last attempt in the field of the 'realistic' novel, since *The Well-Beloved* is most definitely allegorical. When Pierston's desire dies he gives up the pursuit of the chimera and settles down as a 'proper bourgeois' to wait for death. If he does not meet with the same fate as Tess or Jude it is because 'his novel' does not conform to the same conventions. Time and space are abolished, and when they reassert their rights the allegorical hero is no longer there. This change from the emblematic hero to the 'realistic' character is symbolised by his long illness. When he recovers Marcia has taken for good the place of the chimera which will no longer torment him.

This staging of the death of desire is the farewell of our author to realistic literature which has no place for an author inclined to anarchy. As for Hardy, he is too attached to his heroes of desire to continue leading them to the slaughterhouse. He is visibly tired of this kind of literature which feeds on death, thus illustrating the closed cycle, life–death–revival. He knows that if he insists stubbornly on depicting heroes of desire, he will be obliged to make them the scapegoats of a society which is based on the expulsion or the destruction of any force considered to be anarchic. And yet it cannot be said that the characters who are carriers of desire are, initially, forces of destruction. Tess, Giles or Jude are life and love. Tess and Giles will perhaps live on in the memories of Angel, Liza-Lu or Marty, but no-one will go and meditate on Jude's tomb. Thus his death is not the starting point of the circulation of meaning since he sinks into chaos and oblivion. In a word, there is neither order nor truth. Pierston gives up the idea of catching the chimera for the artist cannot be the *flash* of *light*, Bellerophon, mounted on his horse Pegasus. When (in the first version) he throws himself into the waves he lets himself be

engulfed by the chaos which absorbs those who want to bring
order to the 'unorderable', the unassignable or the unnamable.
The artist is not the one who re-knows what he already knew but
the one whose journey transforms. This journey, or transforming
Will, brings about a dissonance in memory, which is the home of
Holy mimesis. The narrator is often the only person able to say
what was and what is, as is confirmed by the poem 'Memory and
I'.[6] On the other hand, we often see characters praying to be
forgotten. Henchard and Jude are the best-known examples, but
we must also remember the poem 'Tess's Lament', in which Tess
is supposed to express a similar desire.

This passage from the geometrical line or the traditional novel
to the cloud of steam or the atoms/letters of poetry is summed up
as follows by Hardy in his autobiography:

> After looking at the landscape ascribed to Bonington in our
> drawing-room I feel that Nature is played out as a Beauty, but
> not as a Mystery. I don't want to see landscapes, i.e., scenic
> paintings of them, because I don't want to see the original
> realities — as optical effects, that is. I want to see the deeper
> reality underlying the scenic, the expression of what are some-
> times called abstract imaginings.
>
> The 'simply natural' is interesting no longer. The much decried,
> mad, late-Turner rendering is now necessary to create my
> interest. The exact truth as to material fact ceases to be of
> importance in art — it is a student's style — the style of a period
> when the mind is serene and unawakened to the tragical
> mysteries of life; when it does not bring anything to the object
> that coalesces with and translates the qualities that are already
> there, — half hidden, it may be — and the two united are
> depicted as the All.[7]

What Hardy refuses here is no less than a drawn or drawable
world, that is to say a world in keeping with Euclid's laws and
geometry. This world of mechanical forms is that of the architect
who draws the plan and has a house built according to the
pre-established plan. The architect, or the realistic novelist (or
naturalist), affirms the existence of a universe in which the *subject*
is the master, the eye which arranges things according to the laws
of perspective. It is a world of lines, circles, pulleys, winches,
levers, an objective world of power and balance of power, men,

machines and work which dispels chaos. The primacy of identity
defines it as a world of representation in which, in keeping with
the humanistic model, man is at the centre, standing straight,
holding his head high, facing in the 'right direction'. The devil is
represented upside down, as he is subversion, that is to say,
disorder and madness. This homogenous space is what Deleuze
calls 'the space of **pillars**, streaked by the fall of bodies, the vertical
of weight, the distribution of matter into parallel slices, the flowing
away, in strips or layers, of what makes up the flood' (my
emphasis).[8]

It is this space which we find in the earliest works, in which the
classical house triumphs over ruins and cracks (*Desperate Remedies*),
in which the tree triumphs over disorder (*Under the Greenwood
Tree*), in which the woman/cloud becomes a sarcophagus (*A Pair
of Blue Eyes*), in which the coffin is closed over the hot-house flower
which is guilty of transgression (*An Indiscretion in the Life of an
Heiress*), in which the Good Shepherd triumphs over the forces of
dissolution (*Far from the Madding Crowd*). In this last work Boldwood
is compared to a 'tower' (ch. 18), Troy to a 'pillar' and Bathsheba
to a 'statue' (ch. 16, ch. 28). The four poles of this stable closed
universe are represented by the four buildings which sum up
Weatherbury: the manor, the church, the malthouse and the barn.[9]
In a word, here the universe is that of the rectangle and its lines,
where the wheel triumphs over the uncertain whirlpool of passion:

> The river would have been seen by day to be of that deep
> smooth sort which races middle and sides with the same gliding
> precision, any irregularities of speed being immediately corrected
> by a small whirlpool. Nothing was heard in reply to the signal
> but the gurgle and cluck of one of these invisible wheels . . .
> (ch. 11)

The collapsing of one of the pillars of this universe begins with an
incident about a 'letter' and 'chance' which is to undermine the
'square-framed perpendicularity' of one who knew nothing about
women:

> To Boldwood women had been remote phenomena rather than
> necessary complements — comets of such uncertain aspects,
> movement and permanence, that whether their orbits were as
> geometrical, unchangeable, and as subject to laws as his own,

or as absolutely erratic as they superficially appeared, he had not deemed it his duty to consider. (ch. 17)

In the following chapter Boldwood's state of mind before the untimely intrusion of Bathsheba's letter is described in the following way:

> That stillness, which struck casual observers more than anything else in his character and habit, and seemed so precisely like the rest of inanition, may have been the perfect balance of enormous antagonistic forces — positives and negatives in fine adjustment.
> (ch. 18)

Is there a better definition of the universe of geometry (or of 'the master'), that is to say statics, in which rest is defined in terms of balance of forces? Boldwood's force is shown by the perpendicularity of his features, his shoulders and his stronghold, which knows nothing of the whirlwind, that is to say the fire of desire:

> When Bathsheba's figure shone upon the farmer's eyes it lighted him up as the moon lights up a great tower. A man's body is as the shell, or the tablet, of his soul, as he is reserved or ingenuous, overflowing or self-contained. There was a change in Boldwood's exterior from its former impassibleness; and his faced showed that he was now living outside his defences for the first time, and with a fearful sense of exposure. It is the usual experience of strong natures when they love. (ch. 18)

The fall of Boldwood is linked to that of Troy, who is the red or the fire of passion. It is this double failure of passion/madness which enables Gabriel Oak to achieve the triumph of Reason, the organised subject, the tree and reference, for the collapsing of a 'tower' does not necessarily mean the end of the space composed of pillars. In a word, *Far From the Madding Crowd* is a painting by Bonington in which the romantic overflowing of passions remains controlled by form, which gets the better of matter.

When Hardy mentions Turner for the first time in his autobiography, it is to tell his readers that he prefers his paintings to those of Bonington, as we have seen. The second reference to Turner is dated 9 January 1889:

'January 9. At the Old Masters, Royal Academy. Turner's water-colours: each is landscape *plus* a man's soul . . . What he paints chiefly is *light as modified by objects*. He first recognizes the impossibility of really reproducing on canvas all that is in a landscape; then gives for that which cannot be reproduced a something else which shall have upon the spectator an approximative effect to that of the real. He said, in his maddest and greatest days: 'What pictorial drug can I dose man with, which shall effect his eyes somewhat in the manner of this reality which I cannot carry to him?' — and set to make such strange mixtures as he was tending towards in 'Rain, Steam and Speed', 'Approach to Venice', 'Snowstorm and a Steamboat', etc. Hence, one may say, Art is the secret of how to produce by a false thing the effect of a true . . .[10]

There is a third reference to Turner in Chapter 28: 'I prefer late Wagner, as I prefer late Turner, to early (which I suppose is all wrong in taste), the idiosyncracies of each master being more strongly shown in these strains.'[11] Thus it is not the painter of 'Dido and Aeneas' or 'Apollo and the Sybil' that Hardy likes, but definitely that of 'Rain, Steam and Speed' which is, strictly speaking, the crowning point of Turner's long career. The works of the last 15 years of Turner's life call illusionism into question radically. Turner dismisses the referent at the end of his career. His clouds (as in 'Venice and la Salute', 'Venetian Scene', 'Light and Colour', 'Seastorm and a Burning Wreck' and many others) invade the whole canvas. In 'Rain, Steam and Speed' the referent has not yet been eliminated since it is easy to make out a train and a viaduct. The spectator is, however, integrated into the picture in so far as s/he cannot be contented with just looking at it passively like a finished object. It is because they display their irreferential pictorialness that Turner's works bring about a break with illusion and representation. It is not the line of the finished form, fixed for eternity, that interests him, but the way in which matter changes. In other words, the message of one of Turner's paintings is a physical — and not a metaphysical — message. If the matter changes it is because the world has a history. The painters of illusion say exactly the opposite since they claim to restore true, perpetual forms. In modern painting one can find only the abstraction of a Kandinsky, which reminds one of the whirlwind and the cataclysms of Turner. We are thinking particularly of

'Improvisation' which Jean Clay describes in the following way:

> In portraying the filamentous wave, the amoebic turbulence of
> transforming organisms, Kandinsky's aim is to represent the
> moment at which matter — lava, ice — is not yet (or no longer
> is) a participant in the order of separate reigns and structural
> objects. 'The implacable gyration of the stars' (Gaëtan Picon)
> carries away in a centrifugal movement of melting substances.
> As far as the artist from Munich is concerned, these cosmic
> driftings refer expressly to a set of religious themes: the Flood,
> the Apocalypse, the Parousia. His painting is not simply the
> description of a gestation or a dissolution, it is itself the resoun-
> ding clash between different worlds, intended to create the new
> world, within their struggle or outside their struggle, between
> themselves . . .[12]

Like Hardy, Turner began as an architect's designer. Both Hardy
and Turner visited Venice and were dazzled by their journeys.
Turner breaks away from the tradition of Claude Gellée and
the Dutch masters and then from all discipline. He completely
abandons romanticism with its balance of masts and sails and turns
to painting matter and its transformations under the heat of fire.
In his chapter in *Hermes III: Translation* entitled 'Turner translates
Carnot', Michel Serres sees in Turner the first real genius of the
new science of fire, that is to say thermo-dynamics, with its two
sources, the hot and cold, fire and water. When Turner paints a
black and red tugboat, spitting forth fire, it is to proclaim the
victory of the new science over geometry, symbolised by the masts
of the 'Fighting Temeraire', reduced to the shadow of a grey ghost.
In 'Rain, Steam and Speed', the engine has taken the place of the
tugboat:

> Turner sees the world through water and fire, as Garrard saw it
> through figures and movements . . . The fire divides the cold
> canvas into two halves, one in the atmosphere and the other
> reflected in the water. The axis of fire, bellowing, on a green
> volume. Result: blazing fire, water, the hot and the cold, melting
> matter, the drawing lost in favour of chancy matter, undefined,
> grouped statistically in bundles, in the clouds of the frozen on
> one hand and of the incandescent on the other; Carnot, almost
> Maxwell, almost Boltzmann, Turner has understood this and

shows the new world, the new matter. *The perception of the stochastic takes the place of the drawing of form* . . . The world disappears, it is the work of man which requires the two sources, red fire and green cold. Hope and death . . . Man has built a nature-object, the artist shows the entrails of this object, stochastic bundles, dual sources, the flashing of fires, its material entrails, which are the very womb of the world, sun, rain, ice, clouds and showers. Sky, sea, earth and thunder are inside a boiler. And this boiler cooks the matter of the world. At random.[13]

Hardy follows a similar path since it can be noticed that, as early as 1876, *The Hand of Ethelberta* was to disturb the beautiful layout of the space of pillars. Admittedly, Ethelberta fails in that she, in her turn, lets herself be shut up in a sarcophagus by Lord Mountclere, but her tribulations as a poetess are a first attempt to open the Ark or the tower. The end shows her as the jealous guardian of the horn of plenty, but what happened to her remains. *The Return of the Native* marks a turning-point in the Hardyian production, with the poetical creation of the Heath and of Diggory Venn, called the 'reddleman'. Water does triumph over the fire of desire and the blind sun does hold forth from the top of the mountain, but this allegory nevertheless brings about an important breakaway from the realistic code. We then come to *The Trumpet Major*, which is a forerunner of a number of themes of *The Dynasts* in that the triumph of Bob is that of the forces of disorder. It all happens as if the smooth surface of the sea triumphed over the streaked space as Bob is the sailor who comes back alive from the naval battle in which the ships are reduced to dust under the volley of fire, whereas the 'worthy' hero dies under the Spanish sun.

With *A Laodicean* the new energy makes a very conspicuous entrance. The heroine is nicknamed 'Miss Steam-Power' as she is the daughter of one of the railway contractors. The ruined castle is destroyed at the end of the novel by the fire set alight by William Dare, and all the lines twist in the heat of the fire. This time Hardy goes, like Turner, from Lagrange to Carnot, from mechanics to thermo-dynamics. Paula marries Somerset, or the 'setting sun', that is to say the architect who was unable to restore the ruins of the castle which was the symbol of shape, enclosure, geometric lines, and in the de Stancys' house, one can see huge, rusted keys which have become useless.

This opening made in the tower is at the centre of the following novel, since it is called *Two on a Tower*. Admittedly Viviette dies, but the beautiful child, as fair-haired as the nomad/astronomer, is the figure of hope that another mother (Tabitha Lark, the musical artist) is going to bring up.

The Mayor of Casterbridge is perfectly in keeping with the works which precede it as the fall of Henchard is that of a man who wanted to assert himself without *the mother*. His melting away on the heath at the end is a reaffirmation of the rights of matter which had been denied.

The Woodlanders is the novel of the wood, that is to say a smooth space similar to that of heathland or the sea. The death of the Tree does not mean the death of the wood, but that of the Tree/Cross, the Ark, the Tower, the mast of the bark, ship or the island of certitude. Fitzpiers and Grace are the water and the fire and their circulation is that of the new energy. In the eyes of the woodmen Fitzpiers is hand in glove with alchemy, fire or the devil, that is to say new knowledge. The world no longer belongs to a deserving man like Giles, but works in an uncertain way, according to the fire of desire which undermines the foundations of the old order, and the victory of Fitzpiers over Giles expresses the fusion of the beam, or the wooden framework of the carpenter's son.

Tess of the d'Urbervilles is a lyrical work which reaffirms, in a tragic form, the rights which are denied to matter. This character of blood and milk is the tongue of fire whose movement is the mark of materialistic writing. This is what Jacques Darras has to say on the subject:

> Tess is the character through whom the Wessex region comes most completely in the order of the imaginary. Tess, who is an ancillary creature — in that she is first the soil, the space which writing kneads, cultivates, tills, before being a socially exploited character. Not only would it be a reduced vision to interest oneself solely in the historical aspect of her destiny, but it would also be the worst misinterpretation possible. Tess *is* space, as space is the raw material which is the novelist's concern. At the very moment that the engineer Verne, with the formal stiffness of a clerk of the court, notes that the universe is closed, Thomas Hardy praises the infinite potentialities of a material feminine imagination in the remarkable microcosmic area of Dorset.[14]

The death of the Name (of the Father) expresses the end of the signs of personal identity which is at the centre of the humanistic model. Nevertheless, Tess dies because the new energy has passed into the hands of the men from the North who refuse to recognise the rights of the natives. They refuse to talk with the country folk who suffer from the infernal rhythm imposed by the machine. Moreover, Hardy describes them as the slaves of 'their Plutonian master':

A little way off there was another indistinct figure: this one black, with a sustained hiss that spoke of strength very much in reserve. The long chimney running up beside an ash-tree, and the warmth which radiated from the spot, explained without the necessity of much daylight that here was the engine which was to act as the *primum mobile* of this little world. By the engine stood a dark motionless being, a sooty and grimy embodiment of tallness, in a sort of trance, with a heap of coals by his side: it was the engineman. The isolation of his manner and colour lent him the appearance of a creature from Tophet, who had strayed into the pellucid smokelessness of this region of yellow grain and pale soil, with which he had nothing in common, to amaze and to discompose its aborigines.

What he looked he felt. He was in the agricultural world, but not of it. He served fire and smoke; these denizens of the fields served vegetation, weather, frost and sun. He travelled with his engine from farm to farm, from county to county, for as yet the steam threshing machine was itinerant in this part of Wessex. He spoke in a strange northern accent; his thoughts being turned inward upon himself, his eye on his iron charge, hardly perceiving the scenes around him, and caring for them not at all: holding only strictly necessary intercourse with the natives, as if some ancient doom compelled him to wander here against his will in the service of his Plutonic master. The long strap which ran from the driving-wheel of his engine to the red thresher under the rick was the sole tie-line between agriculture and him. While they uncovered the sheaves he stood apathetic beside his portable repository of force, round whose hot blackness the morning air quivered. He had nothing to do with preparatory labour. His fire was waiting incandescent, his steam was at high pressure, in a few seconds he could make the long strap move at an invisible velocity. Beyond its extent the environment might be corn, straw, or chaos; it was all the same

to him. If any of the autochthonous idlers asked him what he
called himself, he replied shortly, 'an engineer'. (*Tess*, ch. 47)

The subject of this long passage is none other than the diversion
of the new energy taken over by the power which is symbolised
by the men who have come from the cold. There is no exchange
between the two sources, instead there is a return in strength of
mechanics which triumph over modern knowledge with the *machine*
or the auto-motor. Thanatocracy wins again and Tess is *hanged* (as
will be Little Father Time later on) by a cord which stands for the
pulley, the winch, the *gallows*. The cords, the wheels and the
chains are the symbols of the machine, of the balance of forces in
which the Master is always better placed. In a word, *Tess of the
d'Urbervilles* is a warning against those who use bodies or the
Other to refuel the boiler of their monster, the auto-motor. The
mineralisation of the *flow* marks the victory of weight or of the fall.
When Tess is hanged the *plumbline* does its job and, as the
expression says, everything goes back to 'normal'.

Jude the Obscure is simply the second part of a diptych of which
Tess is the first. The universe into which we penetrate is no longer
that of the cloud, of the exchange, of the two sources or of
materialistic writing, but a world which is governed by geometry
and statics. The water is imprisoned in the well at Marygreen and
is lacking at Christminster, which is a symbol of the North, that is
to say the place where speech freezes. Jude wanders about between
the well and the tower/fortress which is guarded by the guard-
dogs of the Holy Necropolis without ever being able to take part
in any exchange. Energy is once again prisoner of the mortiferous
enclosure. Vilbert uses the child's legs, that is to say his energy or
his force. Jude is expectation killed by the lack of heat, as is shown
by his agony in the freezing rain. He is the fire of desire and hope
which goes out for lack of *water*. The phthisis which consumes
him makes the character an oven or a forge which cannot work
without the other source, that is to say water and its uncertain
whirlpools, for Jude's world is a world in which water has frozen.
He tries to put an end to his life by jumping into the pond in
which his mother had committed suicide but the *ice* will not break.
To put it briefly, Jude suffers because the men from the North have
diverted, to their own advantage, the water or flow imprisoned by
stone. This inveiglement is that of *Stonehenge* where Tess is
mineralised on the sacrificing stone, for the sun gods are always

thirsty and, when they drink the blood of the earth in long gulps, the fire of expectation dies.

Indeed, Hardy *is*, like Turner, the bard of the new energy which, to circulate, needs *two sources* and a *gap* between them so that there can be some exchange between the two poles. What circulates is neither water nor the sun, but the clouds of steam or atoms of the multiple, which Michel Serres talks about in *Genèse*:

> The noisy, anarchical, cloudy, spotted, striped, mottled, mixed multiple, crossed by a thousand different colours and tones, is the possible itself. It is a set of possible things, it is perhaps the set of possible things. It is not strength, it is the exact opposite of power, but it is ability. This noise is the opening. The Ancients were right when they said that chaos gaped. The multiple is open, from it is born nature, which is for ever being born.[15]

When the single prevails over the multiple the cloud melts away and the mortiferous concept (or Sign) sets to work. The victory of the gods is that of stone and death. Henchard thinks he's an archangel and turns back to dust. Man is neither god nor angel, nor stone, nor death, but a sum of things, a multiple or a series of possibles. Without the cloud there is no liberty but the walls of concepts/fortresses. The novels of Hardy are a series of aggressive butts delivered with ever-increasing force against the thick walls of the One. Nevertheless, the dream of an opening was not to become reality until *The Dynasts* in which the atomic explosion reaffirms the rights of the cloud, the end of borders and the futility of genres.

Notes

1. This is what Jean Clay has to say about the principle of specular fidelity to the visible world:

   > Precision, reproduction: a painting is well executed when it imitates outside appearances so well that one 'cannot tell the difference.' It can be compared to a window . . . the same claim to accuracy, in varying forms, is to be found from one age to another throughout the history of Western art. One can go back as far as Vitruvius, who explained that 'painting is the representation of things that exist or can exist, as of a man, a building, a boat or any other object whose

shape or expression can be imitated.' For Alberti, in the XVth century, 'the artist's job is to define and to paint on a board or a given wall, using lines and colours, the visible surface of all kinds of body, in such a way that, seen from a certain distance and under a certain angle, all that is represented appears in relief and looks exactly like the body itself.' According to Leonardo, 'The painting which is closest to the object it imitates is the one which deserves the most praise.' Diderot exclaimed on seeing a landscape, 'This isn't a canvas, it's nature, it's a piece of the universe that I have in front of me'. Ingres, like an echo, repeats, 'Art is never at such a high degree of perfection as when it looks so much like nature that it is taken for nature.' And Whistler calls out to his model, Robert de Montesquiou, 'Look at me just one more minute and you will look for ever.' And this goes as far as Zola who, in 1866, imagines that he can recognise in Manet's works 'the acrid, wholesome scent of true nature.' (Jean Clay, *De l'Impressionisme à l'art moderne* (Paris: Hachette Réalités, 1975), pp. 9–10 — My translation).

At the other extreme Marcel Proust considers the artist Elstir to be close to Turner and, in a *A l'ombre des jeunes filles en fleur* (I, p. 839), speaks of 'the effort of Elstir not to show things as he knew they were but according to the optical illusions which are at the base of our first perception'. Proust, like Hardy, is among those who understood that Turner's art is a radical questioning of illusionism. One can also mention an interesting reaction of J. K. Huysmans who stresses the great extent to which a painting by Turner is above all matter worked by gesture or gesture invested in matter, and not the image of a referent:

One is placed before a mixture of pink and burnt sienna earth, of blue and white, rubbed over with a cloth, sometimes with circular movements, sometimes in straight lines or long zigzags. It is like an engraving swept across by soft bread-crumbs or by a mass of delicate colours spread with water over a sheet of paper which is folded then rubbed over energetically with a brush; this shows a series of surprising shades, especially if a few spots of white gouache are scattered on the sheet before folding it . . .' (J. K. Huysmans, *Certains* (Paris: Plon, 1889), p. 201).

2. R. Barthes, *Le degré zéro de l'écriture* (Paris: Editions Gontier, 1953–64), p. 30. (My translation.)
3. Concerning Newton's theories, see George Gusdorf, *Principes de la pensée au siècle des lumières* (Paris: Payot, 1971), pp. 151–779; and *Fondements du savoir romantique* (Paris: Payot, 1982), ch. 15 'Le procès de Newton', pp. 205–39.
   One can also read Judith Schlanger, *Les Métaphores de l'organisme* (Paris: Vrin, 1971); and, above all, the excellent work by A. Koyré, *Etudes newtoniennes* (Paris: Gallimard, 1968).
4. I. Prigogine and I. Stengers, *La Nouvelle alliance* (Paris: Gallimard, 1979), p. 71. (My translation.)

5. M. Serres, *Feux et signaux de brume: Zola* (Paris: Grasset, 1975).
6. James Gibson (ed.) The Complete Poems of Thomas Hardy (London: Macmillan, 1981).
7. F. E. Hardy, *The Life of Thomas Hardy 1840–1928* (London: Macmillan, 1962).
8. G. Deleuze & F. Guattari, *Capitalisme et schizophrénie*, p. 458.
9. On this subject, see the article by C. J. P. Beatty, '*Far From the Madding Crowd*: A Reassessment', in F. B. Pinion (ed.), *Thomas Hardy and the Modern World*: a symposium (Dorchester: The Thomas Hardy Society, 1974), pp. 14–36.
10. Hardy, *Life*, p. 216.
11. Ibid., p. 328.
12. Jean Clay, *De l'Impressionisme à l'art moderne*, p. 284. (My translation.)
13. Michel Serres, *Hermes III: La traduction* (Paris: Editions de Minuit, 1974), pp. 237–9. (My translation.)
14. Jacques Darras, 'Pour en revenir à Thomas Hardy', *Critique: Victoria Station*, no. 405–6 (February–March 1981), p. 324. (My translation.)
15. Michel Serres, *Genèse* (Paris: Grasset, 1982), p. 45. (My translation.)

Index

226